Park Benjamin

The Age of Electricity

From amber-soul to telephone

Park Benjamin

The Age of Electricity
From amber-soul to telephone

ISBN/EAN: 9783744790437

Printed in Europe, USA, Canada, Australia, Japan

Cover: Foto ©ninafisch / pixelio.de

More available books at **www.hansebooks.com**

THE

AGE OF ELECTRICITY

From *Amber-Soul to Telephone*

BY

PARK BENJAMIN, PH.D.

" Ariel and all his quality."
The Tempest.

NEW YORK
CHARLES SCRIBNER'S SONS
1889

PREFACE.

THIS little work is not a technical treatise, nor is it addressed in any wise to the professional electrician. It is simply an effort to present the leading principles of electrical science, their more important applications, and of these last the stories, in a plain and, it is hoped, a readable way. There are no formulas in the book. Only such technical terms as have now made their way into every-day use are employed; and the more strictly scientific branches of the subject, such as measurement, testing, etc., are omitted altogether.

It is a singular fact, that probably not an electrical invention of major importance has ever been made, but that the honor of its origin has been claimed by more than one person. There was a dispute over the Leyden-jar, and a long and acrimonious controversy about the galvanic battery. Franklin's discovery of the identity of lightning and electricity is still claimed for French philosophers; the title of "the father of the telegraph" is given to Wheatstone in England, and to Morse in the United States, although to neither of these inventors, but to Joseph Henry, the lasting gratitude of the world belongs; Dal Negro, McGawley, Page, and Henry have all been named each as the first and only original inventor of the electro-motor; Davidson, Davenport, Lillie, Jacobi, Page, and Hall are each credited with the invention of the electric railway; Page and Ruhmkorff dispute the invention of the induction coil; Jordan and Spenser, and others beside, waged a bitter war over their respective claims to the discovery of the electro-deposition of metals. Planté, as the inventor of the secondary battery, becomes deposed by the prior work of Ritter; Gramme finds his ring armature in the dynamo anticipated by Pacinotti. Professor Hughes had no sooner announced his microphone than Mr. Edison claimed it. Hjorth, Varley, Siemens, and Wheatstone share the honor of originating the self-exciting dynamo. Contests are still in existence over the incandescent electric lamp, with Edison and Swan and Sawyer in the front. And as for the present telephone war, — the greatest conflict of all, — this is fast becoming not merely a question of whether Reis or Drawbaugh or Gray or Bell or Dolbear, or any other of the numerous claimants, was or was not the inventor of the electrical transmission of speech, but a national issue involving the rights of the people against corporate monopoly, and perhaps also in some degree the integrity of our patent system.

Where it has been necessary to deal with these disputed matters, the author has endeavored to present the facts without partisan bias. The reader will, no doubt, notice that the names of many electrical inventors now celebrated are not mentioned, or but briefly referred to. This is because their inventions — when theirs — are but improvements in details remarkable rather for quantity than quality; or else require descriptions too technical for these pages.

For the most part, all historical data have been gathered from publications contemporary with the date of first production of the several discoveries and inventions, and in many cases from the original writings of the inventors and discoverers themselves. As for sources of information in general, the author can only say that there lie before him, at this writing, the first book on electricity ever written in the English language, — Robert Boyle's modest little pamphlet of 1675, — and the latest numbers of the electrical journals, fresh from the press; and that he has ranged throughout the whole field of electrical literature anywhere and everywhere, in the most arbitrary manner, between these limits.

In a few instances, however, it would be ungracious to deny special credit: and therefore acknowledgment is made for aid from Prof. S. P. Thomson's excellent "Elementary Lessons in Electricity and Magnetism," Mr. J. H. Gordon's "Treatise on Electric Lighting," Messrs. Preece & Sivewright's "Telegraphy," and Prof. J. T. Sprague's latest and best treatise on "Electricity," among modern works; and from Dr. Priestley's grand "History of Electricity," among those of the last century. Free use has been made of the files of "The Scientific American," of "The Journal of the Franklin Institute," and

the special electrical journals of this country; and of
those of "Engineering" and "The Mechanics' Magazine," and electrical periodicals abroad.   In the preparation of the chapter on Telegraphy, Mr. Alfred M. A.
Beale has rendered valuable assistance; and several of
the engravings in the chapter on Galvanic Batteries have
been kindly supplied by Messrs. John Wiley & Sons, from
Niaudet's work on that subject.

New York, May 15, 1886.

CONTENTS.

viii   *CONTENTS.*

THE AGE OF ELECTRICITY.

THE AGE OF ELECTRICITY.

CHAPTER I.

THE MYTH OF THE AMBER SOUL.

SOME years ago, there was found in a tomb in Egypt an alabaster vase, the sole contents of which were a few dry, hard, and blackened seeds. These the discoverer brought to England, and planted them in the rich loam of his garden, more from curiosity than from any belief that they actually would germinate. To his surprise, in due time fresh young sprouts appeared which grew and flourished; and finally, in the harvest season, ears of wheat, as many as fifteen or twenty from a single stalk, were gathered. So it was proved that despite their having been sealed in the ancient tomb for nearly three thousand years, the seeds, to all appearances as lifeless as the huge stones which surrounded them, had retained all their vitality; and we might imagine, that if, during these many centuries, wheat had disappeared from among the earth's products, it would have been possible in time from these few grains to cause all the lands again to teem with golden harvest.

A suggestive parallel exists between the history of the wheat kernel shut up in the Egyptian tomb, and that of a mere atom of human knowledge which for nearly as long a period remained as unfruitful and buried in the minds of men. Indeed, among all the wonders of that strangest manifestation of the energy which pervades all nature, and which we call electricity, there is nothing more remarkable and more impressive than the growth of the single, simple, and uncoördinated fact, — namely, that amber, when rubbed, behaves in a curious way, — into the great science which underlies the telegraph, the electric light, and the telephone.

How rapid this growth has been, is within the remembrance of most of us. Of the vastness of its extent, we have on all sides ocular proof. What farther progress may be made, no one can predict. Conjecture too often outstrips reason : impossibilities and impracticabilities become confounded ; and each new advance only reveals a new horizon, beyond which who knows what fields may lie?

There is a familiar old Greek legend, which tells how Phaethon, son of the Sun, once rashly undertook to drive his father's chariot through the heavens. As the story goes, the horses despised their driver, and refused to be guided by him, so that the blazing chariot approached too near the earth, and living things thereon were burned. Then Jupiter, very wroth, hurled his thunderbolt, and killed the charioteer. When his body, which fell to the earth, was found by his sisters, the Heliades, they mourned long and bitterly, until at last the Father of Gods, pitying them, changed them into ever-sighing poplars, and their tears into translucent amber.

And so, perhaps because of this legend, the Greeks looked upon amber with superstitious reverence, and even thought that it had a soul. For when it was rubbed, it seemed to live, and to exercise an attraction upon other things distant from it. They likened it to the magnet ; and yet knew it to be different from the loadstone, for in the latter the property of drawing other things to itself was inherent, whereas amber could only be brought into life and activity. It was easier to conceive how a natural body might have its own peculiar properties, however incomprehensible, — just as a tree might grow, — than to imagine how this strange substance, at one time inert, could be brought to life by the same process which would restore vitality to a limb benumbed by cold. Thus they speculated upon an amber life, and an amber soul as its essence.

In the light of our modern knowledge we might perhaps trace farther the chain of ancient speculation. Jupiter's thunderbolt was but another name for the lightning-stroke, and the sequence of events following the tragedy resulted in amber. From amber we can reproduce the lightning in miniature ; so that by some stretch of the imagination we might suppose that the Greeks had a crude conception of electrical storage, and traced the manifestations derived from amber to imprisoned lightning. It is quite certain, however, that those who were initiated in the mystic rites of the ancients clearly understood many of the principles of electricity and magnetism which have been re-discovered within recent years. Professor Schweigger considers that the Vestal fire was electrical, and points out that the "twin fires from the electrical spark are sketched in a very natural manner in the representations of Castor and Pollux on ancient coins." So also it is believed that the ancients knew of the therapeutic effects of electrical currents, and the polarity of electricity and magnetism.

Although these mysteries were jealously guarded from public comprehension, and hence all knowledge of them died with its possessors, Ennemoser in his History of Magic says that "it was not forbidden to make known every thing: some things were explained to the uninitiated. For instance, the uninitiated were made acquainted with amber, and with its property when rubbed." We can conjecture that the uninitiated were thus favored because in any event they would be reasonably certain to find out the phenomenon for themselves. Amber was constantly worn as an amulet and in jewellery; and the friction of garments would produce sufficient excitation to cause it to attract lint or other fine particles which would dim its lustre, and so draw the wearer's attention. And of course, inasmuch as explanations naturally would be sought, it perhaps suited the policy of the magi to attribute the fact to the supernatural qualities of the substance. It is remarkable, however, to note that the knowledge of the electrical properties of amber survived for centuries, doubtless, because the whole world had it, while the great mass of facts which the priests and magi collected fell into utter oblivion; and that this is exactly the reverse of the conditions under which the great bulk of learning which was handed down from antiquity through the dark ages maintained its existence. The mediæval monks and scholars treasured their knowledge of natural science while dwelling amid rude and barbarous peoples, in order that it might be handed down to posterity. The Greek and Egyptian priests, on the other hand, in the midst of the most cultivated peoples that had ever lived, surrounded their discoveries with every sort of misleading myth, until finally they faded into oblivion.

As the world grew older, here and there in the writings of the philosophers reference to this strange property of amber appears. Thales (600 B.C.) mentions it, and, being the earliest writer who has been found to do so, is too often credited with the discovery. Some three hundred years later Theophrastus notes that another body, called *lyncurium*, — supposed to be either tourmaline, or the hyacinth, which looks like amber, —acts in like manner; and Pliny (B.C. 70) refers to the same.

Then there is a great gap of sixteen centuries, with hardly a published word to show that all had not been forgotten. Beckmann quotes from an edition of John Serapion, " Lib. de simplicibus medicinis," published in 1531, a reference to a red stone, "Hager Albuzedi," found in the East, " which when strongly rubbed against the hair of the head attracts chaff as the magnet does iron ;" and perhaps other references exist. The fact however, remained, and was supposed to · be peculiar to amber. No one attempted to explain it. The superstition of the amber soul faded and was forgotten. The phenomena which Pliny called the " awful mysteries of nature " puzzled men's souls; yet to inquire into them suggested only impiety. " A star," says Seneca, " settled on the lance of Gylippus as he was sailing to Syracuse ; and spears have seemed to be on fire in the Roman camp." "About that time," Cæsar records, " there was a very extraordinary appearance in the army of Cæsar. In the month of February, about the second watch of the night, there suddenly arose a thick cloud, followed by a shower of stones ; and the same night, the points of the spears belonging to the fifth legion seemed to take fire." Aristotle, Pliny, Oppian, and Claudius were fully acquainted with the shocks produced by the torpedo. Eustathius, who lived in the fourth century of the Christian era, says that a freedman of Tiberius was cured of the gout by a shock from this fish ; the first-known instance of the application of electricity to medical purposes, and if authentic much more successful than its application in modern times. The same authority asserts that Wolimer, king of the Goths, was able to emit sparks from his body. But all these were wonders beyond human ken and control. The whole science lay in the knowledge of the single fact, that excited amber attracted certain light bodies.

CHAPTER II.

THE DISCOVERIES OF THE EARLY EXPERIMENTERS.

IN the year 1600 Dr. William Gilbert of London, a surgeon to Queen Elizabeth, published his famous work " De Magnete," and then made known that the attractive property of amber, when rubbed, was not inherent to that substance, but existed in some twenty other bodies, such as the precious stones, glass, sealing-wax, sulphur, and resin. Inasmuch as these all acted like amber, Gilbert called them *electrics;* and he described the peculiar phenomenon itself as electricity, deriving the term from the Greek word for amber, *elektron.* It has recently been pointed out, that the Elektra of the Homeric legends possesses certain qualities that would tend to suggest that she is the personification of lightning, and that the resemblance between the names Elektra and *elektron* cannot be accidental. Whether, however, Gilbert was thus anticipated or not, is immaterial. The publication of his work marks the true beginning of the progress of the science ; and its immediate effect was to incite philosophers everywhere to efforts to extend his list of electrics.

Singularly enough, this remarkable treatise was severely condemned by Bacon in the " Novum Organum." Not content with singling it out for citation as a peculiarly striking instance of inconclusive reasoning, and of truth distorted by " preconceived fancies," he elsewhere alludes

to the " electric energy concerning which *Gilbert has told
so many fables.*"   A century and a half later, as we shall
see, these " fables " assumed the form of realities.   The
sweeping censure of so high an authority seems to have
produced its natural effect, and may have had much to do
in materially retarding the development of the infant
science.

To Gilbert's category, Cabæus, an Italian Jesuit, added
the gums, white wax, and gypsum. Then Robert Boyle
got the first glimpse (it was no more) of the electric light,
by noting that a diamond when rubbed became luminous
in the dark.   Then Otto von Guericke, burgomaster of
Magdeburg, and inventor of the air-pump, discovered that
electricity was manifested by repulsion as well as by attraction, and that a globe of sulphur after attracting a
feather repelled the same until the feather had again been
placed in contact with some other substance.

Guericke contrived an apparatus for rotating his sulphur
globe, and succeeded in obtaining sparks therefrom ; and
that was the real genesis of the electric light.   By this
time the attention of the scientific world was aroused,
and other philosophers joined in the investigation of the
curious phenomena.   Boyle, then contemporary with von
Guericke, proved that a suspended piece of rubbed amber, which attracted other bodies to itself, was in turn
attracted by a body brought near it ; and he even went
so far as to maintain that an electrified body threw out
an invisible glutinous substance which laid hold of light
bodies, and, returning to the source from which it ema-
nated, carried them along with it.   Sir Isaac Newton, by
rubbing a flat glass, caused light bodies to jump between
it and the table, and noticed that electric attraction was
thus transmitted through the glass.   A sea-captain named
Grofton excited the dismay of mariners by asserting that

a violent thunder-storm had reversed the polarity of the compass-needles aboard his vessel. Dr. Wall, in 1708, made experiments with large pieces of amber rubbed by wool, and found that " a prodigious number of little crack-lings" was produced, each accompanied by a flash of light. " This light and crackling," says Dr. Wall, " seem in some degree to represent thunder and lightning."

Probably every one has observed the peculiar crackling which follows combing of the hair during dry, cold weather, and the tendency of the " knotted and combined locks to part" under the electrical excitement following the rub-bing of the comb.

Robert Boyle appears to have discovered this ; and he wrote in 1675 this amusing description — intended to be perfectly serious and scientific — of his original experi-ment on " Locks (false) worn by two very Fair Ladies that you know : " " For at some times I observed that they could not keep their Locks from flying to their Cheeks and (though neither of them made any use or had any need of Painting) from sticking there. When one of these Beauties first shew'd me this Experiment, I turn'd it into a Complemental Raillery, as suspecting there might be some trick in it, though I after saw the same thing happen to others Locks too. But as she is no ordinary *Virtuosa*, she very ingeniously remov'd my suspicions and (as I re-quested) gave me leave to satisfie myself further by desir-ing her to hold her warm hand at a convenient distance from one of these Locks taken off and held in the air. For as soon as she did this, the lower end of the Lock which was free applied itself presently to her hand : which seemed the most strange because so great a multitude of Hair would not have been easily attracted by an ordinary Electrical Body."

In this way, for more than a hundred and twenty years

after the publication of Gilbert's work, and at long intervals, isolated phenomena were observed, and a fact here and there gathered. A variety of curious theories had been formulated. Cabæus, in the quaint language of Robert Boyle, "thinks the drawing of light bodies by Jet, Amber, etc., may be accounted for by supposing that the steams that issue, or if I may so speak, sally, out of Amber when heated by rubbing, discuss and expell the neighbouring air;" and that these "Electrical Steams . . . shrinking back swiftly enough to the Amber do in their returns bring along with them such light bodies as they meet with in their way." Then there was the hypothesis "proposed by that Ingenious Gentleman Sir Kenelm Digby, and embraced by the very Learned Dr. Browne," that "Rayes or Files of unctuous steams" were emitted, which became cooled and condensed, and so "shrinking" back, carried light bodies with them. Newton supposed that the excited body emitted an elastic fluid which penetrated glass; and Gravesande and other writers maintained that electricity was fire, which, being inherent to all bodies, became manifest by friction.

In 1720 Stephen Gray, a Charterhouse pensioner, that "most meritorious philosopher" as Tyndall calls him, began a series of investigations which terminated only when he died sixteen years later.

In 1729 Gray experimented with a glass tube stopped by a cork. When the tube was rubbed, the cork attracted light bodies. Gray states that he was "much surprised" at this, and he "concluded that there was certainly an attractive virtue communicated to the cork." "This," says Professor Tyndall, "was the starting-point of our knowledge of electric conduction;" and the same authority gives the following account of Gray's most remarkable experiment: —

"He suspended a long hempen line horizontally by loops of pack-thread, but failed to transmit through it the electric power. He then suspended it by loops of silk, and succeeded in sending the ' attractive virtue ' through seven hundred and sixty-five feet of thread. He at first thought that the silk was effectual because it was thin ; but on replacing a broken silk loop by a still thinner wire, he obtained no action. Finally he came to the conclusion that his loops were effectual, not because they were thin, but because they were *silk*. This was the starting-point of our knowledge of insulation."

Gray died in the midst of his work ; and the report of his last experiments was dictated by him from his death-bed, to the secretary of the Royal Society.

In 1733 Dufay, a French physicist, while experimenting with an electrically excited body, found that a piece of gold-leaf floating in the air was repelled if the excited substance was glass, and attracted if the excited substance was resin. And hence he recognized two kinds of electricity, which were for a long time known respectively as *vitreous* and *resinous*. There is no such real distinction, because by changing the rubbing material the electricity of resin can be obtained upon glass, and *vice versa*. But what we now know as plus or positive electricity is that produced by rubbing glass with silk ; and negative or minus electricity, that due to the rubbing of resin with flannel.

The electrical apparatus of 1730 was, as may readily be imagined, very crude. We reproduce from Dr. Gravesande's treatise of that date, the accompanying representation of an electrical machine of the period. It consists simply of a glass globe G, supported on tubes which are revolved by a belt from the large pulley R, which is rotated by the handle M. One of the tubes has an

open end, and is provided with a stop-cock E.   Through
this tube the air can be exhausted from the interior of

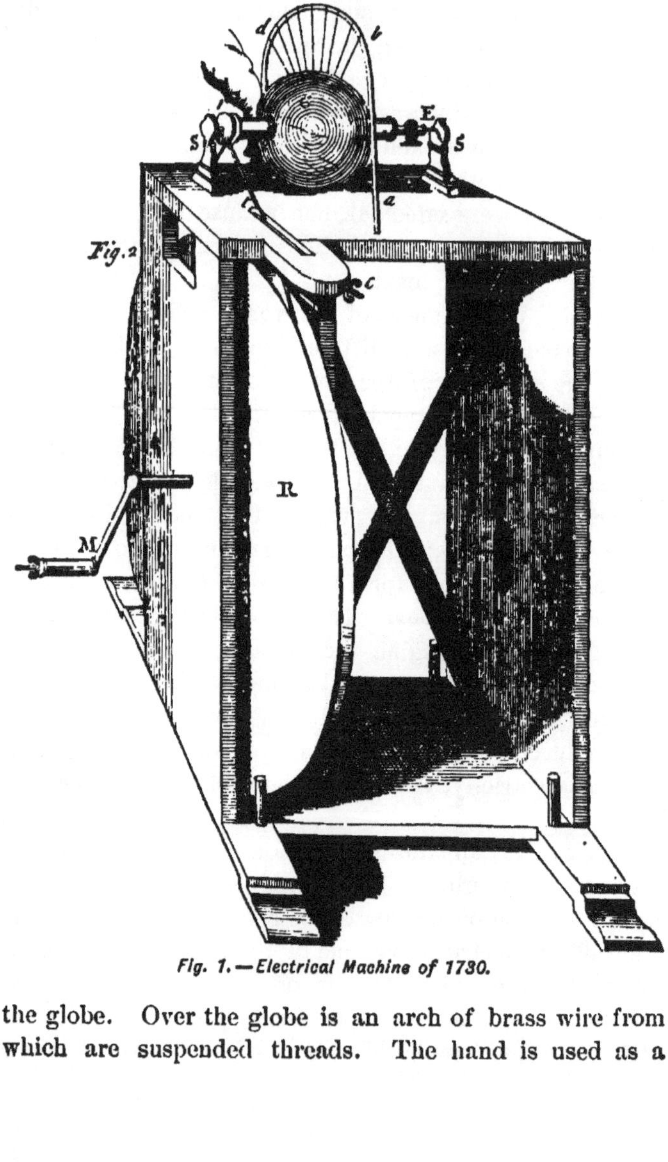

Fig. 1.—Electrical Machine of 1730.

the globe.   Over the globe is an arch of brass wire from
which are suspended threads.   The hand is used as a

rubber, and the machine as shown is intended to demonstrate the following experiment: —

" Whirl the globe, and apply the hand, and immediately the threads will be moved irregularly by the agitation of the air ; but when the glass is heated by the attrition, all the threads are directed toward the centre of the globe, as may be seen in the figure ; and, if the hand be applied a little on one side, or nearer the pole of the globe, the threads will be directed toward that point of the axis which is under the hand. If the air be drawn out of the globe, this whole effect ceases."

This machine had a very disagreeable habit of exploding by reason of the expansion of the air within the glass globe, caused by the heating of the latter by friction.

We have already stated that Otto von Guericke made his electrical machine from a globe of sulphur. For the sulphur globe, Hawksbee and Winkler substituted the glass globe represented in the engraving. The prime conductor, at first a tin tube supported by resin or suspended by silk, and nearly equal in importance to the glass insulator which is to be excited, was not invented until ten years after by Boze of Wittenberg (1741) ; and Winkler of Leipsic suggested a fixed cushion instead of the human hand as a rubber. Still later Gordon of Erfurt substituted a glass cylinder for the globe ; and in 1760 Planta introduced the circular plate of glass still used.

In the year 1745 a discovery was made, which in point of importance overshadowed every thing that had been previously accomplished. And it seems as if the time had come for some great advance. The electrical machine had reached a form in which, with little variation, it has since remained. Large pieces of electrical material had been used to produce manifestations sufficiently potent to suggest thunder and lightning ; and certain properties of the electric fluid, or aura, or whatever it might be, had been more or less perfectly recognized.   Yet, after all, what practical advantage to mankind had been gained?   Curious things had been developed, as wonderful as any thing the conjurers could do; but beyond gratifying the natural taste for the marvellous, and furnishing food for the speculations and material for the lecture-room experiments of a few philosophers, all that had been done had added nothing, so far as then appeared, to that knowledge which directly contributes to human welfare.

CHAPTER III.

THE CAGING OF THE LIGHTNING.

On Oct. 11, 1745, Dean von Kleist of the cathedral of Camin, in Germany, made an experiment which on the following 4th of November he describes in a letter to Dr. Lieberkuhn of Berlin, in the following terms : —

" When a nail or a piece of brass wire is put into a small apothecaries' phial and electrified, remarkable effects follow ; but the phial must be very dry and warm. I commonly rub it over beforehand with a finger on which I put some powdered chalk. If a little mercury or a few drops of spirits of wine be put into it, the experiment succeeds the better. As soon as this phial and nail are removed from the electrifying glass, or the prime conductor to which it hath been exposed is taken away, it throws out a pencil of flame so long that with this burning machine in my hand I have taken about sixty steps in walking about my room ; when it is electrified strongly I can take it into another room, and then fire spirits of wine with it. If while it is electrifying I put my finger or a piece of gold which I hold in my hand to the nail, I receive a shock which stuns my arms and shoulders."

This was the first announcement of the possibility of accumulating electricity.

In the following year Cunæus of Leyden made substantially the same discovery. It caused great wonder and

dread, which arose chiefly from the excited imagination.
Musschenbrock felt the shock, and declared in a letter to
a friend, that he would not take a second one for the crown
of France. Bleeding at the nose, ardent fever, a heavi-
ness of head which endured for days, were all ascribed to
the shock. Boze, on the other hand, seems to have coveted
electrical martyrdom; for he is said to have expressed a
wish to die by the electric shock, "so that an account of
his death might furnish an article for the Memoirs of the
French Academy of Sciences."

Winkler, his coadjutor in the improvement of the electrical machine, "suffered great convulsions through his
body," which "put his blood into agitation;" and his wife,
who took the shock twice, was rendered so weak by it that
she could hardly walk. Nothing daunted, this adventur-
ous lady (who shall say whether from scientific interest or
feminine curiosity?) persisted in being shocked for the
third time; and then her previous ailments were augmented
by the nosebleed.

After the philosophers had got through administering
shocks to themselves and to their immediate relatives, and
had recovered in some measure their mental as well as personal equilibrium, — and it might equally well be added,
their moral balance, for as a matter of fact their reports
as to the force of the shock and its attendant disastrous
effects were all more or less grossly exaggerated, — they
set about seeing what this extraordinary discovery really
amounted to. What Von Kleist actually did was simply
to insert a nail through a cork into a phial into which he
poured a little mercury, spirits, or water. Why this simple contrivance should produce the observed effects, Von
Kleist did not know; but Cunæus and the other Leyden
philosophers solved the problem, and in this way Von
Kleist's apparatus came to be known as the Leyden-jar.

Subsequently the jar was constructed by Dr. Bevis in the form shown in Fig. 2, which is that which it has ever since had. In charging the jar, the outer coating, usually of tin-foil, is connected with the earth; and the inner coating of the same material, by means of the central wire and knob, receives the sparks from an electric machine. The positive electricity from a glass electrical machine, passing to the inner coating, acts inductively across the glass upon the outer coating, and is supposed to at-tract only its negative electricity, while the positive electricity there resident is repelled into the earth, with which the outer coating is connected. In this way two opposite and mutually attracting electricities are separated by the glass. But if a path be provided by which these two electricities can flow to one another, they will do so, and the jar will be discharged. If the outer coating be grasped with one hand, and the knuckle of the other hand be presented to the knob of the jar, the body will then form a conducting path over which this flow can take place; a bright spark will pass between the knob and the knuckle, with a sharp report; and at the same moment a convulsive "shock" will be communicated to the muscles of the wrists, elbows, and shoulders.

Fig. 2. — Leyden-Jar.

In Von Kleist's apparatus, the water or mercury formed the inner conducting coating, and his hand, grasping the bottle, the outer coating which was thus connected to earth through his body. When he touched the nail with his disengaged hand, he completed the path between the inner and outer coatings through his body, and thus received the shock.

Scientists everywhere now began to investigate this phenomenon. Graham caused a number of persons to lay hold of the same metal plate, which was connected with the outer coating of a charged Leyden-jar, and also to grasp a rod by which the jar was discharged. The shock divided itself equally among them. Abbé Nollet procured a detail of one hundred and eighty soldiers, stood them up in a line, and sent shocks through the whole battalion, — a significant commentary on the strength of military discipline, which could make ignorant men face manifestations which disconcerted and agitated the philosophers themselves. But the monks outdid the soldiers : seven hundred and fifty Carthusians formed a line 5,400 feet long, an iron wire extending between each two persons ; when the abbé caused the discharge, the entire company of ecclesiastics "gave a sudden spring, and sustained the shock at the same instant." Apparatus was constructed so that large quantities of electricity could be accumulated, and results hitherto unexpected were obtained. Dr. Watson made experiments to discover through how great a distance the electric shock could be propagated, and in 1747 conveyed it across the River Thames at Westminster Bridge, and finally concluded that " the velocity of the electric matter in passing through a wire 12,276 feet in length is instantaneous." Other investigators killed small animals and birds with powerful discharges from the Leyden-jar.

In 1745 Mr. Peter Collinson of the Royal Society sent a jar to the Library Society of Philadelphia, with instructions how to use it. This fell into the hands of Benjamin Franklin, who at once began a series of electrical experiments. On March 28, 1747, Franklin began his famous letters to Collinson, regarding which Priestley says, " Nothing was ever written upon the subject of electricity which was more generally read and admired in

all parts of Europe. It is not easy to say whether we
are most pleased with the simplicity and perspicuity with
which they are written, the modesty with which the author
proposes every hypothesis of his own, or the noble frank-
ness with which he relates his mistakes when they are
corrected by subsequent experiments." In these letters
he propounded the single-fluid theory of electricity, and
referred all electric phenomena to its accumulation in
bodies in quantities more than their natural share, or to
its being withdrawn from them so as to leave them minus
their proper portion. A body having more than its natural
quantity, he regarded as electrified positively, or *plus;* and
one having less, as electrified negatively or *minus.* On
this theory he explained the action of the Leyden-jar as
it has already been explained above ; and he conceived
the idea of connecting together a number of Leyden-jars,
the outer coating of each being connected to the outer
coating of the next succeeding one, and thus produced
his famous "cascade battery," in which the strength
of the shock was enormously increased. He also discovered that the connecting coatings of the Leyden-jar
"served only, like the armature of the loadstone, to unite
the forces of the several parts, and bring them at once to
any point desired ;" and that the electricity in fact existed
only upon the glass. One of Franklin's letters to Collinson is celebrated for his quaintly humorous proposition
of an "electric feast" to be held on the banks of the
Schuylkill. Whether this ever occurred, is questionable ;
but Franklin's description of it is well worth quoting.
"The hot weather coming on," he says, "when electrical
experiments are not so agreeable, it is proposed to put
an end to them for this season, somewhat humorously,
in a party of pleasure on the banks of the Schuylkill.
Spirits, at the same time, *are to be fired* by a spark sent

from side to side through the river without any other conductor than the water ; an experiment which we some time
since performed to the amazement of many. A turkey
is to be killed for our dinner by the *electric shock*, and
roasted by the *electric jack* before a fire kindled by the
electric bottle; when the healths of all the famous electricians of England, Holland, France, and Germany are
to be drunk in *electrified* bumpers, under a discharge of
guns from the *electrical battery.*" If Franklin's proposal
bordered on the absurd or grotesque, it proves how near
the ridiculous in thought may be to the sublime ; for at
that same period he was formulating the speculations
which ultimately culminated in one of the most audacious
yet most brilliantly successful experiments ever made by
man. More than forty years before, Wall had compared
the crackling from his rubbed amber to thunder and lightning ; Nollet in France had not long before quaintly
said, "If any one should take upon him to prove from a
well-connected comparison of phenomena, that thunder is
in the hands of Nature what electricity is in ours, and
that the wonders which we now exhibit at our pleasure
are little imitations of these great effects which frighten
us ; I avow that this idea, if it was well supported, would
give me a great deal of pleasure." Meanwhile the facts
derived from experiment were rapidly multiplying, which
showed the similarity between the powerful sparks of the
Leyden battery and the lightning flash. The exaggerated accounts of Musschenbroek and others who had
received the shocks went to prove that increase in force
or strength would cause death. Experiments upon birds
and small animals did produce death as sudden as that
due to the lightning stroke. Franklin himself was twice
struck senseless by shocks ; and he afterwards sent the
discharge of two large jars through six robust men, who

fell to the ground, and got up again without knowing
what had happened, neither feeling nor hearing the discharge.

While all these facts convinced Franklin of the identity
of lightning and electricity, they demonstrated at the
same time to him the imminent danger which must attend
any experiment which would serve as proof. One scarcely
knows which to admire most, the lucid reasoning wherein
he states his convictions to Collinson, or the cool courage
with which he faced not only possible death, but the
ridicule of the world, which would be heaped upon his
memory in event of failure. The result would brand him
as a madman and a suicide, or raise him to the topmost
pinnacle of human fame. The account given by Dr.
Stuber of Philadelphia, an intimate personal friend of
Franklin, and published in one of the earliest editions of
the works of the great philosopher, is as follows : —

"The plan which he had originally proposed was to
erect on some high tower, or other elevated place, a sen-
try-box, from which should rise a pointed iron rod, insulated by being fixed in a cake of resin. Electrified clouds
passing over this would, he conceived, impart to it a
portion of their electricity, which would be rendered evident to the senses by sparks being emitted when a key,
a knuckle, or other conductor was presented to it. Philadelphia at this time offered no opportunity of trying an
experiment of this kind. Whilst Franklin was waiting
for the erection of a spire, it occurred to him that he
might have more ready access to the region of clouds by
means of a common kite. He prepared one by attaching
two cross-sticks to a silk handkerchief, which would not
suffer so much from the rain as paper. To his upright
stick was fixed an iron point. The string was, as usual,
of hemp, except the lower end which was silk. Where

the hempen string terminated, a key was fastened. With this apparatus, on the appearance of a thunder-gust approaching, he went into the common, accompanied by his son, to whom alone he communicated his intentions, well knowing the ridicule which, too generally for the interest of science, awaits unsuccessful experiments in philosophy. He placed himself under a shed to avoid the rain. His kite was raised. A thunder-cloud passed over it. No signs of electricity appeared. He almost despaired of success, when suddenly he observed the loose fibres of his string move toward an erect position. He now pressed his knuckle to the key, and received a strong spark. How exquisite must his sensations have been at this moment! On his experiment depended the fate of his theory. Doubt and despair had begun to prevail, when the fact was ascertained in so clear a manner, that even the most incredulous could no longer withhold their assent. Repeated sparks were drawn from the key, a phial was charged, a shock given, and all the experiments made which are usually performed with electricity." And thus the identity of lightning and electricity was proved.

Meanwhile, Franklin, in his letters to Collinson, had already outlined his proposed experiments. Collinson offered the letters to the Royal Society for publication, but encountered a contemptuous refusal. The suggestion that pointed rods would "probably draw the electrical fire silently out of a cloud before it came nigh enough to strike, and thereby secure us from that most sudden and terrible mischief," was received with open derision. But some years later the Royal Society elected Franklin an honorary member, and decreed him their highest honor, the Copley medal. Franklin's letters were, however, published by Dr. Fothergill. They went through five editions in London, and attracted the attention of all Europe.

An incorrect French translation falling into the hands of Buffon, that celebrated philosopher repeated the experiments successfully, and commended them to his friend M. d'Alibard. A report of the wonderful results reached Louis XV., then King of France; and at his request further experiments were undertaken. The notice of the king now acted as a stimulus to the French scientists; and three of them, Buffon, De Lor, and D'Alibard, erected apparatus for attracting the lightning at different localities. It is a curious fact, that despite the eagerness of these philosophers, each to outstrip the other in being the first to obtain actual results, disappointment awaited them all. D'Alibard employed an old soldier, named Coiffier, to help build his apparatus, and subsequently to watch it. It so happened that the long-expected thunder-storm came along during D'Alibard's absence; and Coiffier, who had no idea of the danger of receiving the spark, determined to experiment on his own account. Accordingly, he mounted the insulated stool which had been prepared, and presented a wire to D'Alibard's rod, obtaining a fine spark, — and then another. He at once called all his neighbors, and some one ran in search of the parish priest. The latter was seen making his way to the apparatus in such undignified haste, that it was immediately surmised that the daring Coiffier had fallen a victim to his bold experiment; and accordingly the good father found himself the leader of a miscellaneous mob of villagers. Regardless of the pouring rain and hail, the crowd surrounded the machine, and there in open-mouthed wonder watched the priest himself draw sparks from the rod. Both the clergyman and the soldier managed to get lightly struck, — so lightly, that, in their absorbed attention to the sparks, they scarcely noticed the occurrence until afterwards, when each, feeling stinging pains in his

fore-arm, searched for the cause, and found bright red
stripes on the flesh just as if a few sound lashes had
been administered. It is very likely that the villagers
saw no good in these supernatural manifestations; and
when they all perceived about the persons of the priest
and his companion the marked odor of the ozone generated, somewhat sulphurous in character, they were con-
firmed in their idea that the powers of the nether world
had been invoked. To Coiffier, however, remained the
honor of being the first to receive the spark. This was
on May 10, 1752, about a month before Franklin's famous experiment; and, in many French works, priority as
the original discoverer is for this reason patriotically
claimed for D'Alibard. There is no doubt, however, that
D'Alibard obtained his instructions from Franklin's letters, as he himself afterwards frankly admitted that he
merely followed the track which Franklin had pointed
out.

The European philosophers now remitted experiments
to find out how strong the shock of the Leyden-jar was,
and turned with increased enthusiasm to measuring the
power of the lightning stroke. And then the caged lightning found its first victim. In the engraving of the old
electrical machine, Fig. 1, there are shown a number of
threads which hang from a curved support over the glass
globe, and which are attracted by the globe when excited
so as to assume an inclined position. Professor Richmann
of St. Petersburg had constructed an " electrical gnomon "
on this same principle; his idea being, to measure the
strength of the lightning discharge by observing the angle
of inclination assumed by a suspended thread electrified
thereby. He arranged on the roof of his house an iron
rod which he insulated from the adjacent part of the building; and to this rod he fastened a chain which led down

into his laboratory, and was connected to an insulated support from which hung his thread, the end of which extended over a dial. Richmann had invited an engraver named Solokow to witness the working of the apparatus ; and as a thunder-storm gathered, the two men eagerly watched the movement of the thread. Suddenly a peal of thunder of terrific loudness was heard. Richmann bent forward to observe his thread more closely ; and "as he stood in that posture, a great white and bluish fire appeared between the rod of the electrometer and his head. At the same time a sort of steam or vapor arose, which entirely benumbed the engraver, and made him sink to the ground." The apparatus was torn to pieces, the doors of the room thrown down, and the house violently shaken. Richmann's wife, running into the room, found her husband sitting on a chest which happened to be immediately behind him. He was stone dead, bearing no mark beyond a red spot on his forehead. His shoe was ripped open and his waistcoat singed, showing that the deadly current had passed through his body. Solokow was removed insensible, but subsequently recovered. The luckless experimenter had forgotten to provide an earth connection whereby the charge might have passed harmlessly to the ground. In the absence of this, the enormous electromotive force of the current was sufficient to enable it to leap over the interval of air between the electrometer and Richmann's head, and so to be led through his body.

Of course there were not wanting emotional people to draw all sorts of warnings from Richmann's fate. Franklin's proposition to erect lightning-rods which would convey the lightning to the ground, and so protect the buildings to which they were attached, found abundant opponents, who agreed with Abbé Nollet, that it was "as impious to ward off Heaven's lightnings as for a child to

ward off the chastening rod of its father." Others, whose
religious scruples did not carry them quite so far, went to
the opposite extreme, and concluded that if there was any
impiety about lightning-rods, it lay in the fact that they
invited the "chastening rod," and that it was madness
to "tempt Providence" in any such way. Nevertheless,
public opinion became settled, that whether lightning-rods
were impious because they opposed the decree of Providence, or suicidal because they induced Providence to
make decrees, the fact remained that they did protect
buildings ; and as long as they did that, the theological
questions raised might be left to time for settlement.
Then the philosophers raised a new controversy as to
whether the conductors should be blunt or pointed ; Franklin, Cavendish, and Watson advocating points, and Wilson
blunt ends. That wise monarch whose scientific acumen
stood nonplussed before the problem of how apples are
got into dumplings, graciously considered the question, because it affected his own royal abode, Buckingham Palace,
and, after much balancing of the pros and cons, reached
the sage conclusion that the pointed conductors "were a
republican device calculated to injure his Majesty,"
whereupon he ordered them removed from the palace, and
ball conductors substituted. The same public opinion
which ran counter to him when he tried rather fruitlessly
to repress, some years later, numerous other republican devices calculated to injure his Majesty on the opposite side
of the Atlantic, asserted itself here. "The king's changing his pointed conductors for blunt ones," said Franklin,
" is a small matter to me. If I had a wish about them,
it would be that he would reject them altogether as in-
effectual. For it is only since he thought himself and
his family safe from the thunder of heaven, that he has
dared to use his own thunder in destroying his innocent

subjects." The logic of experiment, however, showed the advantage of pointed conductors ; and people persisted then in preferring them, as they have done ever since.

We have now traced, though very briefly, the progress of knowledge of electricity, from the germ of the science which lay hidden for thousands of years in amber, like the insects so often found in that substance, — and yet unlike them, for it possessed immortality, — up to the first practical application of that knowledge to human use and benefit. The lightning had been caged. The mighty force, which since the creation of mankind had aroused but feelings of awe and terror, could now be confined and examined, or diverted at will from its path of destruction. The wise men of the eighteenth century had captured the electrical Pegasus : it remained for the wiser men of the nineteenth to yoke him to the plough.

CHAPTER IV.

ELECTRICITY IN HARNESS.

THE death of Richmann, and the potent effects of even small discharges of electricity upon the human body, caused, as may be well imagined, much speculation as to the part which an electric discharge could be made to take in curing the ills that flesh is heir to. The electric machine was of course the only available means of artificially producing the current; and the modern practitioner can easily figure to himself the unhappy experiences of patients who were subjected to its unregulated and powerful discharges.

Between those who sought to use electricity as a nostrum for the cure of all ailments, and those who investigated its action physiologically, there was a wide difference. Through the latter class of investigators many discoveries of great value were made, and, finally, one of the utmost importance. Beccaria and others meanwhile observed the effects of the electric discharge upon the muscles, and had noted that those of the leg of a cock were strongly contracted when a shock passed through them.

In 1786 Luigi Galvani, medical lecturer at the University of Bologna, while engaged upon investigations similar to those of Beccaria, prepared some frogs' legs, with the object of observing whether any effect would be produced upon them by the electricity of the atmosphere. To this end, after carefully skinning the legs, he hung them upon a hook which protruded from the railing of his balcony. He stood watching them for some time, but no results showed themselves. Finally, disappointed, he lifted them from the hook; and then, while in the act of so doing, he noticed to his astonishment that the very effects, the peculiar muscular contractions, which he expected the atmospheric electricity would cause, were taking place. As it was evident that the surrounding atmosphere had no part in the phenomenon, he at once sought for the concealed cause; and finally he found that the limbs contracted whenever the iron railing touched their moist surface, their contact meanwhile with the hook, which was of copper, being still maintained. Conjecturing that the hook and railing, of course, as such, had nothing to do with the matter, he made a metallic arc, formed of two pieces of iron and copper; and with this he soon found that it was necessary simply to bring one metal into contact with a nerve or with the end of the spine, and the other into contact with a muscle of the leg, to produce immediately muscular contractions.

Galvani came to the conclusion that the electricity of which he had observed the effects resided in the muscles, which received their supply from the nerves and blood; and in 1791 he published his celebrated work on the subject. If people believed that electricity was a valuable remedy before this, they now began enthusiastically to accept the shock as a universal panacea. Du Bois Reymond says, that wherever frogs were to be found, and where two different kinds of metal could be procured, everybody was anxious to see the mangled limbs of frogs brought to life in this wonderful way. The physiologists believed that at length they could realize their visions of a vital power. The physicians whom Galvani had some-

what thoughtlessly led on with attempts to explain all
kinds of nervous diseases, as sciatica, tetanus, and epi-
lepsy, began to believe that no cure was impossible.

It is a curious circumstance in matters of invention,
that discoveries of the most important nature have been
frequently made by people, who, being unable to realize
their importance, have passed them by, leaving them to be
made over again by others.   The electrical effects of dissimilar metals upon animal substance had been observed
by Sulzer, a German investigator, some twenty-three years
before Galvani made his experiments.   Sulzer applied the
two metals, one above and the other below the tongue,
and then on bringing them into contact perceived the
peculiar sour taste.   He ascribed this sensation to some
vibratory motion, excited by the contact of the metals,
and communicated to the nerves of the tongue ; and then,
content with this loose and fanciful explanation, he announced the fact in 1767, in a work entitled "The General
Theory of Pleasures," where it remained wholly unnoticed
until long after Galvani's discovery had aroused the attention of the world.   Galvani's discovery was also to some
extent anticipated by Cotugno, a Neapolitan professor of
anatomy, who in 1786 published the curious statement
that one of his pupils, feeling a sharp pain in the lower
part of his leg, clapped his hand upon the spot, and 'captured a mouse which had bit him.   The little animal, after
being killed, was made a subject for dissection.   During
this proceeding the pupil " accidentally touched the dia-
phragmatic nerve with his scalpel, and then received a
shock strong enough to make him snatch away his hand."
Cotugno's report attracted considerable attention throughout Italy, and, it is said, caused further investigations to
be made by Vassalli, who formulated the odd theory that
nature accumulates electricity in certain parts of animals,

and that they can draw upon this supply at will. It is quite certain, however, that the work of both Cotugno and Sulzer had been forgotten when Galvani's discovery was made; and the meagre suggestions published by them detract nothing from the honor due the Bolognese philosopher. But Galvani reaped neither profit nor glory in his lifetime. The Cisalpine Republic ordered him to take a certain oath entirely contrary to his political and religious convictions, and, on his refusal, stripped him of his positions and titles. Thus reduced to poverty, he retired to his brother's house, and, it is said, fell into a state of lethargy, whence the tardy retraction by the Government of its unjust decree failed to arouse him, and in which he died. Only six years ago, Bologna erected a statue to his memory, in one of her principal squares, and so made that usual reparation of the public to unappreciated genius.

Some two years after Galvani's results and theories had been published, Alessandro Volta, a professor in the University of Pavia, strongly opposed his deductions.

Volta was then one of the foremost electricians of the day. He had invented the electrophorus and the electrical condenser by which small charges of electricity were accumulated. Volta maintained that Galvani's pretended animal electricity was developed simply by the contact of two different metals; and thus began a controversy which lasted long after Galvani's death in 1798. Its outcome was the invention of the voltaic pile, which was contrived by Volta as a means of proving his theory. He soldered together two disks, one of copper (c) and one of zinc (z).

Fig. 3. — Volta's Pile.

Between these he placed circular pieces of woollen cloth (h), moistened with a solution of common salt or diluted sulphuric acid. Several sets of disks thus arranged were

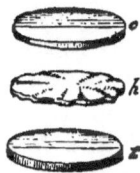

placed one above the other; each pair of disks in the pile was separated from the next pair by a moist conductor. A pile composed of a number of such pairs of disks will produce electricity enough to give quite a perceptible shock, if the top and bottom disk, or wires connected with them, be touched simultaneously with the moist fingers.

Volta's next step was the invention of the cup form of battery. He arranged a number of cups, filled either with brine or dilute acid, into which dipped a number of compound strips, half zinc and half copper; the zinc portion of one strip dipping into one cup, while the copper portion dipped into the other. In each cup, therefore, there was a copper plate and a zinc plate, separated by a conducting fluid; and this is in substance the voltaic cell of to-day.

In discussing the sources of electricity, we shall advert to the theory and operation of this great invention which marks the beginning of a new era in the progress of electrical science. Even as Von Kleist and Franklin may be said to have caged the lightning, so Volta tamed it. He made electricity manageable. He reduced the infinite rapidity of the lightning stroke to the comparatively slow but enormously powerful current, which in the future was destined to carry men's words from one end of the world to the other, and to produce the dazzling light inferior only to the solar ray; and the recognition accorded him might well have satisfied his highest ambition. In marked contrast to the fate of the broken-hearted Galvani, it was Volta's fortune to be called to Paris by Napoleon, then nearing the zenith of his glory, in order to explain his discoveries before the assembled philosophers of France. The First Consul himself presided; and when Volta's demonstration was completed, it was Napoleon who proposed that the rules of the Academy should be suspended, and that the gold medal of the Institute immediately should be awarded Volta in testimony of the gratitude of the French nation. On the same day two thousand crowns were sent to Volta from the national treasury; and, as a final and lasting honor, Napoleon founded the award of an annual medal of the value of three thousand francs for the best experiment in electricity, and a prize of sixty thousand francs to him who should give electricity or magnetism, by his researches, an impulse comparable to that which it received from the discoveries of Franklin and Volta.

And yet, singularly enough, we speak almost instinctively of the galvanic, seldom of the voltaic, cell, — as if posterity had been guided by sympathy for the unfortunate, rather than by a sense of justice to the favored, discoverer. Such words as "galvanize" and "galvanic," possessing even a figurative meaning, are in every-day speech. Volta's name is embalmed only in the technicalities of the science.

Among those who had studied deepest into the phenomena of galvanic electricity was Hans Christian Oersted, a Danish physicist, and professor of physics in the University of Copenhagen. Oersted's researches led him to suspect the identity of magnetism and electricity, but for a long time no means of experimentally proving the fact revealed itself. The expedient had been tried of placing the two poles of a battery, as highly charged as possible, in a parallel line with the poles of a magnetic needle, without results. In one of the reports of the Smithsonian Institute, the story of his discovery is thus graphically told: "Fortune, it might be said, ceased to be blind at the moment when to Oersted was allotted the privilege of first divining that it was not electricity in repose accumulated at the two poles of a charged battery, but electricity in

movement along the conductor by which one of the poles
is discharged into the other, which would exert an action
on the magnetic needle.   While thinking of this (it was
during the animation of a lecture before the assembled
pupils), Oersted announces to them what he is about to
try : he takes a magnetic needle, places it near the electric
battery, waits till the needle has arrived at a state of rest ;
then seizing the conjunctive wire traversed by the current
of the battery, he places it above the magnetic needle,
carefully avoiding any manner of collision.   The needle —
every one plainly sees it — the needle is at once in motion.
The question is resolved.   Oersted has crowned, by a
great discovery, the labors of his whole precious life.''

On July 21, 1820, the discovery was announced, that a
galvanic current passing through a wire placed horizontally
above and parallel to an ordinary compass-needle, will
cause that needle to sway on its axis to the east or west,
according to the direction of the current through the wire.
Oersted's discovery may be said to have pointed the way
to the great applications of electricity to human use ; for
it showed that energy in the form of electricity could be
converted into energy in the form of mechanical motion.

The discovery of the electro-magnet lay but a step beyond, — a short step, — and it was quickly taken.   And
then opened the era of electricity at work, — the era when
the discoverer too frequently finds his sole reward in the
applause of his compeers, and when the world lavishes its
honors and wealth upon the fortunate inventor.   This is
the era in which we live.

CHAPTER V.

THE GALVANIC BATTERY, AND THE CONVERSION OF CHEMICAL ENERGY INTO ELECTRICAL ENERGY.

WHAT is electricity? No one knows. It seems to be one manifestation of the energy which fills the universe, and which appears in a variety of other forms, such as heat, light, magnetism, chemical affinity, mechanical motion, etc. For the purposes of convenient thinking, it is well to consider the electrical current as a fluid, because it apparently follows certain laws of fluids.

In its usual form, the galvanic cell consists of any two dissimilar conducting substances subjected to the action of a third substance capable of chemically attacking but one of them, or of attacking one in less degree than the other. There is a containing vessel, in which is placed a liquid called the electrolyte; and in this liquid are plunged the two conducting substances, usually in solid form, which are called the elements, one of which is attackable by the liquid, and the other non-attackable or less attackable. When the two conducting bodies are connected by a wire of conducting material, then an electrical current will circulate, and will proceed from the body that is attacked to the body that is not attacked, by way of the liquid, and thence back to the attacked body by the wire. The path thus traversed by the current is its circuit. If the circuit is anywhere interrupted, the current stops.

The diagram (Fig. 4) will make this quite clear. Here the wires are attached to the two bodies, immersed in a liquid which will chemically attack one of them. The current then circulates in the direction of the arrow, from *A* the attacked body to *B* the non-attacked body, and thence back through the connecting wire.

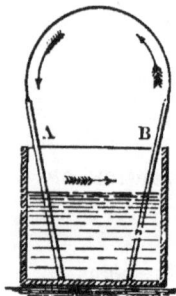

Fig. 4.

Almost every branch of science nowadays has its own language, made up of its technical terms, which in time become absorbed into general speech. This is fast becoming the case with the language of electricity. Amperes and volts and ohms are no longer possessed of meaning only to the initiated, but are taking their place among such every-day standards as pounds and gallons and inches. Although this little work makes no pretence to be a treatise, it is believed that a plain statement of some significations will be of service to the reader as a help to a clearer comprehension of the applications of electricity hereafter described.

If we run or walk, or saw wood or pump water, we are conscious after a time of having exerted ourselves. We have apparently expended certain of our bodily energy in accomplishing something against an opposing force. That is to say, we have done work. Before beginning the task, we were conscious of an ability to undertake it. At the end of the task, comes a sense of fatigue which may be sufficiently strong to demonstrate our inability to repeat the same labor until a period of rest and recuperation intervenes. At the outset, therefore, we possess a power, ability, or *potential*, to exert so much energy. After the exertion, we have not this power, because we have expended the energy in the form of bodily motions, against the opposing forces of friction or gravity. As we have already stated, electricity is simply one form of energy, and when it is exerted against opposition it does work. But, like ourselves, in order to do work, it must acquire a certain condition.

If an athlete is about to enter into an exhausting contest, he trains himself to that end ; and by dint of exercise, judicious fare, etc., he brings his muscles and other organs into a condition competent to the great exertion before him. His *potential*, his capacity to do the work, is thus enhanced. And so in general, any sort of education, whether mental or physical, simply has for its object the raising of the potential of the brain or the muscles, to accomplish certain ends. We have constantly before us examples of natural forces under varying potential. A hot iron must acquire a high temperature before it will burn inflammable bodies, a still higher one that it may be welded, and still higher that it may melt. Water must be carried to a high elevation before, by its fall, it can turn a wheel. The steam in a boiler must reach a certain pressure before it can move the engine piston. And so also electricity, before it can do work, must reach a certain condition, analogous in some degree to temperature and pressure.

Suppose we had a tank of water at *A* (Fig. 5), elevated above the ground. If we connect a pipe *B* to it, the water will run down. What determines the flow? Simply the elevation of the water. Again, take two tanks, one not as high as the other, but both higher than the ground. The water of course flows from the highest one *A*, to the lower one *B*, and so to the earth. The water flows from *A* to *B* simply because of their difference in height ; and this difference determines the flow of water from one tank to the other, or from either tank to the ground. Therefore we say of water, that its ability to do work by exerting pressure (its *potential*) depends on its elevation.

So of electricity. A body may be electrified up to a certain potential. For convenience the earth is considered as of zero or no potential. ·Then, if by any material capable of conducting electricity we connect the electrified body to the earth, the conditions will be the same as in the case of

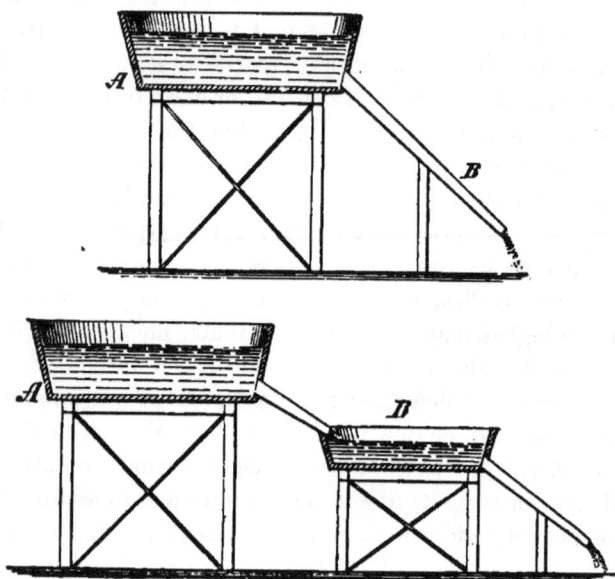

Fig. 5.

the tank of water (Fig. 5) : the electricity will flow from the electrified body to the earth. Again, if a body electrified to a high potential communicate with one electrified to a low potential, then the electricity (as in the case of the water between the tanks *A* and *B* in Fig. 5) will flow from the body at high potential to the body at low potential. There is a force which moves the electricity from one point to another, analogous to the force of gravity which makes water run down hill. That force is commonly called *electro-motive force*, or, as it is sometimes termed, electrical pressure.

We have said that work is energy exerted against an opposing force, or, in other words, against a resistance. This resistance, in the case of water, may be due to friction against the sides of a pipe, or to the opposition to the flow offered by an interposed water-wheel which drives machinery. Electricity in motion in the same way does work, and that which opposes its motion is technically called the *resistance*.

Certain bodies, as glass and India rubber, offer very great resistance to the electric flow : these are known as *insulators*. Others offer very little resistance, and these are termed *conductors*.

In order to maintain a constant flow or current of electricity, there must, as we have seen, be a difference of potential between two points between which a conductor extends ; and this difference of potential must be kept up, otherwise the current would simply equalize itself at both points, just as water will rise to its own level and then cease flowing. The current is urged along the conductor by its electro-motive force, and it is opposed by whatever resistance lies in its path. The greater the electro-motive force in proportion to the resistance, the greater will be the strength of the current ; or, to use the water analogy again, the more gallons of water (for example) will flow through the pipe in a given time. Conversely, the greater the resistance, the more opposition the current will meet, and hence the weaker it will be.

This simple relation of electro-motive force and resistance is the fundamental law of electricity in motion, discovered by Professor Ohm, a distinguished German physicist.

Consequently there are three things about any electrical current to be known : namely, its electro-motive force, or pressure ; the resistance which it encounters ; and the strength of the current, which depends upon these.

We measure steam or water pressure in pounds per square inch, heat by thermometric degrees, distances by feet and inches, and so on. Electro-motive force is measured in volts. A *volt* is very nearly the pressure yielded by a certain standard galvanic cell, usually the Daniell hereafter described. The term has also a very accurate mathematical signification, which need not be discussed here.

Resistance is measured in *ohms*. A column of mercury one millimetre in cross section, and 106.2 centimetres in length, has a resistance of one ohm ; but, for convenience, it may be remembered that ordinary iron telegraph-wire has a resistance of about 13 ohms to a mile.

An electrical current having an electro-motive force of one volt, traversing a resistance of one ohm, is said to have a strength of one ampere.

Here we diverge a little from the water analogy. If we referred to water, we should say that water under so many pounds pressure per inch, going through a pipe of a certain diameter, is delivered at the rate of so many gallons (for example) per minute. If we had some one word which meant " gallons per minute," that would correspond to *ampere*. When a current of one ampere strength flows for one second, the quantity of electricity delivered is called one *coulomb*. A current of the strength of one-tenth ampere will not yield a quantity of electricity equal to a coulomb until it has flowed ten seconds.

To recapitulate in briefer terms : Electro-motive force means electrical pressure. Resistance has its obvious meaning. Electro-motive force is not measured in pounds per square inch like steam or water pressure, but in volts; and a volt is the pressure given by one standard cell.

Resistance is measured in ohms, and an ohm answers to the resistance offered by four hundred and sixty feet of ordinary telegraph-wire, approximately. Strength of current is measured in amperes. Speaking of a water-wheel, we say we need a current flowing at the rate of so many gallons per minute to drive it. Speaking of an electric lamp, we say we need a current of from one to fifty amperes to keep it glowing. The term "coulomb" is far less employed in practice; but it may be in the end most familiar of all, for when the electric light comes into use in dwellings, we shall pay for our electrical supply at so much per thousand coulombs, for example, as we now pay for gas at so much per thousand cubic feet.

To return now to the galvanic battery: It is not necessary here to review the various theories suggested to account for its behavior. These are all in the regular treatises; and whether the current be due to contact of dissimilar substances, or to chemical action in the cell, was a subject warmly discussed by the grandfathers of the present generation. It is better for present purposes to take the facts as we find them, and look upon the cell in the light of what we see happening in it; and, of these happenings, the principal ones necessarily attend the development of the current, and essential thereto is the chemical action on one of the bodies, or so-called elements, therein. In fact, any chemical re-action which occurs between conducting substances may be utilized to generate electric currents. The chemical affinity both supplies and measures exactly the electro-motive force.

There are some very curious but important facts now to be noted about galvanic cells and their currents. The size of the cell has nothing to do with the electrical pressure

yielded, — the electro-motive force. A cell the size of
a percussion-cap will give just as high an electro-motive
force as a cell as big as the distributing reservoir in New-
York City. Electro-motive force, as we have stated, depends on difference of potential ; difference of potential
exists in all dissimilar electrified bodies. Whether they
are large bodies or small ones, is beside the question : just
as the fact that the pressure of water, due to its flow from
a reservoir to a plain beneath, is not influenced at all by
the area of the reservoir, but by the height of the water-
level above the plain. Water-pressure is the same per
foot of vertical height, no matter whether the column is at
its base a square inch or a square mile in area. The two
connecting bodies in the cell, when one is attackable and
attacked by the liquid, are at different potential : that of
the attacked body is the highest. The current then flows
to the non-attacked body through the conducting liquid,
and then back by the wire to the attacked body. The
constant chemical attack keeps the current flowing. A
current of water will flow from a high place to a low place
by gravity, but it will not flow up hill again unless work
is done to force it up. So, in a cell, the current will flow
from high potential to low potential, but not back again.
Work is required to send it back, and this the chemical
action supplies.

When we warm our houses, or drive a steam-engine, we
know that the amount of heat we get in the first case, or
power in the second, depends upon how much coal we
burn, other things being equal. The burning of coal is
simply the chemical action between the carbon of the fuel
and the oxygen of the air. So, in a galvanic cell, we burn
the attacked element. As we convert coal into ashes of
no further use in the furnace, to produce heat, we convert
the zinc of the cell into another substance of no further

use in the cell to produce electricity. Through the steam boiler and engine we can convert chemical action into mechanical work, which we can apply to drive locomotives or steamships or machinery.

The galvanic cell converts chemical action into electricity. The amount of work realized in one case, and of electricity in the other, depends on the amount of fuel, whether coal or zinc, consumed. If, then, in the galvanic cell we burn twice as much zinc in a given time, we shall have a current twice as strong. We can do this by making the attacked body in the cell larger, so as to expose double the area to the attack.

Hence it appears, that, while the size of the bodies in the cell has no bearing on the pressure of the current, it has a very material bearing on the strength of it. It is, as we have said, so far as the pressure is concerned, immaterial whether two water columns of the same height press on bases of a square inch or a square mile in area; but the strength of the two currents, the gallons flowing down per minute, will be enormously different. Consequently, when we want high-pressure electricity, we put into the cell bodies which are, or will be, of widely different potential; we look to the nature of the bodies. When we want great strength of current, we look to their dimensions.

In practice, however, we do not make huge cells, chiefly because of their cumbrousness and difficulty to handle. We can increase either the electro-motive force, or the strength of the current, by using several cells of convenient size, and connecting them together differently. Thus, in Fig. 6, each cell is supposed to give an electro-motive force of one volt. If we connect the wire of the attacked element in one cell to the unattacked element in the next, and so on, we shall add together the several electro-motive forces of each, and obtain an aggregate pressure of four volts, while the strength of the current

Fig. 6.

will remain the same as that of one cell. If, however, we connect all the attacked elements together by one wire,

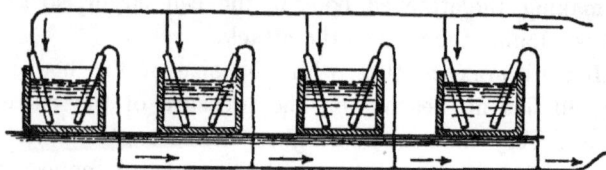

Fig. 7.

and all the non-attacked elements together by another, as in Fig. 7, then we shall really have quadrupled the size of the elements; and we shall have a current four times as strong, while its pressure will remain at one volt.

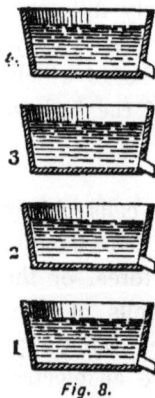

Fig. 8.

Take the water analogy again. Suppose we start with a tank of water at the level marked 1 in Fig. 8. Then the water will flow out with a certain pressure, depending on the elevation of the tank. So in a given cell the current will flow out with a given electro-motive force, dependent on the materials of the cell. Let us now elevate the tank to position 2, then we have doubled the water pressure; if we carry it to the position 3, still higher, we may make the pressure three times, and if to position 4, four times, as great. We do the same thing electrically by adding cells as shown in Fig. 6. The quantity of water or of electricity yielded remains the same, but its pressure increases. Suppose, however, that we start again with our tank of water, which, however, contains say but ten gallons, which it will discharge completely in a minute. If we place beside it three other tanks of equal capacity, and at the same elevation, each one will discharge ten gallons a minute, or all together forty gallons a minute. This is the parallel case to that of connecting the cells as in Fig. 9. The pressure of water or electricity re-

Fig. 9.

mains the same; but more water or electricity is discharged in a given time.

Or, to put this in a more practical form, suppose we have a pipe plenty large enough to carry all the water we need, in a given time, to the top of a house, but find the water will not come up. We increase the water pressure, and the water rises to the desired height. That is the first case. Suppose, again, that we have a water-wheel to turn, but only a little stream delivered, say, from a small pipe, with great force. We increase the size of the pipe, and get more water. That is the second case. This makes the foregoing facts easy to remember.

When the current in a cell travels from the attacked element to the non-attacked element, through the liquid in the cell, it meets with resistance; and so, also, when the current travels around from the non-attacked element to the attacked element, by the wire outside the cell, it meets with still further resistance.

Here, then, are two places where the current will meet obstacles; one inside the cell, and the other outside of it. The resistance offered by the liquid inside the cell is called the internal resistance; and that of the circuit outside the cell, the external resistance, — as illustrated in Fig. 10.

Fig. 10.

The external resistance we control. It may be due to many miles of telegraph-wire, or to the coils of an electric motor, or the filament of an electric lamp, or to any other path which we provide for the current, in traversing which it does the work we desire.

The internal resistance, however, is peculiar to the cell itself; and whatever work the current has to do to get through this may be taken as wasted energy. Consequently it is necessary to make the internal resistance of the cell as small as possible; and to do this there are several ways.

It requires much less work to swim ten feet than twenty: so in like manner, if we shorten the path of the current through the liquid, it will have less liquid to go through, and hence meet less resistance. Therefore we bring the two solid bodies, or elements, in the cell, as near together as possible without touching.

If, however, for any reason we find it impracticable or undesirable thus to bring the plates close together, we can leave the thickness of the intervening liquid as it is, but increase the size (surface area) of the plates. Then more of the attackable body will be attacked in a given time; and, as we have already seen, we shall have a stronger current, which will more easily overcome the resistance.

In the first case, therefore, we actually diminish the resistance by diminishing the thickness of the liquid, the strength of the current remaining the same. In the second case, we neither increase nor diminish the resistance; but we augment the current strength, so that the obstacle is more easily overcome.

It is very like journeying by railway from one place to another. We can take a slow train by a short road, or a fast train over a long road.

There is one more very important fact about the galvanic cell, which is yet to be noticed. If we make a simple cell, say of a plate of copper (the unattacked element), a plate of zinc (the attacked element), and water, we shall find, that after a very short time the electromotive force of the cell runs down, and that the current very perceptibly weakens, or stops altogether. When this happens, if we examine the copper plate carefully we shall find it covered with minute bubbles of gas. This gas is hydrogen, which in all cells, although generated at the surface of contact of the attacking liquid and the attacked element, nevertheless appears on the surface of the non-attacked element.

This hydrogen is responsible for the weakening of our cell: first, because it is a very bad conductor, and thus opposes a high resistance to the current; and, second, because it may be itself attacked more readily than the attackable element, so that a reverse current is set up, flowing in the opposite direction to the one originally generated. When a cell thus becomes weakened, or rendered inoperative, it is said to be polarized. It is therefore of great importance to prevent this polarization; because, no matter how high the electro-motive force of the current at the start, if the current is not constant the battery is of little value.

We can now recognize the essential conditions of a good galvanic cell ; and these are, —

1. It should have high electro-motive force.

2. It should have low internal resistance, so that no energy should be wasted within the cell.

3. It should give a constant current, and therefore polarization should be prevented in it.

Beyond these, are the further requirements, that there should be no action in the cell when the circuit is open ; that it should emit no disagreeable fumes ; and, finally, it should be made of cheap and lasting materials. No one form of cell fulfils all these conditions ; but, as there are very many varieties, it is possible to select certain cells as especially adapted to particular purposes.

Galvanic cells are usually classified with regard to their construction, and to the depolarizing agent employed. Thus there are (1) one-fluid cells with no depolarizer, (2) one-fluid cells with solid depolarizer or liquid depolarizer, and (3) two-fluid cells.

The simple cell of Volta, with its zinc and copper plates plunged in acidulated water, is an example of the first class. One of the best forms is that known as Smee's battery, in which the copper is replaced by platinum or platinized silver. The rough surface of the platinum gives up the hydrogen bubbles, and so diminishes polarization. The ordinary arrangement of Smee's cell is shown in Fig. 11. The plate of platinum or platinized silver is suspended from a wooden bar which supports two plates of amalgamated zinc. Single-fluid batteries of the above type are subject to three defects :

Fig. 11.

(first) their electro-motive force is weakened by polarization, and they have (second) neither a constant current,
nor (third) a constant resistance.

To the second class of cells
above enumerated, belong the
well-known Grenet (liquid
depolarizer) and Leclanché
(solid depolarizer) forms.
The Grenet cell (Fig. 12),
or, as it is sometimes called,
the "bottle battery," contains a plate of zinc suspended between two plates
of carbon. The zinc is usually affixed to a rod, so that
it can be conveniently raised
out of the solution when the
cell is not in use. The liquid
here contains bichromate of
potash, sulphuric acid, and water. This solution chemically acts upon the hydrogen bubbles, to destroy them
while they are in a nascent state. This cell has a high
electro-motive force at the beginning, and yields a powerful current.

Fig. 12.

The Leclanché cell, which is very much used on
telephone lines, and which is represented in Fig. 13,
contains a carbon plate, against which are fastened
by rubber bands blocks of solid agglomerate, composed
of black oxide of manganese, carbon, bisulphate of
potassium, and gum lac. These agglomerate blocks act
as depolarizers. The zinc element is in the form of a
rod.

Complete depolarization is obtained only in two-fluid
cells, which constitute the third class of battery above

noted. Of these the most prominent examples are the Daniell and the Bunsen.

The Daniell cell (Fig. 14) consists of a containing-vessel in which is placed a porous earthenware jar or cup. Within the porous jar is a plate of amalgamated zinc, and a dilute sulphuric acid. In the outer vessel is a plate of

Fig. 13.

copper; the entire vessel is often itself made of that metal, and the liquid here is a saturated solution of sulphate of copper. When the circuit is closed, the zinc is attacked, forming sulphate of zinc, and liberating hydrogen. But this gas, in this cell, cannot as in other cells appear on the copper plate; because, in meeting the sulphate of copper, the hydrogen combines with the sulphur to form sulphuric acid, while the copper is deposited in the metallic state on the copper plate. There is consequently no polariza-

Fig. 14.

tion, and the cell is constant; but it has a high internal resistance, and hence does not give a powerful current. The gravity cell, based on the Daniell, is very widely used

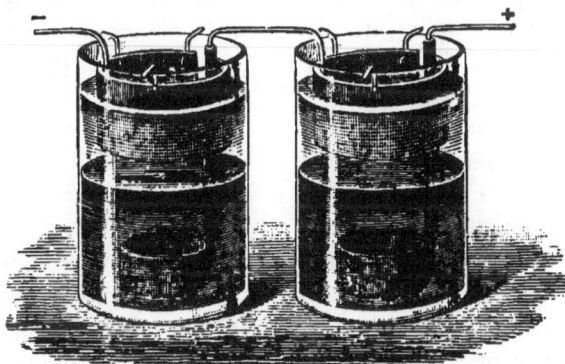

Fig. 15.

for telegraphic purposes. Fig. 15 represents the Callaud form, in which the zinc, in the form of a cylinder, is suspended by hooks from the rim of the jar. The copper element, a thin strip of rolled metal, rests on the bottom. The solution of sulphate of copper is at the bottom of the jar, and remains there because it is heavier than the sulphate of zinc solution which floats upon it.

Bunsen's battery is represented in Fig. 16, and consists of a glass vase *V*, in which is placed a cylinder *Z* of amalgamated zinc, immersed in a mixture of water and sulphuric acid. Within the zinc cylinder is a porous jar *D* of earthenware, which contains a rod or plate of carbon *C* immersed in bichromate solution such as is employed in the Grenet single-fluid cell above described.

Fig. 16.

Of the different forms of batteries above enumerated, the Daniell, for its constancy, is usually taken as the standard. Taking its electro-motive force as unity, or one volt, the electro-motive forces of the other cells mentioned are approximately as follows: —

Smee, about .47 volt.

Leclanché, 1.48 volt.

Grenet, 2 volts.

Bunsen, 1.9 volt.

These forms are mentioned here merely as typical. The actual number of different galvanic cells known to electricians reaches into the hundreds. Experiment with the hope of finding a cell which will be more constant, of higher electro-motive force, or which will consume a cheaper material than zinc, is constantly going forward.

As compared with the steam boiler, *plus* the engine and the dynamo-electric machine, as a means of generating electricity, the battery is most attractive. It costs but a trifle to construct; it needs no fire, and no attendance: these are its advantages. On the other hand, zinc costs twenty times as much as coal, and, other things being equal, generates one-seventh the energy.

Yet we know that the consumption of zinc in the cell is combustion, differing not essentially from the burning of coal in the furnace. Why, we ask ourselves, from the combustion of the expensive substance can we get a direct current of electricity, and not from the combustion of the cheaper material? Wherever there is oxidation, there, in some degree, an electric current is generated. But oxidation in air is oxidation in the most perfect of electrical insulators. The current will not travel from the attacked body to a convenient conductor *via* the air, as it will *via* water; and so, up to the present time, we have found no way of collecting the electricity which may be developed in our grates and furnaces.

Why, then, if we can consume one oxidizable material in the battery, cannot we consume another? If zinc, why not carbon? In the Bunsen cell, and in a great many others, carbon already enters into use as the non-attacked element. Is it not possible to use with it some other substance, which the attacking material will not re-act upon so readily as it will upon carbon? Attempts in this direction have not been wanting. M. Jablochkoff has made a cell in which one element is of coke, and the other of cast iron. His liquid is melted nitrate of potash or nitrate of soda. Here the coke, the carbon, is burned at the expense of the oxygen of the nitrate, while the cast iron remains unattacked. Immense volumes of carbonic acid are produced. The current yielded is powerful. But the cell has no practical utility, save as a mile-post on a road toward perhaps the most important electrical invention that can be made; namely, the consumption of carbon directly in the battery, at low temperatures.

A curious improvement upon Jablochkoff's battery has been contrived by M. Brard of La Rochelle, France, which he calls an electro-generative combustible. It is, in fact, a fuel which produces electricity; or, rather, a piece of prepared carbon, which when thrown into the fire produces electricity by its combustion. Each so-called slab is about six inches long by two inches wide and an inch thick. It is composed of a prism of carbon, a prism of nitrate of potash, and between these a plate of asbestos which acts like the porous partition in ordinary cells. The nitrate of potash is mixed with ashes to prevent too rapid combustion and melting, and in this part of the slab is embedded a sheet of copper which serves as one pole. In the carbon are embedded several strips of brass or copper which are connected to a single sheet, which forms the other pole. It is necessary simply to throw the brick into the fire, previously attaching wires to the poles, to obtain a continuous current for an hour or two. The current of a single slab will actuate an ordinary electric bell.

The galvanic battery, we have defined as an apparatus for converting the energy of chemical affinity into electrical energy. In most cases the force of chemical affinity exerts itself as soon as the ingredients of the cell are put together; in others, as in the instance of the Jablochkoff carbon nitrate-of-potash battery, the constituents of the cell must be heated before the chemical re-actions can occur. Of course, in the latter case, the resulting electrical energy should represent not merely the energy of chemical affinity, but also the heat energy employed in setting free the latter. In fact, however, the energy produced is in no wise commensurate with the energy expended; and all thermo-galvanic cells, so far as now known, are exceedingly wasteful. The thermo-galvanic cell should not be confounded with the thermo-electric cell or thermo-pile. There is a broad distinction between them, in that the thermo-galvanic cell converts heat energy into electrical energy, through the medium of the energy of chemical affinity; while there is no perceptible chemical re-action in the thermo-pile, and the heat applied is directly converted into electricity.

The thermo-electric battery was discovered by Professor Seebeck in 1821. He soldered together a piece of bismuth and a piece of antimony, connected their free ends to a galvanometer which would show when a current passed, and then heated a joint between the metals. He found that when the temperature of

Fig. 17.

the joint was greater than that of the remainder of the circuit, a current traversed the circuit, apparently moving from the bismuth to the antimony as shown in Fig. 17; whereas, if the joint was cooler than the rest of the circuit, then the current would move the other way. The electromotive force thus set up maintains a constant current so long as the excess of temperature of the heated point is kept up, heat being all the while absorbed in order to maintain the energy of the current.

Curiously enough, just as the heating or the cooling of the joint will produce a current in one or the other direction, so the passage of a current through the joint will either heat or cool it. Thus, if a current be conducted from bismuth to antimony, the joint is cooled; if it be led in the other direction, the joint is heated. This peculiar phenomenon was discovered by Peltier in 1834, and is known as the Peltier effect. Another remarkable effect was discovered by Sir William Thompson. If a copper wire be heated at one point, and cooled at another, a current passing through the wire from the hot place to the cool place will heat the wire. If the current goes the other way, the wire will be cooled; but if the wire be of iron, then a current from the hot portion to the cold portion causes cooling.

In constructing a thermo-electric pile, it is usual to join a number of pairs of metal, as bismuth and antimony, in series so bent that the alternate junctions can be heated as shown in Fig. 17, at $A A A$, whilst the other set $B B B$ are kept cool. The various electro-motive forces then act all in the same direction, and the current is increased in proportion to the number of pairs of junctions.

Numerous experiments have been made on thermo-electric batteries, chiefly in France; and with an apparatus of six thousand elements, consuming some twenty-two pounds of coke per hour, two arc lights, equal to between four hundred and fifty and seven hundred and fifty candles, have been maintained. The trouble with the thermo-pile is its great waste; the amount of energy utilized being only between two and five per cent of that of the heat supplied. Its best application is that made by Melloni, who constructed many small pairs of antimony and bismuth in a compact form for use as a thermometer. It is employed with a sensitive galvanometer, and produces currents proportional to the difference of temperature between the hotter set of junctions on one face of the thermo-pile, and the cooler set on the other face. If the hand, for instance, be brought near on the one side, a current indicates its radiant power; or, if a piece of ice be brought near, a current is also indicated, but moving in the opposite direction. In Professor Tyndall's admirable series of lectures on "Heat as a Mode of Motion," this instrument is constantly experimentally employed to show minute differences of temperature. It has been proposed to utilize the waste heat of furnace-flues by surrounding them with thermo-electric elements; and the reverse process has also been suggested, of making stoves the casing of which generates electricity, while radiators diffuse the unconverted heat for purposes of warmth.

In the preceding chapters we have seen that the discharge of an electric machine or of a Leyden-jar is a miniature lightning flash. The discharge of a galvanic cell, on the other hand, is continuous, and may flow over a long period of time. The so-called static discharge may be compared to the sudden explosion of dynamite; the so-called dynamic discharge or current, to the gradual flow of steam or water. Both are electrical discharges, and there is no inherent difference in the electricity manifested; although even to suppose such a difference involves the conception of electricity as a corporeal thing, like water, which is not proved. So-called static electricity is simply electricity of little strength, but of enormous pressure. Dynamic or galvanic electricity has immense strength, but little pressure. To borrow Professor Tyndall's illustration: a cubic inch of air, if compressed with sufficient power, may be able to rupture a very rigid envelope; while a cubic yard of air, if not so compressed, may exert but a feeble pressure upon the surface which bounds it. Static or frictional electricity is in a condition analogous to compressed air: its pressure, its electro-motive force, is great. Galvanic or dynamic electricity resembles the uncompressed air: there is a great deal more of it, but its pressure is comparatively minute.

The immense strength of current of the galvanic cell, and consequent quantity of electricity yielded thereby, as compared with the infinitesimal quantity and enormous pressure of the static discharge, was illustrated in a remarkable manner by Professor Faraday. As will be explained hereafter, an electrical current when conducted into water will decompose the same, tearing asunder the hydrogen and oxygen molecules, and of course exerting energy to effect this separation. The quantity of current necessary to decompose a grain of water is very small. It measures 3.13 amperes; and some idea of what it can do will be obtained from the fact that it should keep a platinum wire $\frac{1}{101}$ of an inch in diameter red hot for three and three-quarters minutes. In order to effect this same decomposition by static electricity, there would be required eight hundred thousand charges of fifteen large Leyden-jars: each charge would be fully capable of killing a rat, and if all of the charges could be accumulated into one, the result would be a great flash of lightning. Faraday estimated the electricity due to the chemical action of a single grain of water on four grains of zinc to be equal in quantity to that of a powerful thunder-storm.

By linking cells together, as has already been described, we can increase the pressure of the galvanic current, and make it more nearly approach that of the frictional or static current. Professor Tyndall, however, states that it requires a battery of more than a thousand cells to make the galvanic current jump over an interval of air one-thousandth of an inch in length. An electric machine of moderate power, and furnished with a suitable conductor, is competent to urge its current across an interval ten thousand times as great as this. The magnetic needle will respond to, and show by its deflection, the passage of an almost infinitesimally small galvanic current; but it is only by the aid of arrangements for multiplying the effect that the discharge of a large static electrical machine is enabled to produce any deflection. With 11,000 cells, the aggregate electro-motive force of which was 11,330 volts, Mr. Warren de la Rue succeeded in obtaining a spark but 0.62 inch in length. On this basis, the electro-motive force of a lightning flash a mile long should be over three and one-half million volts.

We have already noted the fact, that wherever a chemical re-action exists between conducting substances, an electric current is produced. This re-action in a great many instances results from oxidation, the combining of the oxygen of the liquid, usually with the substance of the attacked element.

A very ingenious form of gas battery, invented by Sir W. Grove, contains platinum elements in contact respectively with hydrogen and oxygen gases. These elements enter water; and if they are joined by a wire, a current apparently flows from the hydrogen, through the water in which the ends of the elements enter, to the oxygen. The hydrogen plays the part of a zinc plate, being oxidized by the water; and the hydrogen set free appears at the positive element (oxygen), and combines with it.

Various cells have been devised with the object of utilizing the oxygen of the air for depolarizing purposes. Thus currents of air are sometimes pumped into the cell, and against the plate on which the hydrogen is formed; and various cells have been devised, in which the polarized plate is in the form of an endless belt, a wheel, or a series of radial spokes. The wheel or belt is revolved so as to be partly in and partly out of the cell; so that a portion of it is always active while the remainder is in the air, the hydrogen then escaping.

Jablochkoff's auto-accumulator is a cell remarkable for its small size, light weight, low cost, and freedom from deleterious fumes. It consists of a shallow vessel of hard carbon, in which are placed scraps of metal, such as iron, zinc, or sodium amalgam. Above the metal is a thickness of sawdust, or a piece of coarse cloth, impregnated with chloride of calcium. Upon the cloth are laid hollow sticks of porous carbon. The whole forms a cell four inches square and one inch high. The metal scraps and the carbon vessel form a couple, the carbon being polarized or charged with hydrogen. This carbon is in electrical circuit with the upper porous carbons, which absorb oxygen from the air. Thus we have two surfaces of carbon, one charged with hydrogen and the other with oxygen; and these constitute the elements of the cell. As the current flows, the oxygen and hydrogen generally combine; and the action continues until the supply of one or the other of them is practically exhausted. Then, if the circuit be broken, a recuperative process immediately commences: the hydrogen is evolved from the metal, and attaches itself to the one carbon plate; while the other electrode fills its interstices again with oxygen, which will be drawn out when the current commences to circulate. And so the process goes on, — action following rest, and rest following action, as long as the supply of metal is not exhausted, and there remains a small quantity of moisture required for its oxidation. Five of these cells in series will operate a five-candle-power lamp for an hour, the filament being still bright red at the end of that time. This cell is believed to be of great promise as a means of supplying current for domestic electric lighting.

Another curious atmospheric battery, devised by M.

Jablochkoff, consists simply of a small rod of sodium, squeezed into contact with an amalgamated copper wire, and flattened. This is wrapped in paper, and secured to a plate of porous carbon. No liquid is used, the moisture of the air settling on the oxidized surface of the sodium being sufficient.

A battery which appears to be a decided step in the direction of producing electricity from the oxidation of coal, without the intervention of the steam-engine, was devised in 1885 by Mr. J. A. Kendall, an English electrician. Its operation is based upon the well-known phenomenon of hydrogen passing through platinum at a red heat; two platinum plates being used as the poles, one exposed to hydrogen, and the other to oxygen. These plates are arranged in concentric tubes, closed at one end, and are separated by a fluid medium of fused glass. Hydrogen gas is continuously supplied to the inner platinum tube, while the entire apparatus is maintained at a high temperature by means of a furnace. The absorption of hydrogen by the platinum is accompanied by electric generation, and the current is led away by wires connected to the platinum tubes. The inventor has estimated that a ton of coke used in heating the battery, including the hydrogen-producer, will give at least three times the electrical energy that would be produced by the same quantity of coke used in working a steam-engine and dynamo.

There are a great many other forms of galvanic cell, and new ones are constantly appearing. Most of them are mere modifications of certain general types : others, and especially those which involve novel modes of preventing polarization, or which amount to real advances in the direction of consuming carbon, or utilizing the oxygen of the atmosphere, are of great scientific interest. The subject is a most inviting one to inventors.

The battery of the future — and it will be the greatest of electrical wonders, when it is invented — will simply reproduce the conditions existing in every household grate ; that is, it will burn coal, by the aid of the air, to produce electricity. At the present time, however, there are several forms of battery which are worth noting as electrical curiosities. One inventor boldly grasps the ocean, and utilizes it as his conducting liquid. Of " earth batteries," the globe we live on forms a part. These have been used for driving clocks, and many people have supposed that in some way electricity is drawn directly out of the ground. Earth batteries, however, simply consist of plates of different metals, usually zinc and copper, which are buried at a little distance apart in moist soil, the latter acting like the liquid in an ordinary cell. They have a high resistance, and low electro-motive force. The best place for the zinc plate is under a stable, where saline liquids permeate the ground. One inventor thought he had made a tremendous discovery in recognizing that the lead water-pipes and the iron gas-mains buried under city streets constitute a huge earth battery, from which unlimited electricity might be drawn to light the city. The fact that a battery is there is true enough : but, unfortunately, the attackable substance of the couple is the iron gas-main, which would be surely consumed ; and, as the plan did not contemplate any remuneration to gas-companies for gas lost by leakage, it failed to come into practical use.

M. Duchemin has proposed to use the ocean as the liquid in his battery, and submerge in the sea plates of zinc and carbon attached to a floating body. The main object of this battery was the preservation of the iron hulls of vessels, or the iron buoys, from oxidation. Some experiments were made on a small scale, which apparently demonstrated that it was possible in this way to preserve a surface of iron eighteen times larger than that of the zinc electrode used. The investigations were interrupted by the outbreak of the Franco-German war, and have not been resumed. A somewhat similar idea was proposed many years earlier, by Sir Humphry Davy, who suggested the protection of the copper sheathing of vessels, by means of a communicating sheet of zinc immersed in the sea. It was found that an extent of zinc surface, one hundred and fifty times less than that of the copper, was sufficient to protect the latter; but the plan was abandoned for the reason that certain salts contained in the sea-water were decomposed, and the resulting earthy oxides deposited themselves on the copper, roughening the surface, and rendering the same particularly inviting to barnacles, which attached themselves in great numbers, and so materially impeded the speed of the vessel.

It may be mentioned here, that efforts have been made of late years to remove barnacles from ships' bottoms by powerful currents led to the copper from dynamo-electric machines, thence passing to the water. The current seriously incommoded the barnacles, which made such efforts as lie within the limited capacity of the clam, to get out of their shells; but, Nature not having provided them with suitable means for this purpose, they remained, and submitted to the disturbance with their usual equanimity, possibly cheered by the knowledge that on the whole the experiment was a failure.

Probably the largest galvanic battery ever made is that used in the Royal Institution in London. It consists of 14,400 cells of chloride of silver and zinc elements. It is estimated that a lightning flash a mile long could be produced by 243 such batteries.

The battery which will last the longest is the dry pile devised by Zamboni. This consists of a number of paper

disks, coated with zinc foil on one side and with an oxide
of manganese on the other, piled upon one another, to the
number of many thousands, in a glass tube. The electro-
motive force is great, and a good pile will yield sparks.
The current is very weak, but it lasts an extraordinary
length of time. In the Clarendon Library at Oxford,
there is a pile, the poles of which are two metal bells;
between them is hung a small brass ball, which, by oscillating to and fro, slowly discharges the electricity. It
has been continuously ringing the bells for over forty
years.

One of the most curious alleged discoveries concerning
the galvanic battery was that of Mr. Arnold Crosse, who
in the early part of the present century announced the
extraordinary fact that living insects were generated in
the cell. He stated, that while endeavoring to deposit
crystals of silica on a lump of stone, by the agency of the
current, he noticed, after the experiment had continued
for a fortnight, whitish specks on the stone, which at the
end of the twenty-eighth day assumed the appearance of
insects, standing erect on the bristles which formed their
tails, and distinctly moving their legs. The experimenter
was greatly astonished. Instead of a mineral, for which
he had looked as the result of his experiment, he had
found an animal, alive and kicking. It was plain these
were no mere appearances; for in a few days they de-
tached themselves from the stone, and began to move
about. They were, to be sure, not creatures of a very
inviting and attractive character; for they belonged apparently to the genus *acarus*, which includes some of the
most disagreeable parasites of the animal body. But they
continued to increase, and in the course of a few weeks
hundreds made their appearance. Crosse himself hesi-
tated to believe that spontaneous generation could attend

any action of electricity, and conjectured that his cell was simply a favorable place for the hatching of the ova of the insects existing in the atmosphere. He and others at the time made many experiments intended to preclude the possibility of these ova being present, but the insects continued to appear. The phenomenon made a great sensation. Despite the fact of Crosse's own hesitancy in asserting that he could produce life, others flatly maintained the possibility. At the opposite extreme, were those who attacked Crosse for impiety. If he began by creating animals by electrical power, no matter of how inferior sort, who could tell where he might stop? He was called a "disturber of the peace of families," and a "reviler of religion."

The French Academy of Sciences, however, on receipt of a phial of the mysterious insects, treated the whole matter as unworthy of serious consideration; and one member individually pointed out that the means employed by Crosse simply excited and favored the germination of the ova which must have been present. Many years later (1859), Professor Schulze in Germany repeated Crosse's experiments, aided by more modern knowledge of minute organisms, and modes of sterilization, and showed conclusively that none were generated. The controversy had then continued for nearly half a century.

Among other remarkable ideas concerning the galvanic battery, it has been suggested, that, wherever two flavors are habitually formed in cooking and eating, the reason why they mutually improve each other is because a certain amount of electric action is set up between the substances employed to produce them. Mr. Edwin Smith, M.A., has conducted quite an extended series of experiments based on this theory; and has used as elements in a galvanic cell, pairs of eatables which generally go together, such as pepper and salt, coffee and sugar, almonds and raisins. He states that he found a voltaic current, more or less strong, excited in every instance, and that bitters and sweets, pungents and salts, or bitters and acids, generally appear to furnish true voltaic couples, doubtless in consequence of the mutual action of some alkaloid salt, and an acid or its equivalent. Mr. Smith gives quite a long list of substances tested. Among his couples are tea and sugar, raw potato and lemon-juice, nutmeg and sugar, horse-radish and table salt, onion and beet-root, vanilla and sugar, starch and iodine, and tobacco and tartaric acid. The substance first named in each couple takes the place of the zinc, or attacked element, in the cell.

Mr. Smith suggests that the *rationale* of the right blending of flavors "might be found partly, no doubt, in chemistry, but partly also in galvanism."

One of the most curious batteries is that devised by Sauer, which appears to act only in the sunlight. It consists of a glass vessel containing a solution of table salt and sulphate of copper in water; within is a porous cell containing mercury. One element is of platinum, and is immersed in the mercury : the other is sulphide of silver, and is placed in the salt solution. Both elements are connected to a galvanometer. When the battery is placed in the sunlight, the needle is deflected to a certain point, and the sulphide of silver is found to be the negative pole. The action of the battery depends on the effect of the chloride of copper upon the mercury. Sub-chloride is formed, and reduces the sulphide of silver; but this can take place only by the aid of sunlight.

For the heavy work of electric lighting, or the driving of electro-motors, batteries are superseded by dynamo-electric machines, for economical reasons already pointed

out; but where large expenditure of energy is not required, as in the telegraph and telephone, batteries find
a wide utilization. Ultimately they will displace the
dynamo, and in time the steam-boiler. To make them do
this, is the great electrical problem of the century.

CHAPTER VI.

THE ELECTRO-MAGNET, AND THE CONVERSION OF ELEC-
TRICITY INTO MAGNETISM.

THE tide of a great river moving to the sea is the embodiment of mighty volume. The mountain stream, albeit a mere thread of water leaping down from rock to rock, conveys to us the idea of intense energy. The volume of the river, the force of the torrent, unite in the great cataract. All of these conditions find their parallels in the electrical current. From the galvanic battery flows the slow and steady river; from the electric machine, the swift but slender torrent; and from the dynamo, the Niagara.

And, as we have seen, the electrical current moving in its path is governed by laws similar to those which control water flowing in its channel. We can contract the area of the conduit to diminish, or enlarge it to increase, the flow. We can augment or decrease the pressure of either water or electricity, and so send more or less through the appointed path in a given time.

A step farther, and the analogy fails. Water acts directly only upon objects in it or on it. It may float a vessel, or turn a wheel, or break down barriers; but the mightiest flood cannot influence a grain of iron to move one way or the other, if a few feet of air intervene. Suppose a current of water did have all the properties of an electrical current: what might happen? Perhaps, around and above every stream, there would be a viewless atmosphere which we could not penetrate; an atmosphere in which the laws of gravity affecting iron and steel would be set at naught, in which every iron bar would be a magnet placing itself across the flood, — a most strange and mysterious medium, in which things of iron and steel would arrange themselves in curious curves, whorls and whirlpools and vortices of iron; a field of strains and stresses in something not the air yet in and with the air, of lines of forces without breadth and unending.

This sounds fantastic when spoken of water. But it is true of two natural phenomena, — a conductor through which an electrical current is passing, and the magnet. Around the wire through which electricity is passing, and in front of the poles of a magnet, exists this strange aura; not in imagination, but in fact, for we can make it visible.

First, however, let us recall something about magnets in general.

Ages ago, in Magnesia in Asia Minor, were found certain hard black stones which possessed the remarkable property of attracting to themselves bits of iron and steel. These the ancients called magnets, from the name of the locality in which they were found. And as their behavior was altogether incomprehensible, the ancients, in accordance with their usual way of dealing with things which they did not understand, disposed of the problem very easily by ascribing the phenomenon to the supernatural powers. It is a little odd, by the way, that pretty much every thing which the ancients used to attribute to genii and spirits — because unintelligible — is unhesitatingly ascribed by a large section of their posterity to "electricity;" the mere mention of the word being quite sufficient to account for any thing out of the common run, from rheumatism to red sunsets.

The knowledge of the ancients about the magnet seems to have stopped with the fact of its attractive power. The Orientals, with characteristic largeness of imagination, were not slow to conceive of the tremendous things which huge magnets might do. Who does not remember the story of the third calendar in the "Arabian Nights," wherein the story-teller recounts the remarkable fate which befell his ship?

" A sailor from the mast-head gave notice that he saw something which had the appearance of land, but looked uncommonly black. The pilot, on this report, expressed the utmost consternation. 'We are lost!' said he: 'the tempest has driven us within the influence of the black mountain, which is a rock of adamant, and at this time its attraction draws us toward it: to-morrow we shall approach so near that the iron and nails will be drawn out of the ship, which of course must fall to pieces; and as the mountain is entirely inaccessible, we must all perish.' This account was too true. The next day, as we drew near the mountain, the iron all flew out of the ship: it fell to pieces, and the whole crew perished in my sight."

For a great many centuries, the world knew simply that magnets would attract iron. Then somebody — tradition says the Chinese (which is convenient, because everybody knows they were civilized ages ago, and if they did not have modern improvements then, no one can dispute to the contrary) — hung up a magnet by a thread, and discovered that it pointed north and south. After that it was called the loadstone (leading stone), and the mariner's compass came into existence. Now we know the magnet as an ore of iron, mineralogically termed *magnetite*, and chemically $Fe_3 O_4$.

This knowledge, however, useful as it is, has not prevented people from trying to press the magnet into service as a means of solving that long-vexed problem, of lifting one's self over a fence by one's own boot-straps. Wherefore they have invented — or rather failed to invent — magnetic motors, — not electro-magnetic motors, which are quite another thing, but motors depending on the constant attraction of permanent magnets. Every once in a while, some one announces the accomplishment of this feat, which primarily depends on cutting off the attraction of the magnet by causing the latter to move something in the way of a screen between its own pole and the thing attracted. Unfortunately, magnetic attraction refuses to be cut off in any such way. It is as stubborn in this respect as the attraction of gravity, which it very much resembles.

In that same famous work which began the modern science of electricity in 1600, — Dr. Gilbert's "De Magnete," — it was announced that the attractive power of a magnet, when in elongated form, resides at the ends. These, Gilbert called the poles ; and he also pointed out that the intermediate region attracted iron-filings less strongly, while midway between the poles there was no attraction at all. Every magnet, large or small, has these poles : they are inseparable. We may grind a magnet into powder : every grain will be an independent magnet, having its opposite poles. Furthermore, just as there appear to be two kinds of electricity, — high potential and low potential, or positive and negative, — so these two poles appear to have opposite characters ; one tending to move to the north, the other to the south. Hence the poles are commonly called, respectively, the north and the south poles. When the poles of two magnets are brought together, like poles always repel, while unlike poles attract each other.

To Gilbert is due the distinction between magnets and magnetic bodies. A magnetic body is a body capable of being magnetized, — such as a piece of iron. Either pole of a magnet will attract a magnetic body; but two magnets will attract or repel each other, according as unlike or like poles are presented. Gilbert also made the extraordinary discovery that the earth is a huge magnet; that its poles coincide, nearly, with the geographical North and South Poles; and that therefore it causes the freely suspended magnet which forms the compass needle to place itself in a north-and-south position.

And now we reach a fact about magnets which is bewildering, because it tends to upset all our notions about time. If we present a magnet to a bit of iron, we see the iron attracted apparently instantly. We should be ready to assert, by all the evidences of our senses, that absolutely nothing could happen between the instant the magnet is presented and the instant the iron is attracted. Yet something does happen. Before that magnet can attract the iron, — while the iron is yet distant from it, — it must alter the whole magnetic state of the iron mass. The magnet must induce, on the end of the iron nearest it, a pole of opposite name to the pole presented; and at the farther end of the iron, a pole of the same name. In other words, it must convert the magnetic body into a magnet. Having done that, it repels one end, and attracts the other. But this is done before the attraction begins; but in what period of time we do not know, nor could we form the faintest conception of its duration if we did.

Why does a magnet act in this way? What is the mysterious atmosphere surrounding it, which makes it repel or attract bodies, or convert other bodies into magnets? There is a theory, — a very learned one, — which is altogether too deep for these pages, so it is left out; but, without going into that, we can see for ourselves the effects of this atmosphere, in a very satisfactory way.

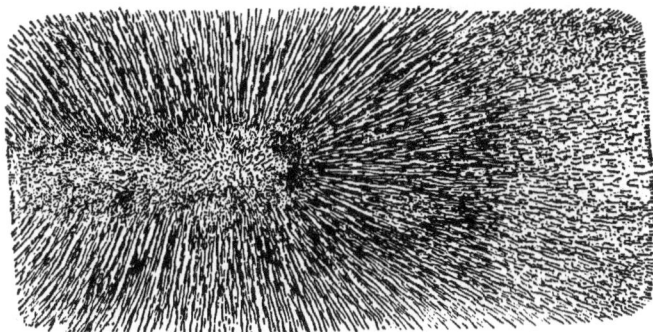

Fig. 18.

If we take an ordinary bar magnet, and place a piece of paper — or, better, glass — over one of its poles, and sprinkle finely sifted iron-filings on the glass, we shall see these filings arrange themselves in curious curves, appar-

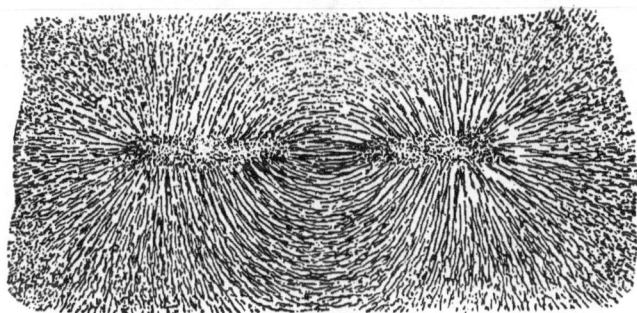

Fig. 19.

ently radiating from the pole, as in Fig. 18. If we substitute for the bar magnet a horse-shoe magnet, and place the glass over both poles, we shall find that the lines

diverge nearly radially from each pole, and curve around
to meet the opposite pole, as in Fig. 19.   If we take two
horse-shoe magnets, and place like poles facing each other,

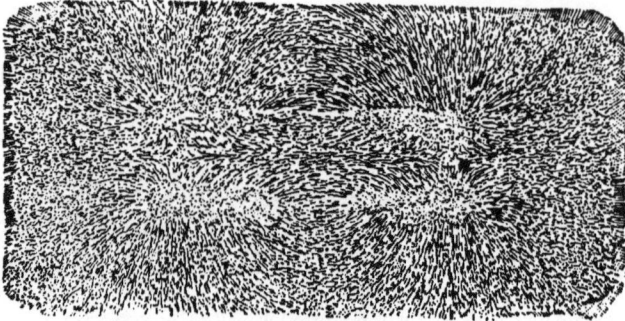

Fig. 20.

then the filings curve away as if repelling each other, as in
Fig. 20 : on the other hand, if we bring opposite poles of
the magnets into proximity, then the filings curve around
from one pole to the other.   The actual appearance of the

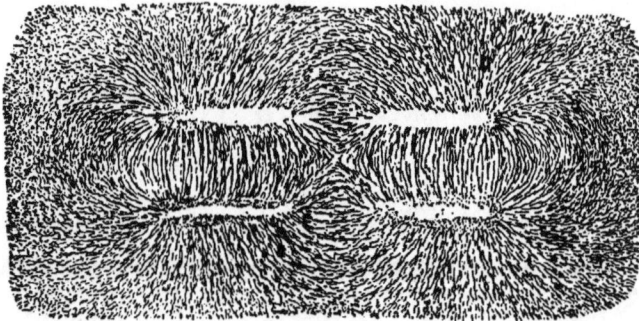

Fig. 21.

iron-filings is here shown, in Fig. 21.   The iron-filings
represented were dusted over glass plates supported on
the poles of the magnets ; and when they had assumed

the positions due to the magnetic influence, they were fixed in place by an adhesive substance, and the plates were used as photographic negatives, whence the engravings were produced.

Now, what does all this mean? Simply, that the magnet is telling its own story, — writing it, in fact, for us to read. We know perfectly well that iron-filings will no more arrange themselves in rows or curves, of their own volition, than books will place themselves in rows on shelves; and that there must be some force which tends to place the filings in these lines. We notice also that the curves are closer together near the poles, and, in fact, the filings resemble a crowd of people massed around some common object of interest: the crowd is thickest around the object, and more scattering as the distance therefrom increases.

It appears, therefore, that around the pole of a magnet exists this strange atmosphere to which we have already referred, — a so-called " field of force," in which exist strains and pulls and pushes as if a host of infinitesimal beings were at work seizing upon the filings, and arranging them to make them accommodate themselves to this new condition of affairs. And the result of it all is, that we recognize seeming lines of force radiating from the pole. It is a wonderful atmosphere, that magnetic field. We have only to move a piece of iron in it, in a peculiar way, to make speech heard miles distant, or to produce the light which is weaker only than the sun in power; and what still stranger things may yet be done, no one knows. Meanwhile these lines of force, which we see mapped for us by the iron-filings, have some singular properties of their own. They never have a free end. The finding of a free end to a magnetic line, and of the place whence the rainbow rises, and the invention of a magnetic motor, are all will-o'-the-wisps together. Every magnetic line that starts gets somewhere. If apparently curving from a north pole, it will end in a south pole, — perhaps the south pole of the same magnet, perhaps the south pole of some other magnet, and perhaps in a south pole induced by itself in a magnetic body.

There must be, however, a magnet or magnetic body; and Gilbert, the reader will remember, — not Gilbert who wrote "De Magnete," but a later Gilbert who wrote "Pinafore" and "Patience," — has very clearly demonstrated this in a pathetic ballad about a magnet which vainly attempted to attract a silver churn. That magnet sent out no lines of force toward the silver churn; and perhaps it may be well to illustrate this sad condition of affairs, just to fix the idea in our minds. No lines of force in Fig. 22 go to the silver churn; but if the churn had been of iron, the result, as we see, would have been very different, and then

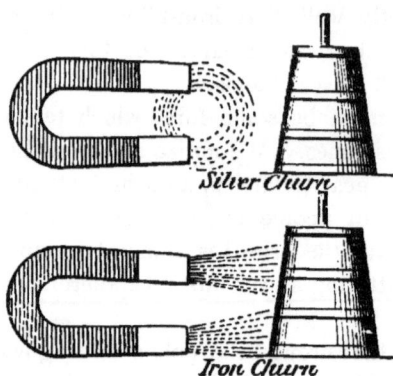

Silver Churn

Iron Churn

Fig. 22.

> "This magnetic
> Peripatetic
> Lover who lived to learn,
> By no endeavor
> Can magnet ever
> Attract a silver churn," —

might not have wasted his rejected fascinations.

And this also, by the way, indicates the reason why the officers of Atlantic steamers show so much uneasiness when young ladies persist in bringing their sewing apparatus into the neighborhood of the compasses. The lines of force from the north pole of a very sedate and responsible compass-needle may find easily a south pole in the frivolous knitting or crochet needle, and, turning in the direction of the latter, may lead the ship miles from her course.

It has been said that a magnet, when it attracts a body of magnetic material, first induces magnetism in the latter. Thus by simply placing a piece of iron in a magnetic field, and taking it out again, we can render that iron magnetic or non-magnetic, as it is termed, by induction. If, however, we wish to render the metal permanently magnetic, we can do so by rubbing it with a permanent magnet in a peculiar way.

We have stated that in two instances in nature this strange surrounding atmosphere is produced. We have seen it proved by the behavior of the iron-filings in the neighborhood of the pole of a magnet. It remains to detect it around the conductor of an electric current. This is easily done. Take a piece of card, or, better, a sheet of glass, through which a hole has been drilled, and pass the wire through which the current is moving, through the hole.

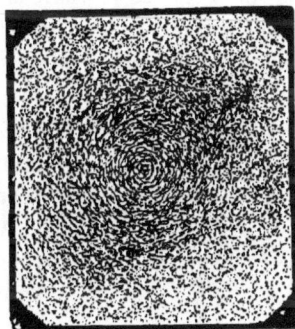

Fig. 23.

Then sprinkle iron-filings around the wire. The filings will arrange themselves in a series of concentric circles, just as if they were controlled by a whirlwind, around the wire. This is beautifully represented in Fig. 23, which has been prepared from a photograph. If the wire is carried parallel to and across the glass plate as in Fig. 24, the filings will arrange themselves in straight lines perpendicular to the direction of the wire and at equal distances from one another : and may be regarded as a number of repetitions of Fig. 23, strung upon a wire, and looked at edgeways.

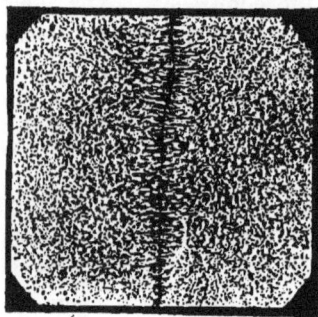

Fig. 24.

This is different from what happens with the magnet. Compare Figs. 18 and 23.

If we suppose the lines of force indicated by the iron-filings to represent a wind blowing, then a flag placed near a magnet would stand as in Fig. 25 ; whereas, if the flag were placed near

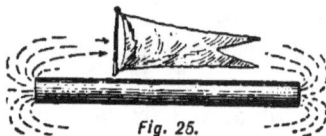

Fig. 25.

the wire, it would stand as in Fig. 26. A suspended magnetized needle would place itself in the same positions with reference to wire or magnet, under the influence of the lines of force.

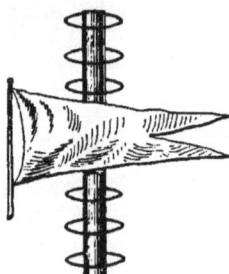

Fig. 26.

A wire conducting a current, therefore, is surrounded by lines of force like those surrounding the natural magnet, but differently disposed. Such a wire is, in fact, a magnet. It will attract iron-filings ; and they will cling to it as long as the current continues, but drop off as soon as the current stops.

Now, suppose we wind our conducting wire into a helix or coil, as in Fig. 27. If the entire length of the wire is surrounded by the whorl of lines of force, clearly a great many of these lines will converge in the space inside the coil, and we shall have there a very strong or concentrated field of force. Into this field we can easily

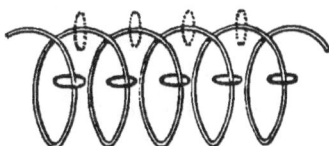

Fig. 27.

insert an iron bar, which will then become very strongly magnetized. That is, just as it would become a magnet if placed in the field of another magnet, so now it becomes a magnet when placed in the field of force of the wire.

This is very perfectly illustrated in Fig. 28. Here the wire is represented with a turn in it, and the lines are thus

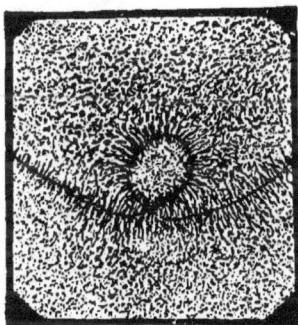

Fig. 28.

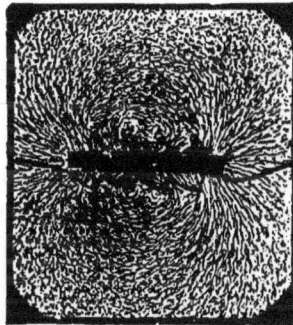

Fig. 29.

perpendicular to the plane of the loop. The filings now form themselves (as far as the plate will allow them) into lines perpendicular to the plane of the paper, and therefore, as seen from above, appear simply as isolated dots or points. Fig. 29 illustrates the lines of force brought into play in the manner above described in the induction

of magnetism in an iron bar when an electric current is
sent through a wire coiled around it. It represents a
small electro-magnet, showing four turns of its coil. In
the actual experiment, the bar was a strip of ferrotype
iron, and the wire carrying the current was threaded
through the eight holes, four being on one side of the bar,
and four on the other.

The iron bar or core of an electro-magnet, as we have
said, temporarily behaves like a permanent magnet. It
has a magnetic field of its own, with endless lines of force,
and, in fact, is a permanent magnet — as long as the
electrical current flows in the coil surrounding it. And
it is worth while to
repeat this very im-
portant distinction.
A permanent magnet
is always a magnet:
an electro-magnet is
not a magnet except
when the electrical
current is passing
through its coil. It is a difficult thing, comparatively
speaking, either to convert a piece of iron into a permanent magnet, or to render a permanent magnet free
from magnetism. On the other hand, an electro-magnet
is energized or de-energized with infinite rapidity, by
simply establishing or stopping the current in the coil.
The poles of a permanent magnet are fixed : those of an
electro-magnet depend upon the direction of the current.
Thus, in Fig. 30, supposing the inner shaded circle to represent the bar, or "core" of the magnet, if the current
moves in the coil represented by the outer circle in the
direction of the arrow in 1, — that is, in the same direction
as the hands of a watch, — the end of the core facing us is

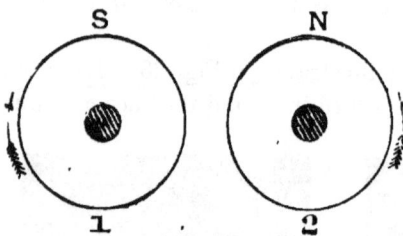

Fig. 30.

a south pole. If the current travelled the other way, as in
2, the same end of the bar would be a north pole. So
that we can not only make and unmake an electro-magnet,
by establishing or breaking the current; but we can
reverse the polarity of the magnet at will, by simply
reversing the direction of the current in the coil.

In Fig. 31 is represented in diagram an electro-magnet
which communicates with a battery ; and a circuit-closing
key, by manipulating which we can establish or interrupt
the current from the battery through the coil of the magnet. In front of the core hangs a piece of magnetic
metal, called the *ar-*
mature; and this is
held away from the
magnet by a coiled
spring fastened at its
opposite end to a
fixed post. In Fig.
31, the key is shown
raised ; no current
then passes to the
coil, and the bar is
not a magnet.

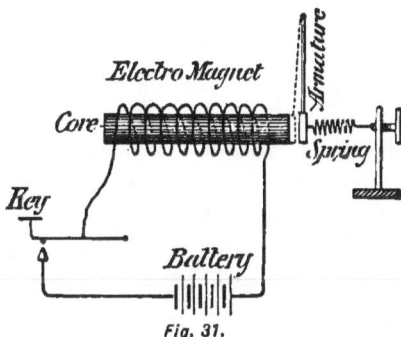

Fig. 31.

If, however, we press down the key, then the current
from the battery will instantly circulate through the coil :
the core will become a magnet, and attract its armature as
indicated by the dotted lines. If we break the circuit
again, the armature, no longer attracted, will be drawn
back by the spring ; and hence we can keep that armature
vibrating to and fro as often as we can make and break
the circuit. As the magnet may be quite strong, it may
attract its armature with much force, so that we can make
the armature drive mechanism. This is how the electro-
magnet converts electricity into mechanical motion in the

great majority of electrical devices, including the telegraph, the electro-motor, and the countless alarms and
kindred apparatus to some of which reference will hereafter be made.

There is still another way in which the electro-magnet
can vibrate its armature; and that is by reversing the

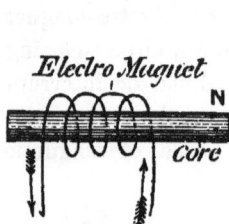

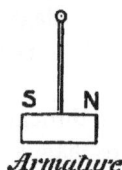

polarity of the core, by
simply changing the
direction of flow of the
current. Suppose, in
Fig. 32, a current cir-
culated around the bar
or core, in the direc-
tion of the arrow; then

Electro Magnet

N   S   N

Core   *Armature*

Fig. 32.

the right-hand end would be the north pole. If, instead
of suspending before our electro-magnet an armature of
magnetic material, we suspended an armature itself a
magnet, having north and south poles, as marked in the
diagram, then, when the nearest end of the electro-magnet
became north, the armature would be attracted, because
unlike magnetic poles would be opposed. But if we
reversed the current, as
shown in Fig. 33, then
like magnetic poles would
be opposed, and the arma-
ture would be repelled.
So that, by simply making

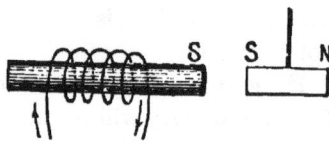

S   S   N

Fig. 33.

the current travel first in one way and then in the other,
we can set a magnet or polarized armature into vibration. If the armature were not polarized, of course the
changing of the current would have no effect on it;
either pole of a magnet attracting a simple magnetic
body not itself a magnet. We shall find this contrivance largely used in the various practical applications

of electricity; although perhaps to not so great an extent as the first-mentioned arrangement,. with which, just as the steam-engine can be controlled by throttling the steam, so the magnet is controlled by throttling the current.

As we shall see farther on, electro-magnets can be made to exert sufficient power to drive locomotives, and do other heavy mechanical work: so that it is quite important to know something as to how they acquire this. A magnet, whether electrical or permanent, has no power of its own. It can only exert whatever energy is put into it. It is like a clock-spring: wind it up, and it drives the clock, not by some inherent clock-driving capacity peculiar to springs, — like the inherent meat-roasting quality ascribed by Martinus Scriblerus to roasting-jacks, — but because it has been wound up. When a body is rendered magnetic, whether by electricity, or by natural means, or by rubbing, energy is imparted to it. When the magnet exerts itself, it parts with some of that energy. If it moves a heavy armature up to its pole, it may expend all the energy it can exert, and will affect other bodies not at all. If a permanent magnet thus draws its armature, it can do no more until the armature is withdrawn. To take away that armature, requires just as much force as the magnet used in attracting it; so that, by this action, the energy expended by the magnet in attracting .the armature is restored to it.

To the electro-magnet, we impart power by the current. The stronger the current, the stronger the magnet, up to a certain point. Eventually, however, the iron of the core becomes " saturated," that is, it reaches a state when it can apparently be no longer affected. If the current is kept constant, and the magnet below saturation, then, the greater the number of turns of wire applied, the stronger the magnet.

An electro-magnet is easily made of a central bar or

core of iron, around which the insulated wire is coiled like
a spool of thread. Usually the core is made in the form
of a horse-shoe, so that both poles may be applied to one
iron armature. The coil is then divided into two parts, as
shown in Fig. 34. In this engraving the magnet is represented as having attracted its armature, — the plate
immediately beneath the coils, — and is sustaining weights

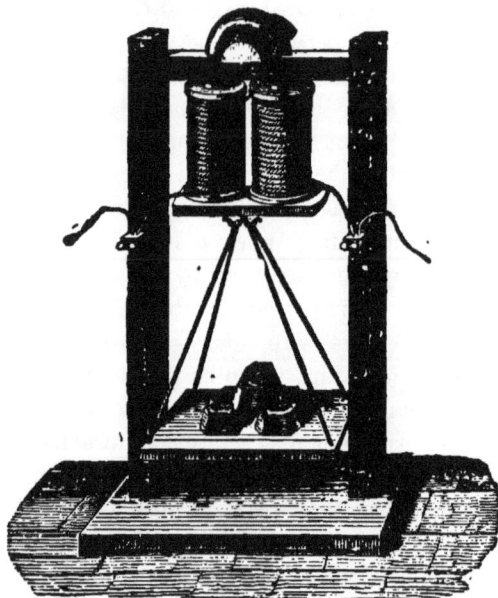

Fig. 34.

on a platform dependent therefrom. An electro-magnet
was designed by Professor Joule, capable of supporting
in this way over a ton, and of exerting an attraction on
its armature of about two hundred pounds per square inch.

The Stevens Institute of Technology possesses one of
the largest electro-magnets in the world. It weighs about
sixteen hundred pounds, and has a lifting force of nearly
forty tons.

It is generally believed that the effect of magnetizing
the iron core is to cause each particle of the iron to try
to set itself at right angles to the direction of the current
in the coil, just as Oersted's needle places itself at right
angles to the wire conveying a current. The result is,
that the irregularly shaped particles place themselves with
their longer axes parallel to the core ; and, as they all do
this, the core as a unit becomes longer and thinner. Of
course it is very hard to realize how this can happen in a
body as dense and hard as iron ; and so it is difficult to
imagine the vibration of the atoms when iron is heated, or
to conceive of the infinitesimal shortness of the paths over
which they must move. Still it is quite certain that this
is what does occur. By actual measurement a rod of iron
magnetized to saturation is found to have increased to the
extent of $\frac{1}{270000}$ of its length. And even if this change
is too small for our eyes to perceive, it is perfectly easy to
hear it ; for the core can be arranged not only so that it
will give out a very perceptible tick when magnetized, but,
if the current be sent from a telephone transmitter, it will
sing and talk, the sounds being produced simply by
changes in the bar itself.

There is hardly a parallel instance, in the history of
electricity, of a discovery being so rapidly turned to practical account as was that of Oersted. He performed his
successful experiment in causing the free needle to be
moved by a current traversing a wire, as we have stated,
in the summer of 1820. Arago and Ampère, in France,
at once began investigations. By the end of the following September, Arago announced that he had ascertained
that iron-filings were attracted " by the connecting-wire
of the battery, exactly as by a magnet," and that he had
magnetized a sewing-needle permanently by the galvanic
current. Ampère reported almost immediately, that a

spiral or helical arrangement of the galvanic conducting-wire was most advantageous for magnetizing needles. Early in November, he "perfectly imitated a magnet by a helical galvanic conducting-wire." Four years later, William Sturgeon made the electro-magnet, using a core of iron bent in horse-shoe form, coated with varnish, and surrounded with a spiral coil of naked copper wire. Shortly afterwards, Professor Joseph Henry made his famous experiments at the Albany Academy, which revealed for the first time the extraordinary power of the electro-magnet. Henry followed the plan, previously suggested by Schweigger, of covering his wire, instead of merely putting the insulating material around the coil as Sturgeon had done. With a magnet wound with twenty-six strands of copper bell-wire covered with cotton thread, — the aggregate length of the core being 728 feet — he had suspended nearly a ton weight. Afterwards, with a small horse-shoe of round iron, one inch in length and six-tenths of an inch in diameter, wound with but three feet of brass wire, he raised a weight 420 times greater than that of the magnet itself. Sir Isaac Newton describes a lodestone weighing three grains, which he wore in a ring, and which is said to have raised 746 grains, or 250 times its own weight. This is the greatest recorded strength of any permanent magnet. Natural magnets, or lodestones, are stronger than those artificially made. The former usually carry a load of about twenty times, while the latter are rarely able to lift a mass exceeding five times, their own weight. Within recent years, however, very powerful permanent magnets, equal to the lifting of twenty-five times their own weight, have been constructed by M. Jamin; the advantage being gained through the use of very thin leaves of thoroughly magnetized steel, bound together to form the magnet.

Let us sum up some of the strange phenomena thus

far briefly outlined. We have seen that the electrical current is competent to produce effects not merely in its channel or conductor, — like water turning a wheel, — but to influence bodies entirely outside of that channel. It causes, around its conductor, a peculiar aura or atmosphere like that around the poles of a magnet, but differing from the latter as a whirlwind differs from a steady gale. It converts the conductor into a magnet, which, like other magnets, is capable of influencing magnetic bodies to become magnets. It also converts magnetic bodies, around which the conductor is wound, into magnets; and a bar of iron in this way is given all the properties which it would have were it normally and naturally a magnet, or piece of lodestone. This is an electro-magnet. But the magnetic state of this bar is controllable. It is a magnet, or not, in accordance as we permit the current to flow, or interrupt it. As a magnet, the bar has different poles, at opposite ends; but these poles change reciprocally in accordance with the direction of the current. By making and breaking the current, we can make the electro-magnet attract and release alternately a piece of magnetic material, placed in front of either of its poles, and called an armature. If, however, the armature be itself a magnet, then we can make the electro-magnet attract or release it without breaking the current, but by simply changing the direction of the current, — this because, when the magnet opposes an unlike pole to the adjacent pole of the armature, the latter will be attracted; but when the magnet presents a like pole, the armature will not be attracted, or, if already attracted, will be released.

Why the magnet, and the conductor carrying a current, produce this singular atmosphere; why other bodies act as they do in that atmosphere; what the medium is which carries this unknown force between the separated magnet and armature, — are all unsolved problems.

CHAPTER VII.

THE DYNAMO-ELECTRIC MACHINE, AND THE CONVERSION OF
MAGNETISM AND MECHANICAL MOTION INTO ELECTRICITY.

Is electricity magnetism? or is magnetism electricity?
Are these phenomena two different forms of energy? or
are they phases merely of the same form? The last is
probably true.

By means of the electric current, a body capable of
being magnetized may be, as we have seen, converted
into a magnet. We have now to note even more extraordinary results following the reverse of this; namely, the
production of electrical currents by magnets.

In the fall of 1831, Professor Faraday announced that
from a magnet he had obtained electricity. On the 8th
of February, 1832, he entered in his note-book: "This
evening, at Woolwich, experimented with magnet, and
for the first time got the magnetic spark myself. Connected ends of a helix into two general ends, and then
crossed the wires in such a way that a blow at a b would
open them a little. Then bringing a b against the poles
of a magnet, the ends were disjoined, and bright sparks
resulted."

Next day he repeated this experiment, and then, as was
his habit, invited some of his friends to see the new light.
He had a piece of soft iron, surrounded by coils of wire
insulated with calico and tied by common string. When

he touched the pole of a magnet with the soft iron, the ends of the coil, as he says, opened a little, and a spark passed between them. An electrical current had been caused in the coil, and Herbert Mayo described it in the following neat impromptu : —

> " Around the magnet, Faraday
> Was sure that Volta's lightnings play;
> But how to draw them from the wire ?
> He drew a lesson from the heart :
> 'Tis when we meet, 'tis when we part,
> Breaks forth the electric fire."

Faraday's experiment is very easily repeated with the aid of the little apparatus represented in Fig. 35. The operator holds in one hand an ordinary horseshoe magnet, and in the other a bar of iron around which is wound a little coil of insulated copper wire. On one end of the coil is a small disk of copper. The other end is sharpened to a point, and brought in contact with the disk. On placing the bar across the poles of the magnet,

Fig. 35.

and then suddenly breaking contact, the point and the disk become separated at the same time, and the spark appears.

Some fifty years earlier, one of those intensely practical individuals who see no outcome in the results of scientific discovery unless the same can be immediately estimated at a money value, rather superciliously asked Franklin what use there was in the facts proved by certain of his experiments.

" What's the use of a baby? " the philosopher retorted.

Faraday's reply to those who saw nothing gained by the development of the little spark, and who demanded its utility, was equally sententious. " *Endeavor* to make it useful," he said. He left to others the immediate work of doing so. Some twenty-five years later, he saw that tiny flash expanded into the magnificent blaze of the famous South Foreland light-house. To-day it illuminates the thoroughfares of the great cities of the civilized world.

The first practical magneto-electric machine was constructed by M. Hippolyte Pixii of Paris, in September, 1832. His apparatus consisted of an ordinary horse-shoe magnet, under the poles of which a powerful steel horse-shoe was rotated by a shaft. On the steel horse-shoe was coiled a wire ; and as the ends of the horse-shoe were moved up to and removed from the poles of the magnet, electric currents were produced in the coil. The best form of this apparatus was probably that produced by Clarke of London, in 1834. This is represented in Fig. 36. It embodies a large permanent magnet AB, beside the poles of which are rotated two pieces, or cores, of soft iron, each encircled by a coil of fine wire, and mounted at the ends of arms supported on a horizontal shaft; the shaft being rotated by turning the large belt-wheel by its handle. When the coils are rotated in front of the magnet, currents are produced in them. The coils are connected to separate metal plates on each side of the shaft, from which plates the current is led, by springs touching them, to binding-posts to which conducting-wires may be attached.

It will be apparent that these machines are merely convenient mechanical contrivances for doing just what Faraday did in the little experiment first described in this chapter. We have, however, by no means recoguized all that Faraday then discovered.

Fig. 36.

As we have seen, he determined that an electrical current was produced in a closed coil of wire when a magnet was brought up to the coil, or the reverse. The coil might be moved in front of the pole of the magnet, as in

Clarke's machine above described ; or the magnet may be moved up to or into the coil, as represented in Fig. 37. In the latter case, the ends *ff'* of the coil may be connected with a galvanometer, which will reveal the presence of the current.

It must not be understood that the mere proximity of the magnet to the coil produces any current, for that is not the fact. It is the motion of the coil to the magnet, or of magnet to coil, which produces the current. The actual mechanical work which we perform in moving either coil or magnet is converted into the other form of energy which we call electricity. But how this is done, is not easy to realize. We have seen that all around a magnet exists the so-called field of force, and that magnetic bodies become magnets on being simply placed therein. Here, however, is a new property of that mysterious atmosphere. If a closed circuit is *moved* in that field, a current will traverse the wire ; or if the field itself, by moving the magnet, be brought nearer to or farther from the coil, the same thing will happen.

It is necessary, however, that the motion should be made in a certain way ; that is, so that, by reason of the change of its position, either more or less of these singular endless lines of force which make up the magnetic

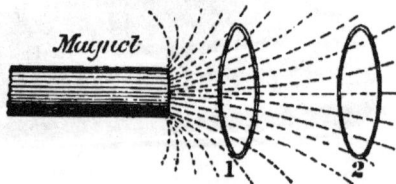

field shall pass through the coil. There are various ways of doing this. We can move our coil from a place where the lines of force are very numerous, — as near the pole of a magnet, — to a place where they are not so numerous, as indicated by the positions 1 and 2 of the ring in Fig.

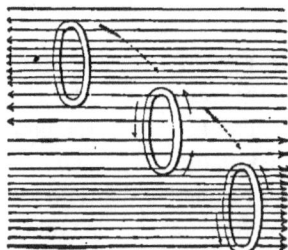

Fig. 39.

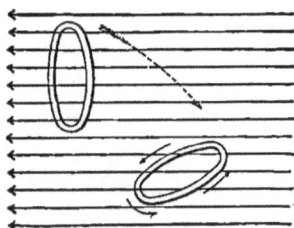

Fig. 40.

38, or 1, 2, and 3, in Fig. 39. Or, we can turn the coil on its axis, as in Fig. 40; in which case, fewer lines of force will pass through it when it lies horizontal than when it stands upright. Or, we can move the coil simply past the pole, as in Fig. 41; the coil here travelling in the

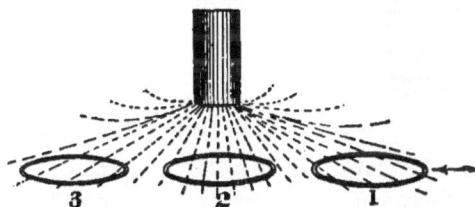

Fig. 41.

direction of the arrow successively into the positions 1, 2, 3, so that it thus moves into and out of the field of the magnet. If, however, the coil should be so moved that the number of lines of force passing through it is not changed, then no current would be produced in its convolutions.

We can easily imagine lines of force extending from the pole *B* of the magnet in Fig. 37; and hence it will be apparent that more or less of these lines will be cut, or, rather, that more or less of them will enter the enclosing coil, whether the magnet be moved into or out of the coil, or, conversely, whether the coil be moved on and off the magnet.

If, for the permanent magnet of Fig. 37, we substitute an electro-magnet as in Fig. 42, the results will be the same. The field of force now produced at the pole or end of the core resembles the field of force of the natural magnet; and the same movements of either coil or magnet, as described with reference to the preceding figure, will cause currents in the large coil.

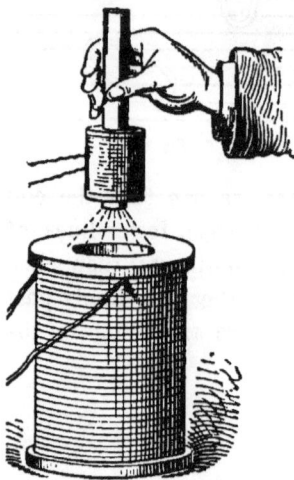
Fig. 42.

Fields of force, however, exist not merely around the poles of magnets, but around wires conveying currents; and the properties of the atmospheres, in either case, are similar. If this be true, then it should follow, that if, in Fig. 42, we remove the magnet bar altogether, and retain simply the wire coil, the current circulating in that coil should produce around it a field of force which should set up a current in another and adjacent coil. This is the fact, and it forms a later discovery by Faraday.

In Fig. 43, the small coil of wire connected with the battery, and hence conveying a current, is introduced into and removed from the large coil connected with the gal-

vanometer. Whenever this is done, the galvanometer
needle swings, proving the existence of a current in the
larger coil.

So far, we have dealt with moving bodies. A magnet,
permanent or electro, *moved* with reference to a closed
coil, produces in the latter a current. The coil, *moved*
with reference to the magnet, accomplishes a like result.
A coil of wire in which a current is flowing, *moved* with
reference to a closed coil in which there is no current,

Fig. 43.

causes a current in the latter: conversely, if the closed
coil be moved. In all of these cases, it is the energy of
motion, as we have stated, which causes the electrical
current.

There is, however, one instance where we can cause a
current in the closed coil, from the coil in which the current is circulating, without moving either of the coils; and
that is simply by starting and stopping the current. The
coils are placed in proximity, as one within the other, and
so fixed. When there is no current in one coil, there is

of course no atmosphere of force to enter the other. The instant the current is established, the atmosphere exists. It comes into being, and affects the outer coil, for example, the same as if the inner coil were moved into it. So, when it disappears, the effect is as if the inner coil were moved out. This is the principle of the inductorium, or induction coil, which is fully described in another chapter.

To recapitulate, therefore : If we bring a closed coil of wire into the strange magnetic atmosphere, we shall cause a current in the coil. So when we take it out. So when we move it from a dense to a thin part of the atmosphere, or *vice versa.* And it makes no difference, in substance, whether we bring the coil into the atmosphere, or move the atmosphere (by moving the thing which it surrounds) into proximity to the coil, or cause the atmosphere suddenly to come into existence around the coil.

Whatever happens is the result either of the coming into or going out of existence, or of proximity, of the magnetic atmosphere, with relation to the coil; or of changes in the position of the coil in that atmosphere. To speak of the coil enclosing more or less of the lines of force, and the current in the coil attending the change, is one convenient way of realizing what occurs. We can express the same idea by saying, that, in order that the coil may have a current in it, it must *cut* the lines of force in its motion, — that is, move across them. These theories are, however, waning. The more modern view is, that the molecules of the wire in the coil are in a condition of equilibrium, liable to instant change ; and this occurs the moment the particles enter the magnetic atmosphere, or field of force, where they become subject to new strains and stresses, which introduce new conditions of balance. In effecting the necessary molecular changes, an expenditure of energy is involved, which results in the current.

This theory has been very fully elaborated by Professor Sprague.

Of course the three theories are, after all, only different ways of saying the same thing. If a coil moves from one part of the field to the other, so that more or less lines of force pass through it, it must cut or pass across lines of force in so moving; and similarly, if, in order to have a current caused in it, it must proceed from one part of the field to another, in which the strains and stresses due to the lines of force shall be different, it follows necessarily that it must go to a place where different lines of force (more or less) exist.

It is not necessary, however, to proceed farther into the realm of theory. For present purposes it is sufficient to recognize that there is a very broad distinction between producing an electric current in a coil of wire by reason of the actual motion of the coil in the magnetic field, or of the field about the coil; and by reason of the establishment or change of strength in a magnetic field about a stationary coil. In the one case, we convert the energy of mechanical motion into electricity: in the other, the energy of one current engenders another current.

With the apparatus wherein the character of the current is changed by the induction of one stationary coil upon another, we have nothing to do in this chapter.

We have frequently referred to the field of force which surrounds the magnetic pole, or current-conducting wire, as an atmosphere. This is a convenient way of thinking of it; but in fact it is nothing material or tangible, as the air, for example, is which surrounds our earth. The same effects are present, even when the most perfect vacuum exists around the magnet; so that it is probable that the magnetic action is propagated through space, by movements or pressure in the ether which is supposed to pervade the entire universe, — to exist between the atoms of all bodies, however solid, as an infinitely thin though jelly-like medium.

One other important fact remains to be noted, before we examine the construction of the machines which produce electricity ; and that is the changes in the direction of movement of current in the coil. In referring to the electro-magnet, in the preceding chapter, we have found that the poles of the magnet depend on the direction of the current traversing the wire, and that we can reverse the pole simply by reversing the direction of the current. The direction of the current of a coil which is moving in a magnetic field depends upon whether the coil is moving from a place where it encloses more lines, to a place where it encloses less lines, or the reverse. The current moves in one direction in one case, in the opposite direction in the other ; and we shall• presently see the effect of this reversal in practice.

In the upper part of the Western Union Telegraph Company's building in New York, there is a large room in which are disposed tier upon tier of galvauic cells. There is no clatter and rush of machinery, no noise except such as rises from the busy street without, or comes from the numberless telegraph-instruments in another part of the building. Here are generated the electrical currents which are to find their way over thousands of miles of wire, and carry the messages of the great metropolis throughout the country.

Not far from the telegraph-offices is the establishment of one of the corporations which provide the electric lights which now illuminate the city thoroughfares ; and here are generated the currents which feed these miniature suns. But now, instead of the perfect silence with which the mighty forces of chemical affinity do their work in the battery, there is the thunder of great engines, the roar of the escaping steam, and the bewildering whirr of the huge dynamos. The visitor is warned away from the wires : it is death to touch them. Here and there are brilliant flashes of light. An odd odor is in the air. But above all there is motion, — as driving, as headlong, as impetuous, as unremitting, as that of the locomotive in its hurried course.

As we become accustomed to the confusion and noise, we find that the source of power is a steam boiler, and that the steam drives a steam-engine, no different from other steam-engines except that it is constructed to run with especial steadiness and uniformity. The work of this steam-engine is to turn the "dynamo;" and in and by the dynamo, the electricity is produced. This is obviously very unlike the production of the current by a battery. There are no chemicals here, no zinc consumed. The engine simply rotates the dynamo shaft; and in the wires leading from the machine the current circulates, and goes to the lamps.

The idea will perhaps occur to us, that, inasmuch as here is a machine which is rotated, and which produces electricity, we perhaps have in the dynamo only some more modern and improved form of the old frictional or static machine, in which the glass or sulphur cylinder is excited by rubbing. This is very wide of the truth. If we could see into the dynamo, — and it is quite possible to do so, in some forms of the apparatus, — we should at once discover that the thing revolved does not rub against any thing, but apparently turns freely in the air. We should also notice that the revolving object is substantially a solid mass ; that there is nothing moving inside of it. On closer examination, we should find it to be a bundle of wires; and if we examined the mass of metal which surrounds this rotating mass of wire, we should find that the same was a magnet or perhaps several magnets.

We thus recognize the dynamo as a machine wherein coils of wire are moved in a very intense magnetic field produced by the encompassing magnets; and, from what has been before explained, we know that it is simply requisite to dispose these coils so that they will be carried through this field, embracing at times more and at times less of the pervading lines of force, to cause in them currents of electricity. This, however, is exactly what is done in the old Clarke magneto machine, represented in Fig. 36; so that there is no difference in principle between the dynamo and the magneto-electric machine as an electrical generator.

But we shall further find, that in lieu of the permanent magnet, for producing the field, the dynamo has an electro-magnet; and we have seen that the strength of an electro-magnet is not a permanent and fixed quantity, but, up to the point of so-called saturation, depends upon the strength of the current in the coils surrounding its core. In this way we can make immensely strong magnets, and, consequently, immensely strong fields of force; and, the stronger the field, the more lines of force there are in it. Hence if we rotate coils of wire through that field, they will cut large numbers of lines of force; and the consequence of this is very strong currents produced in the coils. And thus it becomes possible to obtain, from dynamo-electric machines, currents of electricity far stronger and more powerful than ever could be got from magneto-electric machines.

Let us now analyze this mechanical generator of electricity a little more closely. The two principal parts of the machine are the magnets which make the field of lines of force, — or the field-magnets, — and the body which revolves in that field. This body is called the armature; and it consists of a core or mass of magnetic metal, such as iron, and the coils wound thereon. We have already seen, that, when an armature of iron is placed before the poles of a magnet, the lines of force will apparently run into the armature. Consequently, if we place the coil which is to receive and to cut these lines of force, on an iron body, we place it on something which will apparently draw the

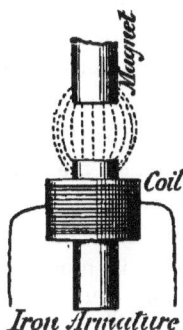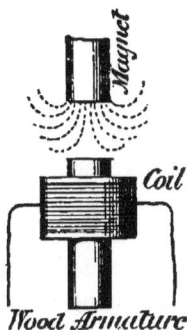

Iron Armature — Fig. 44.   *Wood Armature* — Fig. 45.

lines of force into the coil. If we made the support for the coil of wood, for example, then very much fewer lines of force would pass through the coil. This difference will be clear from Figs. 44 and 45, which show the lines passing to an iron armature, and the lines unaffected by the wooden one.

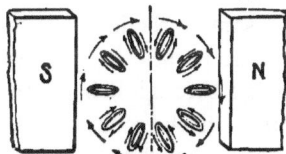

Fig. 46.

Now let us see what happens when a coil — which, for convenience, we will represent by a simple ring — moves around between two strong magnetic poles. In Fig. 46, these poles are represented at *N* and *S;* the ring is supposed to assume the several positions represented. We are going to see a paradoxical state of affairs, which will require some thought — which the reader can avoid, if he chooses, by skipping the next page or so, and reading only the conclusion of the explanation.

The lines of force pass almost directly between the

poles, as represented by the dotted lines. Beginning at the left, the ring at first stands nearly horizontal, so that hardly any of the lines of force thread through it. As it is carried upward and around, in the direction of the arrow, toward a vertical position, the number of lines of force passing through, however, increases ; and a current is set up in the ring, in the direction of the small arrows. As it moves farther, it receives more and more lines ; and finally when it reaches the central point, marked by the vertical dotted line, the number of lines passing through reaches a maximum. Then the ring begins to turn flat-ways again ; the lines passing through it now commence to decrease in number, and the current in the ring changes direction. The decrease in the lines goes on until the ring becomes once more horizontal. Now the ring enters the lower right-hand quadrant, and begins to thread more lines of force. But here the current does not appear to change direction. This is because we have reversed the ring itself, and the lines of force are entering the opposite side from that hitherto presented ; so that, although we have an increase in the lines of force, the current apparently continues in the same direction. This state of affairs goes on until the ring passes the central point, when the lines of force running through it begin to decrease. This reverses the current in the ring, which after passing through the left-hand lower quadrant reaches its starting-point.

It is not particularly easy to understand this, chiefly because it is necessary to bear in mind both the reversal of the current and the reversal of the ring. The current changes in space on passing the pole where the lines decrease or increase, so that there is no variation from the law. But it does not change with reference to the ring. This can be shown rather neatly in the following way:

Let the black circle of Fig. 47 represent the ring, with the currents flowing in it in the direction of the arrows, — that is, in the direction in which the hands of a watch move. Now let the reader hold this page up to the light, and look at the figure from the rear of the page. It will look like Fig. 48. According to the arrows, the current will be moving opposite the hands of a watch, and in just the reverse direction from before. That comes from simply reversing the ring. Suppose, however, that when we looked at the ring reversed by ourselves, the currents reversed simultaneously on their own account : then, instead of the arrows appearing as in Fig. 48, they would appear in the reverse direction as in Fig. 49. But Fig. 49 is just the same as Fig. 47 ; which, as the geometry says, was to be proved.

Fig. 47.

The sum and substance of all this is, that, when the coil is carried around in front of the poles, the current produced in it reverses in direction every time it passes the neutral line between the poles. This is what electricians call an alternating current; and, while it is not particularly important for the non-professional reader to consider very deeply why or how it thus alternates, it is of some moment that the difference between what is meant by an alternating current which is constantly changing its direction like a pendulum, and a continuous direct current which flows but in one way like a river, be understood. From the difference in their capacity to produce either an alternating or a continuous direct current, dynamo and magneto electric machines may be divided into two distinct classes.

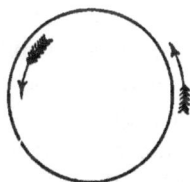

Fig. 48.

Returning now to Fig. 46, it will be apparent, that, if we arrange a number of coils around a circular disk, and between the poles of a magnet, we shall get alternating currents from each coil, and thus a succession of rapid alternations as the coils move swiftly past the neutral points between the poles. If we had but a single coil, then, in addition to the current constantly changing direction, it would, while flowing, vary in strength. This difficulty we overcome, in a measure, by multiplying the coils so that each shall be brought successively into operation, the current beginning in one coil before it has ceased in another.

Alternating currents are very useful in many cases, but for most purposes we need a direct, continuous flow. We find alternating action in mechanical devices very useful in pumps and steam-hammers; but if a locomotive, for example, could be moved only a little way in one direction, and then a little way in the other, it would not be of much use to draw trains.

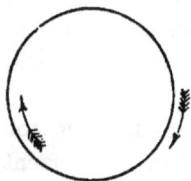

Fig. 49.

Yet this is how the piston in the locomotive-cylinder travels; and the piston, in turn, moves the whole great machine. But the locomotive does not follow the to-and-fro movement of the piston; because, when that movement reaches the wheels, it is converted into a uniform rotary movement by the crank, which pushes the wheel above the hub, and pulls it below, so that the wheel can turn in one direction, and the engine goes straight ahead.

There is a little contrivance connected with alternating-current machines, called a commutator, which does for the alternating current about what the crank does for the alternating steam-pressure. In its simplest form this is represented in Fig. 50, and it can be seen on a small scale in the engraving of Clarke's magneto machine, Fig. 36. This consists of a simple piece of brass or copper tube, slit longitudinally into two portions, and fixed upon the axis of revolution of the armature so as to revolve with it; the two halves of the split tube being fixed upon a small cylinder of ivory or other insulating material. One half of the tube is attached to one end of the wire of the coil,— or, where there are several coils, to like ends of the wires of all the coils, — and the other half to the other end or ends. Against the split tube are pressed two springs or brushes, AA. Suppose the armature carrying the coil or coils to be rotating in the direction indicated by the arrow in the engraving. During one half of the revolution the. current will flow toward the commutator, and during the other half the current will flow from it; because, as we have seen, the current reverses during each revolution of the coil. Now, as each end of the wire is connected to a separate part of the commutator, it follows that while the armature is passing one part of its revolution, — say, the upper part, — the current will flow to the commutator plate which is uppermost; and while the armature is completing the other part of its revolution, the current (reversed) will flow from the other, or lower, commutator plate. Consequently each half of the split tube will, as it passes over the top of its axis, deliver to the upper contact spring or brush the current flowing into it, while the lower contact brush will always (apparently) be feeding the return currents back to the lower half of the split commutator tube. So that, if we connected our

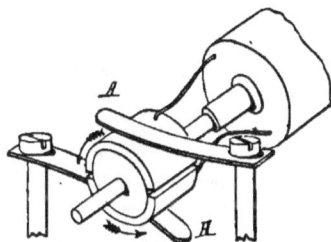
Fig. 50.

circuit wires to the two brushes, or springs, we should have a continuous current flowing in the wire from the upper brush to the lower one.

In general it may be stated, that, in all apparatus of the alternating-current type, there are a number of coils placed on the rim of a wheel which revolves, and is surrounded by fixed magnets. Alternating currents — that is, currents alternately in opposite directions — are produced in the coils, and are either used as alternating currents, or

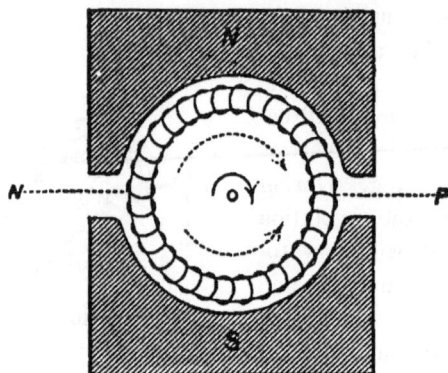

Fig. 51.

are converted into direct currents by being passed through a commutator before they go to the line wire.

There are two types of direct-current machines, known after their inventors as the Gramme and the Siemens forms. A simple diagram of the Gramme apparatus is given in Fig. 51. The armature is a ring of soft iron, around which the wire is wound in a continuous spiral, forming a closed circuit. It revolves between two poles of opposite names, the lines of force from which terminate in the ring; as shown in Fig. 52, which represents a section made through Fig. 51 by a plane in the line NS of Fig. 51 and at right angles to the plane of the paper. As the ring revolves, these lines of force are cut by the

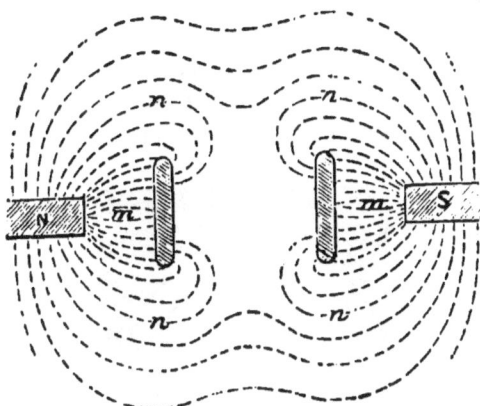

Fig. 52.

moving wires, and electro-motive forces are generated in the two halves of the ring, in opposite directions, so that they meet and op-
pose one another at the neutral points *NP*, as in Fig. 53. As long as no further connections are made, no current is gener-ated. If, however, the *N* points *NP* are connected by a wire in circuit, through a number of lamps, for ex-ample, as in Fig. 54, then a current will flow from *P* to *N*. In order to col-lect the currents from the

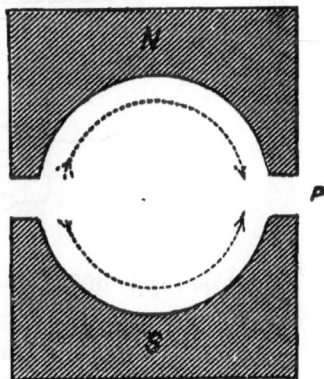

Fig. 53.

ring, a special device, called a collector, is employed. This is usually made of a cylinder of wood or other insulating material, upon which are placed longitudinally a number of insulated metal strips. Each strip or bar is connected by a wire to the part of the spiral coil immediately opposite to it, as represented in Fig. 55. At the points *PN*, where the opposite electro-motive forces diverge and join again, two metal brushes rub against the strips; and with these brushes the external circuit is connected.

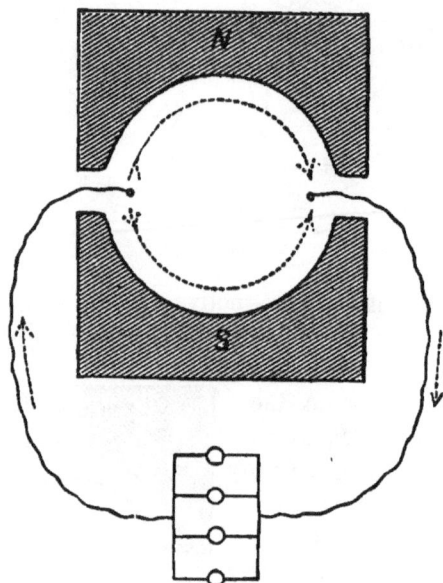

Fig. 54.

The second type of direct-current dynamo employs the Siemens or drum armature, in which the coils of wire are wound lengthways over a drum or spindle; the wire being carried along the drum parallel to its axis, across the end, back along the drum on the side opposite, and so around to the starting-point; the separate turns, or groups of turns, being spaced out at regular intervals all around the drum. This method of winding is illustrated in Fig. 56. In each of the wires, as it rises past the south pole, currents are generated which flow towards the front; whilst in the other half of their revolution, in descending past the north pole, the currents generated in them flow from the front towards the back. The method of joining the coils to the commutator bars insures that the currents shall follow one another, and flow into the upper contact brush.

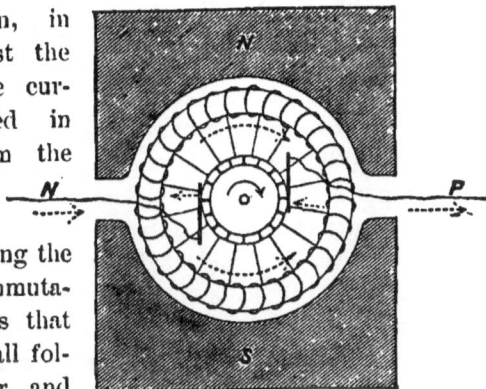

Fig. 55.

We have now recognized the two principal types of mechanical electrical generators, — namely, the alternating-current apparatus and the direct-current apparatus; the difference being in the construction of the armature.

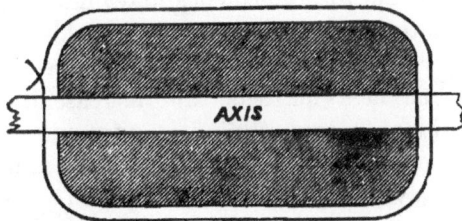

Fig. 56.

The magnets may be either permanent or electro, so that the classification applies to either magneto or dynamo electric machines; but in fact all so far described was invented some years before the modern dynamo may be said to have begun its existence.

The Siemens armature was devised by Dr. C. W. Sie-

mens, in 1856 ; and the continuous-ring armature was contrived by Dr. Pacinotti of Florence, Italy, in 1860. The
compound multipolar armature dates back farther than
either.

In 1867 Mr. H. Wilde replaced the permanent field-magnets by electro-magnets ; and these he excited by means
of a small separate magneto electric machine having
itself permanent steel magnets. This was a very material improvement ; because the small magneto machine
utilized all its current in exciting the electro-magnets of
the larger apparatus, which thus were enabled to produce
a very intense field of force. Following this came the
quadruple yet independent discoveries of Hjorth, Varley,
Siemens, and Wheatstone, that there was no need of a
separate exciting machine, for the generator could be
made to excite itself. This is somewhat paradoxical at
first, but in reality not at all difficult to understand. It
is necessary, to begin with, that the field magnets should
have some little magnetism of their own. A very little is
quite sufficient. If they are magnetic at all, they have
a field of force ; and in the coils of an armature rotating
in that field, there is therefore produced a very weak
current.

Now suppose that the wire which constitutes the armature coil forms also the enveloping coil of the field-magnets : then the current produced on the armature will
circulate around the field - magnets, and increase their
magnetism. Then, of course, their field of force will
become stronger, and so will the current in the armature ; and in this way the cycle will be completed. The
result is, that, in a few seconds after the armature is
set rotating, the field-magnets are magnetized to saturation, — or to as great a degree as they are capable of
reaching. This is called the dynamo electric machine ;

in contra-distinction to the apparatus already described, wherein the magnets are permanent, or always of the same strength.

When the dynamo is intended to produce alternating currents, the separate-excitation system is employed. This is illustrated in Fig. 57. A small separate magneto machine, not shown, energizes the large field-magnets S N by circulating in the coil surrounding the same, as shown

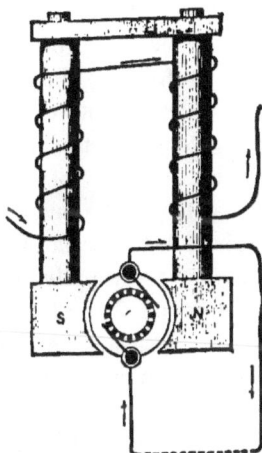 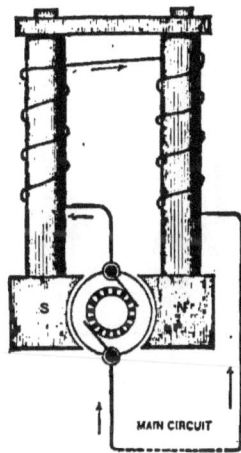

Fig. 57.   Fig. 58.

by the arrows. The current produced by the dynamo, whose magnets are thus excited, moves in a separate circuit, as shown.

Fig. 58 represents a self-exciting dynamo, on what is termed the series system. Here the current, taken at one of the brushes of the commutator, passes around the field-magnets, and then through the main circuit, and so back to the other brush.

Fig. 59 represents a self-exciting dynamo on the so-called shunt system. In this arrangement, the current is divided; part going from the brushes around the magnets by way of the thin line of wire, and part going by the main line to the external circuit.

Various other arrangements of the circuit wires for exciting the field-magnets in dynamos have been invented. The foregoing are, however, the most important.

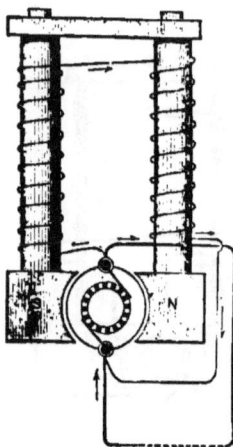

Inasmuch as the currents produced by a dynamo-electric generator depend upon the cutting of the lines of the field of force by the armature, it follows that it is necessary, in order to obtain powerful currents, to cause the armature coils to cut as many of these lines as possible in the shortest time. To this end, the armature is made to rotate very rapidly, and is given a large number of turns of wire, or coils enclosing as much area as possible. In order that the current may not be wasted in overcoming the resistance of the armature coils, these are made to offer as little resistance as possible; and, finally, as the number of lines of force to be cut depends on the strength of the field of force, the field-magnets are placed to concentrate the lines of force as much as possible across the space where the armature revolves.

Fig. 59.

There is an immense variety of forms of dynamo and magneto electric apparatus; and to review them, even in the briefest manner, would far exceed our present limits. Only a few typical machines are therefore given.

Fig. 60 represents the De Meritens magneto-electric

machine. This contains one or more rings carrying coils which revolve between the poles of powerful steel magnets. As the wheel revolves, the polarities of the cores are constantly reversed, and currents are therefore induced on

Fig. 60.

the wires. The ring is of light brass, and the coils are wound upon iron cores. This is an example of an alternating-current magneto machine.

An alternating-current dynamo is represented in the

Siemens machine shown in Fig. 61. This consists of
two fixed iron rings carrying electro-magnets, which are
excited by a small auxiliary direct-current machine. The
polarity of the magnets in each ring is alternately north
and south, and the polarity of each is opposite to that of

Fig. 61.

the magnet facing it on the other ring. Each magnet has
an extended flat pole plate, as shown. Between the two
rings of magnets, revolves a wheel partly of wood, partly
of metal, carrying in its circumference a number of coils
equal to the number of magnets in each ring. As the
wheel revolves, currents are induced in these coils in the

manner already explained. The currents are taken off by springs.

The Brush machine belongs to the same general class as the foregoing, but differs in the construction of its armature, which consists of a wrought-iron ring, around which the wire is wound in the hollow channels, as shown in Figs. 62 and 63. The ring revolves between magnets having extended pole pieces, the two opposed poles at the same side of the ring being of the same name.

The Siemens machine represented in Fig. 64 has an armature in the form of an iron cylinder, around which the wire is wound longitudinally so that the wire is parallel to the axis. The collector consists of a num-

Fig. 62.

Fig. 63.

ber of strips of metal fixed on an insulating barrel. The magnets are bars of wrought iron, straight at the ends and curved in the middle. The current in the magnetizing-coils has such directions that the whole of the curved portion of the magnets at the top of the machine has one polarity, and that at the bottom of the machine the opposite. The outer ends of the upper and lower magnets, which are of opposite polarities, are connected by yoke plates in the usual way.

Fig. 65 represents a large Edison machine. The armature consists of a number of disks of thin iron plate, separated by paper, and grouped together to form a barrel about three feet six inches in length. A number of copper bars are laid on the circumference of this barrel, parallel to the axis. The diameter of the barrel outside the bars is twenty-eight and a half inches. The bars are connected so as to form a continuous circuit, analogous to

Fig. 64.

the longitudinally wound wire in the Siemens machine. The whole armature revolves between the poles of a very large electro-magnet; these poles being immense blocks of cast iron, which nearly meet, but are kept apart by the brass distance pieces seen in the front of Fig. 65. The lines of force from the magnets terminate in the central iron barrel. The magnet coils are twelve in number, and are each eight feet long. This machine will maintain from a thousand to twelve hundred lamps of sixteen-

Fig. 65.

candle power each. Its total weight is about twenty-five tons.

The foregoing examples will suffice to give a general idea of how dynamos are constructed. Of the two principal types, those which give the direct current are the best for general use. For electro-plating and other electrolytic operations, a direct current is, in fact, essential; and it is necessary, of course, to maintain the continuous magnetization of electro-magnets.

Alternating-current machines are simpler in construction; and their current, as will be seen hereafter, is especially adapted to incandescent lamps. They cannot excite their own magnets, nor can they drive existing electromotors. Good dynamo machines will return from seventy to eighty per cent of the power expended in driving them, in the form of electricity. This, however, refers to large machines : small apparatus, intended to be driven by hand, cannot be depended upon to utilize much over one-fifth of the power ; and, in fact, it is better not to use the dynamo on a small scale, but in such case to substitute permanent magnets for the electro-magnets. One of the best forms of machines of this class contains a Gramme ring armature, revolving between cast-iron pole pieces fitted with a form of magnet devised by M. Jamin. The Jamin magnets are exceedingly powerful, and are made of successive layers of hoop-steel let into and riveted to the pole pieces.

CHAPTER VIII.

THE ELECTRIC LIGHT. — THE CONVERSION OF ELECTRICAL
ENERGY INTO HEAT AND LIGHT.

WHEN a current of electricity flows along a wire, it is
opposed by the resistance of the wire ; just, for example,
as a current of water is retarded by its friction against
the pipe which encloses it.   Every one knows that when
a body is rubbed against another body, friction results.
When there is friction, there is heat ; and when there is
much friction, the heat may become intense enough to set
either or both bodies on fire if they are of inflammable
material, or, if not inflammable, to cause them to glow or
become red or white hot.   The ordinary friction-match is
an example of an inflammable body thus set on fire.   The
line attached to a whaler's harpoon, after the whale is
struck, is dragged over the side of the boat so rapidly
that water must be poured on it to keep the wood rubbed
from being set on fire.   The brake-shoes of a railway-
car, rubbing against the wheels when the brakes are put
down, cause, by their friction, brilliant streams of intensely
heated minute particles of iron.   The journals of these
wheels, or of any machinery, become highly heated by
the rubbing friction when no lubricant is present.   A
piece of iron pounded smartly with a hammer becomes
hot.   The striking of a bullet or cannon-ball upon a mass
of iron is attended by intense heat produced at the place

of impact, and a bright flash of light. We apply friction to members of the body benumbed by cold, — rubbing our hands together to warm them.

Of course it should not be understood that there is really mechanical friction between a current of electricity, and the wire through which it passes. As has already been explained, we speak of electricity as a thing, or corporeal substance, merely for convenience' sake in talking about it. Its effect, however, in traversing a conductor, resembles that which might follow the movement of a body through that conductor, despite the apparent solidity of the latter, in that the conductor becomes the more heated as it offers more resistance to the flow. Consequently, the more resistance there is, the more of the energy of the current is expended in overcoming it; the more work is done at the place where it is overcome. Just as the energy of the movement of the hand which strikes a friction-match is converted into the heat which raises the inflammable material to a condition when it bursts into flame, so the energy of the seemingly moving current in overcoming the obstacle offered by the wire raises the temperature of the wire. If the wire is long or thick, this elevation of temperature may be so much distributed as not to be noticeable; but if we make the wire very thin, the heat produced may be sufficient to cause it to become red hot or white hot and so dazzlingly bright, or, if the wire is not of a refractory material, to melt it. If, to illustrate, we connect the poles of a powerful galvanic battery with a short piece of fine platinum wire, — platinum because it will withstand a high temperature, — we shall see the platinum become intensely hot and glow. This is because the energy of the current, opposed by the resistance of the very narrow path through which it is driven, heats its channel.

As a fine red-hot wire will burn its way easily through many substances, instruments containing such wires are used in surgery for the performance of operations in which the cautery of the wire attending its cutting action is desirable; and there have been devices proposed for cutting timber and shearing sheep in the same way. In these cases, the heat of the wire is utilized.

When the heat of a body of metal is greatly augmented, it becomes intensely luminous, — so much so, that it is impossible to gaze upon molten steel in the furnace without the aid of some means for protecting the eyes. The sun itself is in this intensely heated and luminous state. If we use a resisting body which will not melt, we can raise its temperature so high by a strong electric current that it will glow with a brilliancy which is exceeded only by that of the sun; and the luminosity so caused is termed the electric light.

The electric light, therefore, is the direct application of the heat produced by the energy of the electric current. This energy is caused to overcome the resistance, usually, of a short interval of highly resisting material, — short because it is advantageous to concentrate the heat, and so have its utmost intensity in the smallest possible space.

The electric light is not produced from electricity. This sounds paradoxical, but only so because of our false thinking again of the current as a tangible thing. If we start with a certain quantity of electricity, — such, for example, as is generated by the consumption of a given amount of zinc in a battery, — that same quantity will go through its conductor, and may be, so to speak, gathered, wholly regardless of whether it heats the conductor or not. It makes no difference whether it goes straight from the cell to an electro-plater's bath, where it may cause the deposition of a certain amount of copper; or whether, on its way thither, it heats an electric lamp: only it will take longer to go through the circuit in the last case. If we dammed a certain amount of water in a mill-pond, with which to drive a water-wheel, we know perfectly well that all the water will go through or over the wheel which is driven by it. The wheel simply takes the energy of the water. It does not consume the water itself. So in the steam-engine. We heat water to make steam. We use the energy thus imparted to it; and after we are done with the steam, it condenses back to water again. Of course it all ciphers down to the fundamental law that the matter and force in the universe are alike indestructible, and that we can merely change them from one form to another, without addition to or subtraction from the total amount. This, however, is the deep water of science; and this chapter is about the electric light, and not the abstractions of philosophy.

Whenever, then, an electric current meets resistance in its passage, heat is developed. If a body intensely charged with electricity approaches a non-electrified body, then the current tends to pass from the former to the latter. If the energy of the current can overcome the resisting medium between the bodies, it will do so; and in doing so, it will develop heat. Now, air is a substance which offers the highest resistance to the current. Hence, as we have seen, it requires electricity of enormous electro-motive force to pass over a very small air interval. Thus a cloud may become electrified very intensely; and when it approaches a cloud oppositely electrified, or of lower potential, then the current will force its way through the intervening air. In overcoming that resistance, its energy will be converted into heat and light. The flash thus caused we call lightning; and so the electric light existed from the beginning. But think of the fate which would have awaited the impious Roman or Greek, a couple of thousand years ago, who should venture the prediction that the streets of Rome or Athens would one day be lit by Jupiter's thunderbolts, quietly blazing on the tops of long poles!

The first electric light produced by human agency was obtained by Burgomaster Von Guericke, from his revolving sulphur globe. Priestley says that Robert Boyle got "a glimpse of the electric light" before Von Guericke;

Fig. 66.

"for he found that a curious diamond which Mr. Clayton brought from Italy, gave light in the dark when it was rubbed against any kind of stuff; and he found that by the same treatment it became electrical."

In Gravesande's "Mathematical Elements of Natural Philosophy" (1731), appear the engravings Figs. 66 and 67, which are reproduced from that work in facsimile. These represent the earliest methods of production of the electric light, other than by the simple rubbing of amber and like substances by hand. In Fig. 66 is shown a glass globe which is to be "briskly whirl'd in a dark place, the Hand all the while being held against it, to give it Attrition. If the Globe be exhausted of its Air, it will appear all luminous within, but mostly so where the Hand touches the Glass. But if the Globe has Air in it and being whirl'd in the same Manner, the Hand be applied to it, no Light appears, either in the inner or outer surface of the Glass; but Bodies at a small distance from the Glass (as for Example at a Quarter of an Inch, or nearer) become luminous; and so only those Parts of the Hand held against the Glass, which terminate or rather environ the Parts that immediately touch the Globe, are luminous."

Observe the reason : " that Glass contains in it and has about its surface a certain Atmosphere which is excited by Friction and put into Vibratory Motion : the Fire contained in the Glass is expelled by the Action of this Atmosphere," and " this Atmosphere and Fire is more easily moved in a Place void of Air."

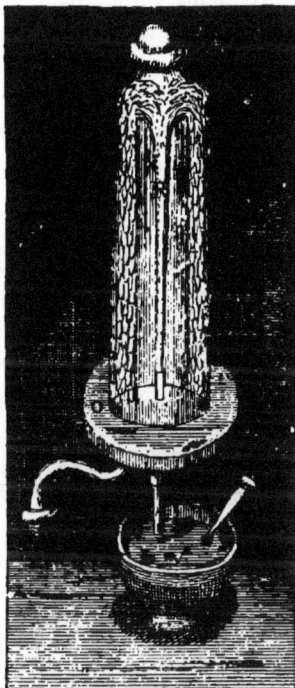

Fig. 67.

. Farther on, the author concludes that quicksilver contains fire; " for if mercury well cleaned be shak'd about in an exhausted Glass it will appear luminous; " and then he suggests the apparatus represented in Fig. 67, which is a bell-glass from which air has been exhausted, and into which mercury is caused to spout by the pressure of the external atmosphere. "The experiment must be made in a dark place, and the mercury will appear luminous."

These experiments were devised by Hawksbee in 1709. He called the mercury jet the "mercurial phosphorus," and did not consider the glass as in any way concerned in producing the light. "The greatest electric light Mr. Hawkesbee produced," says Priestley, "was when he enclosed one exhausted cylinder within another not exhausted, and excited the outermost of them, putting them both in motion. Whether their motions conspired or not, he observed, made no difference. When the outer cylinder only was in motion, he says, the light was very considerable, and spread itself over the surface of the inner glass. What surprised him most was, that after both glasses had been in motion some time, during which the hand had been applied to the surface of the outer glass, the motion of both ceasing, and no light at all appearing; if he did but bring his hand again near the surface of the outer glass, there would be flashes of light, like lightning, produced on the inner glass: as if, he says, the effluvia from the outer glass had been pushed with more force upon it by means of the approaching hand."

For a long time after Hawkesbee, no further experiments on the electric light were made. In fact, the use of the rotating globe machine was discontinued; and to this circumstance Priestley ascribes the slow progress afterwards made in electrical discoveries. Meanwhile the idea that the electric spark could be utilized as a light did not seem to strike any one. The philosophers kept getting shocks from different things, and discovering afterwards that they were electrical. They obtained fine flashes from cats, and pondered long over the problem of why cats gave sparks; until one Waitz, having procured "a dry dog," applied vehement friction to the unhappy ani-

mal, and so found, not only that dogs gave sparks as well
as cats, but that these sparks were electrical. "This,"
remarks Priestley in his most owlish manner, "had been
supposed, but was not accurately ascertained before."
One is tempted to ask why; but Priestley vouchsafes no
further information.

It will be remembered, that in describing the extraordinary effects of the shock of the Leyden-jar upon the
electricians of the period, when it was first produced, we
adverted to the exaggerations of these learned persons.
It is difficult to trace the history of electricity without
experiencing a sense of mild wonder as to whether there
is not, perhaps, some subtle influence of the mysterious
current exerted upon the moral faculties of those who
deal with it, — or, rather, invent around it, — which induces them to view facts differently from most people.
And it is singular how this peculiar obliquity of vision
affects those who have to do with the electric light; not
in these times (as every one who precipitately sold his gas
stock during the electric-light scare of 1879–80 can tes-
tify), but, of course, a hundred years ago.

There was Boze of Wittenberg, who some time before
had wanted to die from the effects of a shock for the sake
of personal advertisement; and who had discovered, by
the way, that water running from a vessel in drops would
escape in a constant stream when electrified, a valuable
idea long afterwards utilized by Sir William Thomson
in his siphon recorder. Boze was a most meritorious investigator, until he became entangled in an electric-light
scheme. He said that *he* gave light, — not sparks of the
cat-and-dog order, but that *he* himself had only to be electrified, and he would become a perfect illumination. He
called it a "beatification;" and furthermore, with all the
vigor of the man who prophesies that by next Christmas

gas will be extinct in every dwelling in the land, he assev-
erated that a glory would form around his head, just like
the rings or miniature auroras represented by painters
about the heads of saints. It is all solemnly recorded in
" Philosophical Transactions." Although the reader may
look in vain through that erudite work, for any reference
to the Boze Electric Light Company (limited), this remarkable announcement — to quote Priestley once more —
" set all the electricians in Europe to work, and put them
to a great deal of expense."

Among these electricians was Dr. Watson; who, having
failed to see why there should be such a thing as Boze
electricity any more than cat electricity or dry-dog electricity, — or, in other words, disbelieving Boze's whole story,
— caused himself to be electrified while perched on a huge
cake of pitch, just as Boze described. He candidly
admitted, that, so far as he was concerned, he felt the
skin of his head tingle, and the rather disagreeable sensation of things creeping over him ; but despite his remaining, with exemplary patience, several hours in the dark,
under these not wholly pleasant conditions, no truthful
person could be found who for a single moment would
admit that any light was visible.

It is perhaps as well that the argument which Watson
thereupon addressed to Boze is not set down. Ultimately,
however, Boze confessed that he had dressed himself in a
suit of metal armor covered with points, many of which
radiated from the helmet, and the sparks were produced
from these in the usual way (brush discharge) when a
strong charge was conducted to them.

There was a poetic justice in the penalty inflicted on
Boze. He claimed afterwards to have discovered that he
could invert the poles of a magnet " by electricity only,
to destroy their virtue, and restore it again." He did not

describe his method: what it may have been, or how far
it may have foreshadowed the electro-magnet, no one
knows. He got no hearing, apparently, from the Royal
Society; and his chronicler contemptuously remarks, that,
" considering that no person in England could succeed in
this attempt, and that we are now (1769) able to do it but
imperfectly, it is hardly probable that he did it at all."
And that was the fate of the first philosopher who pretended that he had an electric light which he did not have,
and who put the other philosophers "to a great deal of
expense."

In 1745 Mr. Gottfried Gummert of Biala, Poland, in
order to observe whether a tube from which the air was
exhausted would give light when it was electrified, as well
as when it was excited, presented one, some eight inches
in length and about a third of an inch in diameter, to the
electrified conductor of a machine. He was surprised to
find the light dart vividly the whole length of the tube.
This light *in vacuo*, Gummert proposed to make use of
" in mines and places where common fires and other lights
cannot be had." This appears to have been the first
announcement of the discovery, that, by rarefying the
air, the discharging distance, or the space over which the
spark will pass, is augmented, while the discharge itself is
caused to pass silently. It is now known that every attenuated gas has its own color when traversed by the discharge, and that the rosy color of the light seen when
rarefied air is used is due to the nitrogen of our atmosphere. The same color appears in the aurora borealis,
which has the same origin. Tubes containing attenuated
gas are called vacuum or Geissler tubes. Their light is
faint, and has not been practically applied as yet to illuminating purposes. Many of the phenomena observed
with these tubes remain unexplained.

Referring to other modes of causing electric illumination, Priestley, writing in 1769, says, " A variety of beautiful appearances may be exhibited by means of the electrical light, even in the open air if the room be dark. Brushes of light from points electrified positively and not made very sharp, or from the edges of metallic plates, diverge in a very beautiful manner, and may be excited to a great length by presenting to them a finger or the palm of the hand."

The first voltaic pile was constructed in 1800. Eight years later Humphry Davy obtained from the battery of the Royal Institution, the first electric light produced by the constant galvanic current. This battery consisted of two thousand cells, arranged in two hundred porcelain troughs. The fluid was a mixture of sixty parts of water with one of nitric and one of sulphuric acid. The plates were zinc and copper, square in form, and thirty-two square inches in surface. " When pieces of charcoal," says Davy, " about an inch long and one-sixth of an inch in diameter, were brought near each other (within the thirtieth or fortieth part of an inch), a bright spark was produced, and more than half the volume of the charcoal became ignited to whiteness ; and, by withdrawing the points from each other, a constant discharge took place through the heated air in a space equal at least to four inches, producing a most brilliant ascending arch of light, broad and conical in form in the middle."

Davy used pencils of common charcoal, which wasted away rapidly ; and as no means of regulating the distance between them had been devised, the light was of short duration. For some thirty years, the production of the voltaic arc remained an interesting though fruitless laboratory experiment. The power derived from available batteries was weak ; their construction was expensive ; and these difficulties were added to the lack of proper carbons and of controlling apparatus therefor. In 1836 Grove's, and in 1842 Bunsen's, batteries were invented. In Grove's cell the attacked electrode is zinc plunged in dilute sulphuric acid, and contained in a porous jar ; in the outer vessel is platinum immersed in nitric or nitro-sulphuric acid. Bunsen's cell has already been described. Both of these batteries give a high electro-motive force ; their currents were therefore better adapted to overcome the resistance of the carbons and the intervening air space than those of any cells previously invented.

In 1844 Léon Foucault replaced the slides of common charcoal, used since Davy's time, with pieces of gas carbon, and employed the Bunsen cell as a current-generator. He also contrived a means of regulating the lamp by hand. With this apparatus M. Deleuil took photographs ; and in French treatises he is often accorded the credit of being the first person to use the electric light for such a purpose. This, however, is not the fact. In November, 1840, Prof. B. A. Silliman, jun., and Dr. W. H. Goode obtained " photographic impressions by galvanic light reflected from the surface of a medallion to the iodized surface of a daguerrotype plate," using the large battery of nine hundred cells belonging to the laboratory of Yale College. Two pictures were obtained : one " made up of a blur or spot produced by the light from the charcoal points, the image of the retort-stand on which a medallion of white plaster rested, and the image of the medallion ; " the other picture was of the medallion only. An interesting account of this experiment was published in the Journal of the Franklin Institute in 1843.

One evening in December, 1844, during a thick fog, the people who were passing the Place de la Concorde in Paris were astonished by suddenly finding that they could see

clearly, although the gas-lamps at a distance of a few yards
were invisible. A very intense light traversed the atmosphere, and illuminated even the remotest corners of the vast
square. This was an electric light, and the occurrence is
believed to mark the first illumination of a public thorough-
fare therewith. The Parisians were more than delighted
with the magnificence of the light. In rapid succession
electric lamps were established on the Pont Neuf to illuminate the Seine beneath, on the Arc de Triomphe, in the
court of the Palais Royal, and at the Porte St. Martin.
It was simply necessary for an inventor to allege that he
had a new form of lamp, to secure a public trial. With
characteristic ingenuity the scenic artists of the opera
seized upon the light as a means of introducing new and
startling effects into the *mise en scène*. Rossini's "Moses"
was put on the stage, on a scale of great magnificence;
and the beams of the electric light were shed upon the
figure of the inspired prophet, investing him with a supernatural radiance. In the final scene, the spectrum of the
light was used to imitate the rainbow. The Israelites
were grouped on the front of the stage; while in the far
distance, the Egyptians, immersed in partial darkness, are
seen perishing in the waters. Moses, upon a high rock,
holds the tables of the Law. The light, gradually increasing, represents the break of day; at the same moment, as
the symbol of the new covenant, a rainbow appears. One
lamp was placed behind the rock in the foreground, and
its light concentrated upon the characters; the rest of the
stage being in obscurity. The beam of a second lamp,
after dispersion by a prism, painted itself as a rainbow
upon the scene at the back.

The mode of producing the voltaic arc is quite simple.
The two rods of carbon are first placed in contact. The

current then passes from one to the other ; and while it is
so passing, the rods are gradually separated. During this
action, the current heats the air, and also vaporizes a portion of the conductor, so that the interval between the rods
becomes filled with carbon probably in a gaseous state.
This carbon vapor, while it conducts the current, offers a
high resistance. It becomes white hot. The plus carbon
— or that from which the current flows — is usually the
uppermost, and, being the more highly heated by the current, burns away most rapidly : particles of this carbon are
carried off, and transferred to the negative carbon, which
thus assumes the form of a pointed cone, while the plus
carbon forms a hollow crater of intense brightness, and
acts as a sort of reflector to throw a large proportion of
the light downward.

The temperature of the arc is immensely high, and is
the most intense of all artificial sources of heat. " Platinum," wrote Davy, in the account which he has left of
his famous experiment, " was melted as readily as wax
in the flame of a common candle : quartz, the sapphire,
lime, magnesia, all entered into fusion." The diamond
— a very refractory body — when placed in the arc becomes white hot, swells out, fuses, and gradually transforms into a black crumbling mass. Carbon itself has been
softened so that it can be easily bent and welded. The
temperature of the arc is estimated at about 8700° Fah. ;
but this is not settled. In point of brilliancy, it is rather
less than one-third as bright as the sun. Its characteristic
color is a bluish white ; the carbons giving a white light,
and the arc a bluish purple. The effect is rather ghastly,
owing to the excess of blue rays. The light may be produced not only in air, but also under the surface of water
and other non-conducting liquids, in oils, and in a vacuum ;
so that it appears to be due to the incandescence, and not

to the oxidation, of the carbon. The pressure of the current required to maintain an arc one-tenth of an inch in length is sixty volts, increasing quickly up to a quarter of an inch, and after that at the rate of fifty-four volts per inch. To supply such high pressure, obviously, a large number of battery cells would be required, with attendant large expense due to the consumption of zinc. All the early arc lamps were thus supplied.

Inasmuch as the carbon rods slowly burn away, it is necessary that one of them should be continuously fed forward by suitable machinery, so as to keep the resistance of the arc as constant as possible. Upon the uniform working of this feeding mechanism, greatly depends the steadiness of the light. A great many different forms of apparatus for this purpose exist. We shall therefore refer to but a few of the most typical forms.

For street illumination, it is important that the lamp should give a steady light. In construction it should be not too heavy to be supported by an ordinary lamp-post, and it is important that the mechanism should all be above the lamp so that no shadows may be cast downward.

In the Brush lamp, the feed is actuated by gravity as will be understood from the diagram of the lamp mechanism (Fig. 69). The upper carbon A descends by its own weight until it meets the lower one B. Then the current, moving in the direction of the arrows, is established, and passes between the carbons, and through the coil C of a hollow electro-magnet. In this magnet is a soft iron. plunger D, which, when the magnet is excited, is drawn upward. Through the intervention of a lever and an ingenious annular clutch at E, surrounding the rod of the upper carbon A like a washer, the upper carbon is lifted away from the lower carbon, and thus the arc is established.

As the carbons burn away, the arc has a tendency to

THE ELECTRIC LIGHT IN NAVAL WARFARE.

become longer ; and this, by reducing the strength of the current, diminishes the supporting power of the coil C. The latter then allows its plunger to descend, thus lowering the carbon, and so shortening the arc until the proper strength of the current is restored, when the rising of the plunger once more holds the carbon in position. There is also an ingenious contrivance whereby each lamp in a circuit is enabled to control itself independently of the action of all the others in the circuit. Ordinary Brush lamps such as are used for street-lighting give a light equal to that of about eight hundred candles ; but very large ap-

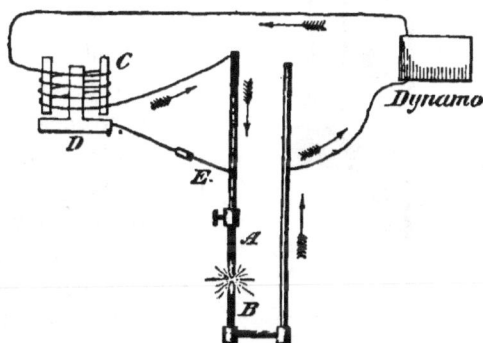

Fig. 69.

paratus of this kind has been made, in which the carbons are three and a half inches in diameter, giving a light equal to that of a hundred and fifty thousand candles. An ordinary Brush street-light such as is used in New-York City is represented in Fig. 70.

The Siemens lamp depends on what is termed the differential principle, which is illustrated in the diagram, Fig. 71. Here the lower carbon B is stationary. The upper carbon A is attached to the end of a rocking arm or lever C, at the other end of which is a core D of soft iron.

This core enters two coils E and F, one above and the other below the lever. The coil E offers a high resistance to the current, because it is of fine wire. The coil F, on the other hand, is of thick wire, and offers little resistance. The current, starting from the dynamo, goes by a wire to the point G. It may now take either of two roads, — through the coil F, the lever C, and the carbons AB, and so by the wire H back to the dynamo, thus completing the circuit; or it may pass through the coil E, and thence by the wire G to the wire H, and so to the dynamo, — in this case, not passing through the carbons at all. Now, the current having two possible paths will divide itself through both, the most current going through the path which offers the least resistance. If we suppose that at the outset the carbons are wholly separated, then there is a very great resistance in the first of the paths above noted: consequently the current will flow around the other path. But in passing through the coil E, it converts that coil into a magnet, which draws up the core D; and when the core D is drawn up, the outer end of the lever C moves down, and thus the carbons are brought into contact. Then the

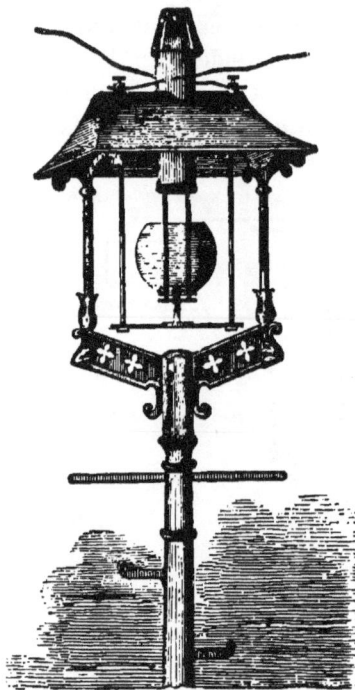

Fig. 70.

current is free to pass through the carbons ; and it does so until they become burned away, too widely separated, and hence the space between them offers so much resistance to the current that the latter again travels through the coil E, and so causes the lever C to bring the carbons nearer together again. When the current passes through the coil F, which it does when supplying the carbons, this coil also acts as a magnet to move the lever in the opposite direction to that in which it is moved by the coil E.

The actions of the two coils balance each other when the resistance of the arc is uniform.

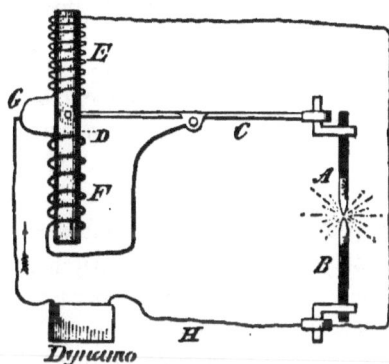

Fig. 71.

The two lamps above described are types of the two principal systems in use. The Brush lamp is based on what is termed the gravity plan, wherein, as we have seen, the weight of one carbon causes its approach to the other, and the magnetism of the current acts against this to separate the carbons. The Siemens lamp, on the other hand, is constructed on the differential system ; the difference between the opposite actions of the two magnets being utilized to control the carbon.

For light-house purposes, it is of course absolutely necessary that the light shall never be extinguished for an instant, and that the mechanism shall be very strong. Expense, weight, and bulk are matters of no moment ; and slight pulsations of the light are not a serious defect. For this use, a comparatively old form of lamp, the

Serrin, is still employed. As the light must be kept in the focus of the reflector, both carbons are fed forward; this being effected by clock-work mechanism actuated by the weight of the upper carbon, so that, as the upper carbon descends, the lower one rises to meet it.

Hitherto we have referred simply to the lamps which are known as "arc lamps," and which, as has been seen, depend upon the production of the voltaic arc between the ends of separated carbon rods. These constitute one principal class. Another class of electric lamp, of much greater importance, — for its applicability is far wider, — is the incandescent lamp, which consists of a thin filament or wire of carbon enclosed in a glass globe from which the air has been exhausted.

The idea of using a body rendered incandescent by the heating action of a current, as a means of illumination, appears to have been first described by Mr. Frederic de Moleyns, who in 1841 patented in England an electric lamp in which a platinum wire enclosed in an exhausted glass globe was to receive a shower of plumbago particles. There is nothing practicable about De Moleyns' idea; and it would doubtless have remained forever in oblivion, had not the English writers on the subject found De Moleyns' patent a convenient peg on which to hang a claim that the incandescent electric lamp is a British invention. The real inventor of the lamp appears to have been J. W. Starr of Cincinnati, O. Starr used an exhausted glass globe in which was a thin strip of graphite held between two clamps affixed to a porcelain rod; the latter being suspended by a platinum wire sealed in the globe. Starr died in 1847, but twenty-five years of age; a victim to overwork, and disappointment in his endeavors to perfect this lamp and a magneto-electric machine to drive it. It gave an excellent light. Starr was evidently a prophet without honor in his own country; for his endeavors to interest others in his invention met with failure, and critics were not wanting who openly asserted that he was simply invoking perpetual motion. This, apparently, because he proposed to utilize a magneto-electric machine to supply his lamp. "The Cincinnati Advertiser" of Sept. 4, 1844, published a letter from a correspondent who stated as follows: —

"1. That this light is magneto-electrical.

"2. That it is produced by permanent magnets, which may be increased to an indefinite extent. The apparatus now finished by the inventors and discoverers in this case will contain twenty magnets.

"3. That it supplies a light whose brilliancy is insupportable to the naked eye.

"4. That a tower of adequate height will enable a light to be diffused all over Cincinnati, equal for practical purposes to that of day.

"5. That this light, when once set in operation, will continue to illuminate without one cent of additional expense.

"6, and lastly. That the inventors in this process have nearly solved the long-sought problem, — perpetual motion. . . . I suppose this light will prove the greatest discovery of modern times. It is needless to add how much it gratifies me, that Cincinnati is the place, and two of its native sons — J. Milton Sanders and John Starr — the authors, of the discovery."

Starr appears thus to have been the first to suggest the lighting of cities by electric lights on high towers. Shortly afterwards, Mr. W. H. Weekes in England proposed supplying lights thus elevated, from earth batteries formed of huge plates of zinc and copper buried beneath the structures. Several years before, he had suggested elevating oxyhydrogen lights in the same way. On the strength of that suggestion, the English journals, as usual, claimed Starr's invention as British; and when Starr's patent appeared, in 1846, they insisted that it was anticipated by De la Rive, who had employed coke cylinders surrounded by rings of metal, between which rings and cylinders the arc passed; and by Grove, who had used platinum spirals. Neither Grove nor De la Rive enclosed an incandescent carbon rod in a globe exhausted of air; but a small difference of that sort did not stand in the way of denying to an American the honor and credit that was his due. It was carrying Sydney Smith's sneering comment, " Who reads an American book? " a little farther by the habitual refusal to believe that any thing good whatever could come out of the Nazareth of the United States.

One of the most extraordinary claims to the honor of the same invention was made not long ago, by M. de Changy, who asserted that as far back as 1838 his friend M. Jobard of Brussels suggested the idea that a small carbon, employed as a conductor of a current in a vacuum, would give an electric lamp with an intense fixed and durable light. Acting on this suggestion, De Changy invented several forms of lamps, using platinum spirals, and even devised systems for the electric lighting of mines, luminous buoys, submerged lamps for fishing, and nautical telegraphy by means of colored tubes containing the incandescent wires. The whole matter was brought before the French Academy of Sciences ; and a commission, of which M. Desprez was the chief, was appointed to examine the invention. De Changy claimed to have succeeded at this time in arranging several lamps in one circuit, which could be lighted simultaneously in groups, or separately without affecting the normal intensity of each.

Desprez wrote for a detailed account of the invention;
which was declined by Jobard, on the ground that the
exposure would affect a pending patent. Thereupon
Desprez — with that singular fatuity concerning patents,
now happily confined to medical practitioners — said that
De Changy evidently desired to make money out of his
invention, and so did not merit the name of *savant*, and
that the Academy had no further interest in his work.
This so disheartened De Changy, that he abandoned his
labors, and as a consequence, — if his statements be correct, — the incandescent light was lost to the world for
more than a quarter of a century. In that interval, however, the Academy changed its views. It decreed the
award of the Volta prize to Mr. Alexander Graham Bell,
upon his claim to the invention of the speaking telephone,
— an instrument which has yet to be given freely to the
world.

The incandescent lamp which forms one of the great
classes of electric illuminating devices, as now constructed,
consists of a thin filament or wire of carbon enclosed in
a glass globe from which the air has been exhausted.
When a current of electricity of suitable strength passes
through the filament, it becomes white hot, or incandescent, and so yields a light of from one to one hundred
candles, according to its surface, and for a given surface
according to the temperature to which it is raised. There
are many forms of incandescent lamps, differing mainly
in detail and more especially in the mode of preparing the
carbon filaments. New forms are constantly appearing.
In all of these, however, the filament is of vegetable fibre,
carbonized by heat. The ends of this filament are connected to two platinum wires which pass through a neck
formed on the globe. These are melted into the glass
itself; and platinum is chosen because it expands by heat

at about the same rate as the glass itself does, so that the latter does not crack in cooling. The exhaustion of the air in the globe must necessarily be as nearly perfect as possible. Without the Sprengel air-pump, it would probably be impracticable to produce an efficient vacuum. This pump consists of glass tubes, down which mercury flows in a broken stream or in drops. Near the top of the tubes are side openings connected to the chamber to be exhausted. Air enters from this chamber, and, becoming compressed between consecutive mercury drops, is carried away; and the process is repeated until the chamber is completely exhausted. While the lamp is still attached to the pump, a current of electricity is sent through the filament, sufficient to raise it to a somewhat higher degree of incandescence than will be used in actual work. All the gas driven out of the carbon is at once removed by the pump, and the lamp is sealed while the current is still passing.

The incandescent lamps in most general use are respectively those devised by Edison and Swan, and these may be taken as typical. Mr. Edison's experiments upon the materials and construction of incandescent lights are probably the most elaborate and far-reaching ever conducted. On the other hand, it is doubtful whether any inventor ever undertook an investigation more abundantly provided with the means for carrying it to successful termination. He began by studying conductors made of an alloy of platinum and iridium, and also of platinum alone; but found that the effect of incandescence upon the wires experimented upon was to produce, all over their surface, innumerable cracks, and in a few hours these fissures united, and the wire fell to pieces. With characteristic ingenuity he contrived a way of heating the wires by a current *in vacuo* so as actually to weld together the edges of these minute cracks ; and finally succeeded in producing metals in a state such as had never been known before, increasing their hardness and density to an extraordinary degree, and raising their fusing-points so high that they remained unaffected at temperatures at which most substances would be melted or consumed, and very many would be converted into vapor. By his process he rendered platinum wire competent to yield a light of twenty-five standard candles ; while the same wire not treated would give a light of not more than four candles before it fused.

Ingenious as this discovery was, it did not solve the problem. The inventor then turned his attention to carbon, — that extraordinary substance which was already playing the principal part in the operation of the speaking telephone, the galvanic battery, and the voltaic arc light. As usual, he carbonized about every thing within reach, — " cotton and linen thread, wood splints, paper coiled in various ways, also lamp-black, plumbago, and carbon in various forms," in his endeavor to make a carbon filament or wire. Later on he settled upon paper, — " Bristol board," — which he punched into narrow elliptical strips. Finally he determined that the carbon should be purely structural in character ; that is, its natural structure, cellular or otherwise, should be preserved unaltered, and not modified by any treatment " which tends to fill up the cells or pores with unstructural carbon, or to increase its density, or alter its resistance." Farther on we shall see that just the opposite view is taken by the inventor of the Swan lamp ; and the curious fact is presented, of two forms of the same apparatus, both fairly successful, yet dependent on radically opposite deductions from experiment.

The fibre now used in the Edison lamps is that of a

grass from South America, called "monkey-bast;" each blade of which is generally round, and composed of a great number of elementary fibres held together by a natural cement or resin, which, carbonizing, locks all the elementary fibres together into a homogeneous filament. The ordinary form of Edison lamp is represented in Fig. 72. The ends of the carbon filament are connected to platinum wires, and these are attached to a screw, and a sole plate stamped from thin copper, and insulated from each other by plaster-of-paris, which surrounds the neck of the envelope, and forms a firm and rigid attachment. The socket into which this fitting screws is simply a counterpart of the thread on the lamp.

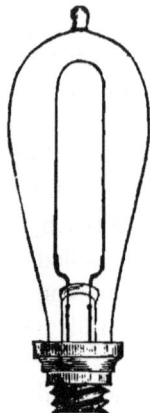

In lieu of using a so-called structural carbon, Mr. Swan in his lamp prefers a filament as far as possible devoid of structure. He steeps a cotton thread in a solution of sulphuric acid and water until the tissue is entirely destroyed, and a horny homogeneous filament is produced, which before carbonization is rendered uniform in density by compression. Fig. 73 represents the present form of Swan lamp.

Fig. 72.

The filament is connected, as usual, to platinum wires, which terminate outside the neck of the globe, in small loops. The globe is entirely separate from the holder; the latter being of ebonite, provided with a screw plug for attachment to the fixture. On the side of the holder are binding posts for the connection of the circuit wires. These posts communicate with platinum hooks, which engage the loops of the globe wire. The neck of the globe rests in a spiral spring, which steadies it, and at the same time causes a slight strain on the hooks, so that the hooks and loops make a very excellent electrical joint. The whole arrangement is about the neatest and most elegant which has thus far been devised for the purpose. The form of the Swan filament is distinctive, it being shaped in a spiral.

M. Muthel, a German inventor, has made an incandescent lamp which requires no vacuum in the globe. He makes a wire of a mixture of bodies which are conductors and nonconductors of electricity, in which fusion is wholly overcome; the non-conducting substances preventing the melting of the metallic parts. It is supposed that the electric spark jumps, so to speak, from one particle to another, and in this way causes a heating of the other substances, which, being brought to incandescence, emit a more intense light.

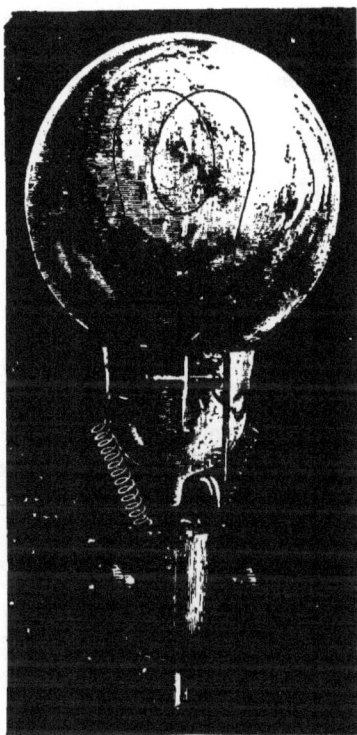

Fig. 73.

There are two ways of arranging electric lamps in order to distribute the current to them. They can be placed one after another in a single circuit or wire connecting the two poles or brushes of the generator; as shown in Fig. 74, where M is the generator or machine, and LL the lamps.

In this case the current requires to have a high electro-
motive force in order to overcome the added resistances
of the whole number of lamps. Such a current is supplied
by the Brush generator or the peculiar form of Gramme
generator employed by Jablochkoff. The other way of
arranging the lamps is to connect them singly or in little
groups by cross wires between two main conductors joined
to the brushes of the generator, as shown at *LL* in Fig.

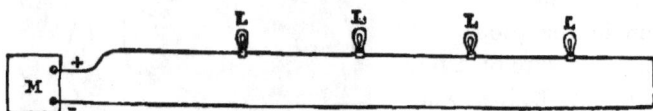

Fig. 74.

75. Then the current, instead of traversing one lamp
after another, splits up between the lamps, part going
through one lamp or group, and part through another.
The resistance of any particular path or channel for the
current is in such a case not very great, and the electro-
motive force of the current need not be dangerously
high. It is on this plan that incandescent lamps are
generally arranged for domestic purposes, and the cur-

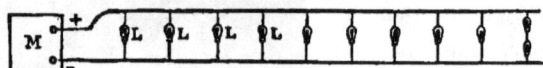

Fig. 75.

rents flowing in the wires about a house would of course
be harmless. These lamps can be mounted on an ordinary
chandelier.

There is still a third form of electric-light apparatus,
which, however, has not come into extended use. This
is known as the incandescence arc system. It is an intermediate arrangement between the arc and the incandescent
lights. The illumination is produced by the passage of

the electric current through a rod of carbon of a diameter
so small that its extremity becomes heated nearly to whiteness. This is one of the oldest forms of electric light.
It was originally patented in England in 1846.

The "electric candle," so called, is a very remarkable form of arc light which on its introduction in 1878 created great popular interest. It
probably did more to turn the attention of inventors to the possibilities of improving the electric
light, after thirty years' neglect of the subject,
than any other recent invention, excepting probably the Gramme dynamo. It was originally invented by M. Paul Jablochkoff, a Russian officer
of engineers; and, as first produced, consisted of
two carbon rods fixed parallel to one another, a
slight distance apart, and separated by an insulating medium which is consumed at the same rate
as the carbons themselves. As soon as the current commences to pass, the voltaic arc plays
across the free ends of the carbons. The adjacent insulating material becomes consumed, and
slowly uncovers the pair of carbons just as the
wax of a candle gradually uncovers the wick.

The usual form of Jablochkoff candle is represented in Fig. 76. There are two cylindrical
carbons about nine inches long by sixteen-hun-
dredths of an inch in diameter. The insulating
material between them is a mixture of sulphate of
lime and sulphate of barytes. As a candle will
last but for about two hours, it is necessary to ar-

Fig. 76.

range several of them in a holder, so that the total period
of lighting may range up to sixteen hours. Whatever may
be the number of candles to be lighted, one after another,
to afford a continuous light for a given time, it is neces-

sary to employ a device by which, as soon as one candle has burnt out, the current feeding it shall be switched off to the one adjacent. This is effected either by hand or by the use of an automatic commutator.

The Soleil light stands midway between the electric candle and the incandescence arc light. It has, however, some remarkable characteristics peculiar to itself. A block of refractory material, such as marble, lime, or granite, has a cavity on one side, shaped like a truncated cone, to the face of which penetrate the carbons, traversing the mass through inclined cylindrical holes. When the arc passes between the two points, it plays on the face of the recess, heats it, and transforms it into a small crater, whence the luminous rays escape in a conical beam. The light is slightly golden in color. It consumes more power than many arc lights, but is very durable and simple.

When a conductor conveying a powerful electric current is suddenly broken, a bright flash, called the extra spark, appears at the point of separation. The extra spark will appear, although the current is not sufficient to sustain an arc of any appreciable length at the point of separation. In order to obtain a continuous light from this spark, Professors Thomson and Houston have devised an apparatus in which one or both of the carbon electrodes are caused to vibrate to and from each other, so as to touch momentarily at each vibration. These motions follow each other at such a rate that the effect of the light produced is continuous; for, as is well known, when flashes of light follow one another at a rate greater than twenty-five to thirty per second, the effect of an uninterrupted glow is produced.

The applications of the electric light are very numerous. The most extensive in point of magnitude which has been proposed is the establishment of an electric sun of eighteen-million-candle power, on the summit of a tower twelve hundred feet high, for the illumination of Paris. For military use, the powerful beams of the arc light are employed to illuminate fortifications under bombardment, or reveal the approach of an enemy. Projectors have been devised whereby the beam can be given a range of eighty-six thousand feet. For submarine purposes, the electric light is of great value: it has been employed in removing sunken obstructions in the Suez Canal; for illuminating the sea depths, and so attracting deep-sea fish; and for lighting floating buoys. This last application is of considerable ingenuity. By the motion of the buoy, due to its rise and fall on the waves, air is compressed within the buoy, which acts intermittently to drive a dynamo, and also to sound a whistle. When the air reaches a certain degree of compression, the dynamo rotates, and the lamp glows brilliantly. On shipboard, arc lamps are used for running lights, and also at the mastheads of steamers; and incandescent lights illuminate between decks. The steamship "Arizona," for example, carries two dynamos capable of supplying six hundred lights; and the Sound steamer "Pilgrim" is fitted with nine hundred and twelve incandescent lamps.

It has been proposed to use a balloon filled with hydrogen, and containing inside an incandescent lamp, for signalling purposes; the whole globe becoming illuminated whenever the lamp glows. For lighting carriages, electric lamps are arranged both inside and beside the coachman's seat, and are conveniently fed by storage batteries. The arc light forms an excellent head-light for locomotives; the jarring action of the vehicle being prevented by controlling the carbons by hydraulic pressure.

Electric lights of immense power are used in lighthouses. The condensed beam of the great light at Souta Point, England, is equal in power to eight hundred thousand candles. The South Foreland lights, two in number, are of one hundred and eighty thousand candle power each.

The incandescent electric light has been found especially useful in coal-mines, where the fire-damp atmosphere renders the presence of any exposed flame exceedingly dangerous.

In medicine the electric light has been adapted with various forms of carrying apparatus, whereby it is used to illuminate the larynx, the stomach, and the cavities of the mouth. Combined with a photographic camera, it allows of accurate photographs being taken of diseased parts which the eye cannot see. Its latest application is to the ophthalmoscope. Fig. 77 represents one of the miniature lamps used for surgical purposes. Water circulates in the space between the lamp itself and an outer glass tube, to keep the lamp cool enough to permit of its introduction into the internal parts of the living body. Miniature lamps have also been set in brooches and shirt-studs, and made to form the petals of artificial flowers. Sometimes they are incased in masses of colored glass cut in facets to imitate jewels.

Fig. 77.

During the political campaign of 1884, as part of one of the torchlight processions, quite a large body of men marched with incandescent lamps on their heads. The participants formed a hollow square, in the middle of which was a large dynamo driven by a forty-horse-power engine, these machines being on trucks. Steam was provided from the boiler of a large steam fire-engine. The dynamo current was conducted through copper wires through a rope some twelve hundred feet long. At intervals of five feet along the rope was an ordinary cut-out, or lamp-receptacle, within which screwed a safety catch carrying two wires which led up the sleeve of the person holding the rope at that point, and through the back of his helmet to a sixteen-candle-power incandescent lamp on the top of it. Other lamps — there were some three hundred in all — were distributed on the trucks and on the harness of the horses. The effect was exceedingly brilliant and novel.

One of the comicalities of the electrical exposition of 1884, in Philadelphia, was a negro who distributed cards, while wearing upon his helmet a very brilliant incandescent light. Two wires led from the lamp, under his jacket, down each leg, and terminated in copper disks fastened to his boot-heels. Squares of copper of a suitable size for him to stand naturally upon were placed at intervals in the floor, and were electrically connected with the dynamo. Folks from the rural districts inquired cost, as useful to have around the house.

For theatrical effects, the incandescent electric light in its various forms is frequently employed. In a recent performance of "Faust" in England, the actor personating Mephistopheles produced the most unearthly colors on his countenance by means of small incandescent lights contained in globes of various colored glass, fastened beneath the visor of his cap. In the duel scene between Faust and Valentine, in which Mephistopheles takes a sinister part, whenever the sword of the demon crossed that of Valentine, a continuous flash of fire appeared. The combatants had a metal plate under foot, connected with a battery; and both Valentine and Mephistopheles wore shoes provided with metal soles, which were connected by a concealed wire with their sword-blades. The continuous discharge of electricity was produced by the saw-like edges of the weapons, each tooth giving off its spark. For ballets and fairy scenes, small incandescent lamps are fastened on the heads of the performers, and are supplied by storage batteries concealed on their persons. In the aquatic circus in Paris, the great circular tank of water, which replaces the usual ring, is illuminated by submerged electric lamps. When all other lights in the auditorium are extinguished, very novel and curious effects are produced by swimmers, representing mermaids, naiads, etc., moving about in the illuminated water.

A series of important experiments were conducted by the late Sir William Siemens, upon the influence of the electric light upon vegetation. He fitted up in his large greenhouses two arc lamps, each capable of emitting a light of about five thousand candle power. Among the vegetables planted were pease, French beans, wheat, barley, oats, cauliflowers, and a variety of berries and flowering plants. It was found that the electric light was capable of producing upon plants effects comparable to those of solar radiation ; that chlorophyll was produced by it, and that bloom, and fruit rich in aroma and color, could be developed by its aid. The experiments also went to prove that plants do not, as a rule, require a period of rest during the twenty-four hours of the day, but make increased and vigorous progress if subjected (in winter time) to solar light during the day and to electric light during the night.

Very beautiful effects can be produced by the aid of the electric light when reflected from below into a jet of water. By simply placing pieces of colored glass before the lamp, the jets can be differently colored, so that the appearance of a fountain of luminous jewels is caused.

It was for a long time believed that electric lights were far inferior to oil or gas lights in their capacity to penetrate fog. Recent investigations have shown, however, that the advantage in favor of oil and gas is not more than one per cent.

With regard to the energy consumed in electric lighting, in Edison's incandescence system, one horse-power of work yields from 99 to 189 candle power light; in Swan's system, about 150 candle power. With existing galvanic batteries, the yearly cost of operating incandescent lamps is about seven times as much as when the dynamo is employed. A good incandescent lamp will last from seven hundred to a thousand hours.

Recent electric-lighting statistics show that at the present time (1886) there are in the United States upwards of ninety-five thousand arc and nearly two hundred and fifty thousand incandescent lamps, distributed in over four hundred cities and towns. Not less than seventy millions of dollars is invested in the business of electric lighting in this country alone. In Paris, in 1878, the cost to the city was at the rate of twenty-nine cents per hour for a lamp of from five hundred to seven hundred candle power. The city of New York, at the present date, pays at the rate of about six cents per hour for a lamp of two thousand candle power.

CHAPTER IX.

ELECTRO-MOTORS, AND THE CONVERSION OF ELECTRICAL ENERGY INTO MECHANICAL ENERGY.

THE electro-motor, or electro-magnetic engine, is an engine driven by electricity; or, more correctly, it is an apparatus wherein electrical energy is converted into mechanical energy. Unscientifically defined, it is one of those contrivances which appear especially to have been "for man's illusion given." It has caused more waste of time, more useless expenditure of money, and more heart-breaking disappointments, than perhaps any other single device evolved by human ingenuity. From the very beginning, it has exercised an irresistible fascination upon the inventive mind. Its possibilities were within easy range of speculation, from the outset. That it might prove a substitute for the steam-engine with its heat and smoke and danger and waste, was apparent. A few pounds of zinc, noiselessly consumed in the battery, would replace the explosive boiler dependent upon coal only to be obtained at an expense increasing as the supply diminished. The tremendous power exerted could be arrested, or set in operation, or governed, by the touch of a child's finger. It could be conveyed anywhere and everywhere, by slender wires, to objects moving as well as stationary. It could drive ships and locomotives, and all the machinery of the world. In brief, as the power of falling water and of the moving wind had supplanted the power of the horse, and as the power of steam in turn had taken the place of the power of wind and water, so in the future electricity would do the work of steam. All this was as plain fifty years ago as it is now. It is far from being a delusion : we are advancing toward its realization with wonderful rapidity. But in that it all could be accomplished by the ways and means of the third and fourth decades of this century, lay the error, — one that still is being repeated, and always with the same result, — loss and disappointment.

The idea of a machine to be driven by electrical power, and capable of doing useful work, followed as a necessary consequence upon the discovery of the immense attractive strength of the electro-magnet. Why, it was argued, should that *ignis fatuus*, that other form of the perpetual motion, — the cutting-off the magnetism of a permanent magnet by a screen of something to be interposed by the attraction of the magnet itself, be further sought, when the electro-magnet could be made to exert its huge strength, or be rendered powerless, instantly and at will, by the mere contact or separation of the ends of a wire? When the current is established in its coil, the electro-magnet attracts its armature : when the current is interrupted, the armature is released to fall back into its original position, or to be retracted by a simple spring. If the current is established and broken alternately, then the armature will reciprocate to and fro like the piston of a steam-engine ; and, like the piston, it may operate other mechanism to produce rotary or any other form of motion.

The lazy boy who was set to work the valve of the old engine, in order to let in steam at the proper time to move the piston in the cylinder to and fro, found out that if he attached the string wherewith he pulled open the valve, to the moving machine, the latter would itself admit the steam at the right intervals. The same idea, applied to the electro-magnet and its armature, made the motor automatic. When the armature is attracted, in moving it may draw apart the ends of the wire whereby the current is led to the magnet. Then the magnet will release the armature. In falling back, the armature again brings the ends of the conductor into contact. Then it will be once more attracted. And thus it will go on vibrating to and fro before the pole of the magnet, as long as the supply of current is kept up.

This idea came to inventors all over the civilized world, at about the same time. Electro-motors varying only in details of construction appeared simultaneously in England, France, Germany, Italy, and the United States. Modern research has shown that probably the first machine was constructed by the Abbé Salvatore dal Negro, professor in the University of Padua, in 1830; although the earliest published description of it appeared some two or three years later. Dal Negro suspended a permanent magnet between the poles of a horseshoe-shaped electro-magnet, in the coils of which the current was alternately reversed, so that the end of the suspended magnet was first attracted and then repelled from side to side. By means of a simple mechanism the swinging magnet turned a wheel slowly and with little power.

Professor Joseph Henry, in this country, constructed an exceedingly powerful electro-magnet, capable of lifting six or seven hundred pounds with a pint or two of liquid and a battery of corresponding size; nor did he desist until, a short time after, he lifted thousands of pounds by a battery of larger size, but still very small. Subsequently Henry constructed an electro-magnetic engine, having a beam suspended in the centre which performed regular vibrations in the manner of the beam of a steam-engine.

Bourbouze in France devised the remarkable machine which is represented in Fig. 78. Here two electro-magnet coils successively attract two pieces of soft iron; and each of these, placed at the extremities of an oscillating beam, is drawn into the interior of the coil. When the current passes into one coil, the iron armature, being drawn down, causes the end of the beam to which it is

Fig. 78.

attached to descend: when the current passes into the other coil, the other end of the beam goes down. The beam in vibrating turns a crank, and so rotates the flywheel. The battery is placed in the base of the machine, and communicates with a special piece of metal, the purpose of which is to interrupt the current and throw it alternately from one side to the other. This arrangement is carried out simply by means of two small bits of iron, separated by a plate of ivory. A metallic spring rests upon the iron and ivory at the end and at the beginning of its course, now on the first bit of iron, then on the second, and so alternating; and thus the current is led first into one coil, and then into the other.

In all mechanical contrivances, where motion is rapidly reversed, there is a great waste of power; this because the momentum of the moving part must be overcome before the direction of motion can be changed. It was soon found that this principle applied very cogently to reciprocating electro-motors.

The first rotary electro-motor was described in "The Mechanics' Magazine" of June, 1833. The apparatus consisted of a bent electro-magnet, "an arc of iron measuring about two-thirds of a circle, and supposed to be armed with a helix of wire, and connected with a galvanic battery." The armature was solid, and upon it were fixed permanent magnets built of steel bars; the poles of the magnets being placed so that they would move "all but in contact" with the poles of the arc magnet. The communication is anonymously signed, but is of especial interest from the fact that the writer describes, with great clearness, an apparatus which embodies every thing that is essential to the construction of electro-motors of the class to which it belongs, and includes features subsequently patented over and over again as original with numerous claimants to the invention.

In the fall of 1835 the Rev. Mr. McGawley exhibited to the British Association a motor in which a pendulum vibrated between two electro-magnets, the poles of which were alternately reversed, so that first one magnet attracted and the other repelled the pendulum, and *vice versa*. This created considerable scientific interest, and was pronounced the "best attempt yet made, of the many schemes that had been proposed for producing motive power by the electro-magnet.'' McGawley's invention, like that of Dal Negro which it very much resembled, is in fact of little value as an electro-magnetic engine ; but it is of much historical importance for the reason that it contained the first automatic circuit-breaker, — wires dipping alternately first into one cup of mercury and then into another. This was subsequently patented in the United States to Professor Page of Washington ; a proceeding difficult to understand, in view of the fact that Page himself had written to Sir David Brewster, — the chairman managing a relief-fund for McGawley's heirs, — conceding in explicit terms the invention to McGawley.

The fortunes of Thomas Davenport with his electro-motor constitute a curious chapter in the history of the apparatus. Davenport was a country blacksmith, living in Brandon, Vt. By accident he became possessed of one of Henry's magnets, and by dint of hard work and perseverance — for he had no special education — he contrived to master the principles involved. This was in 1833. By the summer of 1834 Davenport had invented his rotary motor, which he subsequently patented in this country in 1837. It was substantially like the apparatus described by the anonymous writer in '' The Mechanics' Magazine '' of 1833 ; except that the armature had electro-magnets instead of permanent magnets, and the field magnet was a permanent magnet instead of an electro-magnet, the apparently earlier contrivance being to this extent reversed. Subsequently he suppressed permanent magnets altogether, and used electro-magnets only, both as field and armature. The machine worked well. It was exhibited in Washington before the President, and subsequently in Saratoga, whither great crowds of people flocked to see it, and lost their heads over it. So did the newspapers, scientific and unscientific. '' The American

Journal of Science and Arts " concluded that the " power generated by electro-magnetism may be indefinitely prolonged . . . and increased beyond any limit hitherto attained." Davenport thought that a battery " as big as a barrel " would drive the largest machinery, and that " half a barrel of blue vitriol and a hogshead or two of water would send a ship from New York to Liverpool."

The American people seem to have contented themselves with purely mental speculation as to the future of the machine, and to have declined pecuniary investment. Consequently Davenport sent the apparatus to England. It captivated John Bull at first sight. Abundant funds were subscribed to build a " big machine," — the invariable requirement, since time immemorial, of the investor in new inventions. Accordingly one was constructed having four huge electro-magnets aggregating in weight some three hundred pounds. A battery " as big as a barrel " was made to charge it. It had a cast-iron wheel six feet in diameter, and weighing six hundred pounds, which revolved at seventy-five turns a minute.

Among the scientific men who came to see this new wonder, were Wheatstone (already famous for his inventions in telegraphy), Daniell (equally renowned for his invention of the Daniell battery), and Faraday, then in the zenith of his fame as a discoverer. Wheatstone praised the machine in glowing terms ; Daniell waxed enthusiastic over it, and predicted the time when ships would be run across the Atlantic with the aid of a few sheets of zinc and a little acid, — yea, not even acid, for the waters of the ocean would supply its place.

Faraday came last of all. He looked at the huge wheel flying around, with surprise ; and then fixed his gaze more intently on the great spark which was given off every time the current was broken, yielding enough light to illuminate brightly the whole room. The promoters of the machine stood silent, expectantly waiting the verdict from the foremost scientific authority in the land. After a while, Faraday walked to the nearest corner, and picked up a broom. Then he placed the handle on the periphery of the wheel, and it was seen that under a slight pressure the speed of the wheel became slower. He did not quite stop the motion, but simply and without a word demonstrated how easily this could be done. Then he called the promoters aside into another room, and gently suggested that his opinion, if made public, would greatly injure the sale of the patent. The interested parties thought it wiser not to press him for that opinion, and he left without giving it. He had found, as others did later, that the power yielded was wholly inadequate for practical use.

After this Davenport started a paper in New-York City, called "The Electro-Magnet and Mechanics' Intelligencer," the first number of which appeared on Jan. 18, 1840. He announced it as the first paper ever printed on a press propelled by electro-magnetism. The public regarded the enterprise rather apathetically. In his second issue, Davenport particularly requested "those who would wish to advance the cause of philanthropy to come forward and assist us in our experiment." Perhaps he failed to make clear the connection between his newspaper and the "cause of philanthropy;" or perhaps the public, after three years excitement over his machine, had tired of the subject: at all events, the paper ceased publication, and in the technical journals of the day no further record of Davenport's motor appears.

One of the best of the early forms of rotary motor was that devised in France by M. Froment, which is represented in Fig. 79. Around the periphery of a skeleton drum are arranged eight pieces of iron, which serve as armatures.

In the frame of the machine are fixed six couples of electro-magnets. (The two upper couples are omitted in the engraving.) When the current is diverted into one of these coils, one of the armatures is attracted, and is moved to a position in front of the pole of the magnet. The wheel is so turned over a certain distance. As soon,

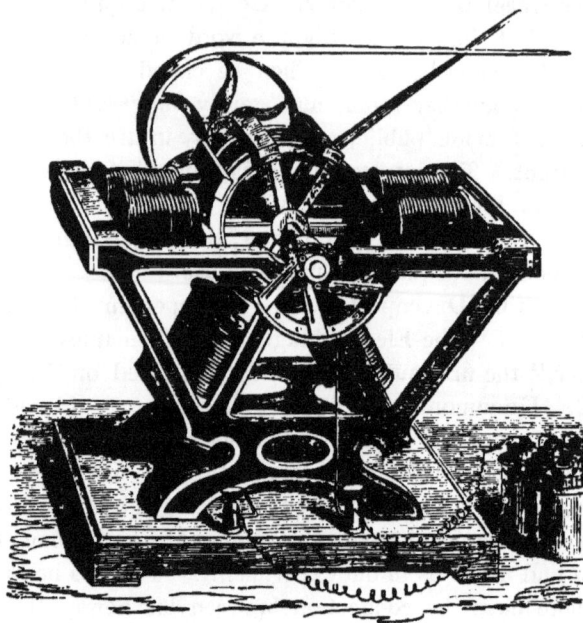

Fig. 79.

however, as the armature has thus placed itself, the current is thrown from the first coil into the next one, which draws the armature to its pole in turn. As all six electromagnets act in this way, the wheel is continuously rotated.

The interest aroused by the exhibitions made by Davenport in London extended over all Europe ; and in the fall of 1838 Professor Jacobi was invited by the Emperor of

Russia to conduct experiments on a large scale, with the object of determining the practicability of the electro-motor for marine propulsion. Jacobi's vessel was a ten-oared shallop, equipped with paddle-wheels, to which rotary motion was communicated by an electro-magnetic engine. In general there were ten or twelve persons on board; and the voyage, which was made on the River Neva, was continued for entire days. The difficulty of managing the batteries, and the imperfect construction of the engine, were sources of frequent interruption, which could not be well remedied on the spot. After these difficulties were in some degree removed, the professor gives, as a result of his experiments, that a battery of twenty square feet of platinum will produce a power equivalent to one horse, but he hoped to be able to obtain the same power with about half that amount of battery surface. The vessel went at the rate of four miles per hour, which is certainly more than was accomplished by the first little boat propelled by the power of steam. Jacobi's boat was 28 feet long and $7\frac{1}{2}$ feet in width, and drew $2\frac{3}{4}$ feet of water. The machine, which occupied little space, was worked by a battery of sixty-four pairs of platinum plates, each having thirty-six square inches of surface, and charged, according to the plan of Grove, with nitric and sulphuric acid. The boat, with a party of twelve or fourteen persons on board, went against the stream at the rate of three miles per hour. This experiment was tried in 1839, and shows what great progress had been made in the period of about one year; for in 1838, when it was attempted to propel the same boat by the same machine, a battery of about five times the size was required. Jacobi's batteries generated so much gas, that the fumes seriously discommoded the operators, and at times compelled them to abandon their experiments; and even the spectators on the banks were forced to retire when the wind blew in their direction.

Jacobi wrote a letter, describing his results, to Faraday; and this, being published, elicited one from Professor Forbes of King's College, Aberdeen, in which for the first time the labors of Mr. Robert Davidson of that place were brought to light. Davidson's most remarkable performance was his locomotive. He used two batteries, arranged at each end of his carriage, which energized a number of large electro-magnets. On the wheel-axles were large cylinders, on the peripheries of which were fastened masses of iron. These masses were attracted by the magnets; and in this way the cylinders were revolved, so rotating the wheels. The carriage, Davidson claimed, was once tested on the Edinburgh and Glasgow Railway, where it ran at the rate of about four miles per hour. It was sixteen feet in breadth, and weighed some five tons. This report has always, as the newspapers say, "lacked confirmation."

Davidson's experiments had, however, gone far to show the disadvantages of carrying the batteries on the locomotive. In the fall of 1845, "The Mechanics' Magazine" published a letter signed "J. M.," which contained this significant suggestion : —

" Now, suppose we have a railway ten miles long, and that at one terminus is placed an enormous stationary galvanic battery, might we not make the rails themselves the conducting lines of the battery? and, the wheels being so arranged as to break the connection where required, a rotating magnet might revolve by the electro-magnetism thus communicated. . . . Perhaps some fertile brain may take the hint, and bring forth soon the ' electric railway.' "

A fertile brain on this side of the Atlantic was already

working on this idea; and it was carried into practical execution by Mr. John B. Lilly, who in 1846 exhibited in Pittsburg, Penn., a model which was driven by a current passing up one rail and down another, and through the magnets on the car. "Heretofore," says "The Pittsburgh Journal" of the time, "the propelling power has been used on the car itself: in this instance, however, the power is in the rails; and an engineer might remain in one town, and with his battery send a locomotive and train to any distance required."

Five years later Professor Page of Washington made a trial trip, with an electro-magnetic locomotive, between Bladensburg and Washington. It was claimed to be of sixteen horse power, and was provided with a hundred cells of Grove's nitric-acid battery, each having platinum plates eleven inches square. It is stated that the progress of the locomotive was at first so slow that a boy was enabled to keep pace with it for several hundred feet; but the speed was soon increased, and Bladensburg, five miles and a quarter distant, was reached in thirty-nine minutes. When within two miles of that place, the power of the battery being fully up, the locomotive began to run on nearly a level plane, at the rate of nineteen miles an hour. This velocity was kept up for about a mile, when some of the battery cells cracked, and their liquids became intermixed. Considerable time was lost in stoppages; but the return trip was safely accomplished, the entire running time being one minute less than two hours. It was found on subsequent trials, that the least jolt, such as that caused by the end of a rail a little above the level, threw the batteries out of working order, and the result was a halt. This defect, it is said, could not be overcome; and Professor Page reluctantly abandoned his endeavors.

In the same year Thomas Hall of Boston constructed

a small locomotive which ran on a track some twenty feet long, and took the current from the rails, the wheels being insulated. It has been claimed for Hall, that he utilized not only a battery to supply his current, but also a dynamo-electric machine.

Some twenty-one years had now elapsed since the first electro-motor — Dal Negro's mere toy — had been produced. In that period both forms of the machine, beam and rotary, had been invented. It had been applied to the propulsion of vessels and of locomotives; the last being operated by batteries carried by themselves, as is the steam-boiler of the modern railway-engine, and by batteries at a distance, which transmitted their current to the motor through the rails. About all the principal adaptations of the electric engine had been made. It had claimed the attention and labors of the most noted scientists of the world. It had been backed by an emperor of unlimited power, and capitalists representing unbounded wealth had endeavored again and again to make it the basis of successful enterprise. And yet when the success of the electric telegraph, which had seemed far the greater impracticability, aroused the wonder and admiration of the world, the electric motor worked usefully for no man. What was the reason?

As we have seen, the inventors of the early machines found no trouble in making them go. The beams vibrated, or the wheels spun around, fast enough to make people with vague ideas about speed and power believe that almost limitless energy could be got out of a pint pot. The early inventors, and those who promoted their projects, are not the only persons chargeable with this delusion. It exists yet, and crops out occasionally. In 1871 a New-Jersey discoverer asserted that he could make a fifty-pound electro-magnet sustain a weight of one hundred and twenty tons with a battery of four Daniell's cells, and drive a five-hundred-horse-power engine by the same means, at an expense of but twenty cents a day. An electro-magnetic engine company — as usual — was organized ; capital, three millions. The engine was to be exhibited on the 4th of July — year indefinite. Also — as usual — there was an element of mystery introduced, in the assertion that the battery was merely a connecting link between the machine and some storehouse of magnetic energy, and therefore, that, while the battery was apparently the source of power, it really was not ; bearing a relation thereto, similar to that of a percussion-cap which fires the charge which impels the cannon-shot. Public interest in this great discovery — or, rather, that section of the public interest which is ignorant enough to give such discoveries consideration — was transferred two years later to the Keely motor ; which was obviously of much greater importance, because it did not even require the pint pot wherefrom to obtain limitless power.

The great vicissitude which invariably came to promoters of electro-magnetic engines driven by batteries, was the discovery that they do not pay ; and no amount of glowing anticipations in prospectuses could prevent stockholders becoming painfully aware of this, in the end. It is much cheaper — besides far easier — to take the mere fuel used in extracting the zinc from its ore, and burn it under a steam-boiler, to drive a steam-engine, and so obtain power in that way, than to go through the roundabout process of extracting the zinc, consuming it in a galvanic cell, and so generating a current wherewith to drive a motor. Zinc, as we have already pointed out, yields about one-seventh the energy of coal, and costs about twenty times as much. Merely comparing the energies derivable from zinc and coal, a steam-engine should be about a hundred and forty times more economical than an electro-motor driven by a battery. But the best steam-engine and boiler can utilize no more than about two-ninths of the energy of the burning coal; all the rest being wasted. This reduces the difference: it is "not so deep as a well, nor so wide as a church-door, but 'tis enough," since it leaves the motor some thirty times as expensive in the production of power as the steam-engine. The efficiency of the motor has no part in this question. The battery is the hopelessly inefficient part of the system; and it will remain so, no matter how much the motor itself may hereafter be improved. According to Professor Joule, the cost of zinc expended in the Daniell battery, to maintain one horse power for twenty-four hours, would be $6.25; in an ordinary steam-engine, the cost of the same power for the same period would be about twenty-one cents. From a "business" point of view, no further argument is necessary to show why electro-motors driven from galvanic batteries, as were all the early machines, could find no place in the world's work.

While one set of investigators and inventors were studying how to convert electricity into mechanical power, another set, almost simultaneously, were endeavoring to convert mechanical power into electricity. The researches of these last culminated in the modern dynamo electric machine. Now, the machines which generate electricity from motion bear a strong resemblance, in point of general construction, to those which generate motion from electricity. Let us repeat one illustration already given, to show this.

Fig. 80 we have already described as a hollow coil of wire, the ends of which are connected to a galvanometer, which shows by the movement of its needle whenever a current circulates in that coil. Into that coil we insert a smaller coil, the ends of which are connected to a battery. We have seen, that, when the small coil is moved to and fro inside the large one, then the galvanometer will show that a current is being generated in the large coil. We are thus converting the energy of the motion given to the small coil, into electricity.

Now, let us simply reverse the arrangement of the battery, connecting it to the ends of the large coil, removing the galvanometer. Let us also join the ends of the

Fig. 80.

small coil together. Then when the current passes through the large coil, on holding the smaller coil in the position shown in the engraving we shall feel the large coil pull the smaller one into it, release it when the current is broken, and, if we draw out the small coil, on re-establishing the current it will be pulled back again, so moving to and fro. Here the electricity circulating in the large coil is converted into motion.

The same thing can be done with the arrangement represented in Fig. 81. We have seen, that, when the permanent magnet is moved into and out of the coil, a current is caused in the latter. If the current be sent directly through the coil in one direction, the magnet will be drawn in: if in the opposite direction, it will not be attracted. Or if, instead of the magnet, we use simply a piece of soft iron, then, whenever the current is established, the iron will be drawn inward, and when broken it will be free to be moved out, — as by a spring, for example.

Fig. 81.

If the foregoing be compared with the engraving of Bourbouze's electro-magnetic engine on p. 155, it will be seen that that apparatus depends exactly on the operation last described. An electro-motor is in fact a dynamo or magneto electric machine reversed. If a dynamo is rotated by mechanical power, it will produce an electric current. If an electric current be conducted into a dynamo, its armature will be rotated. Good dynamo machines, in fact, make the best motors; and the latter, like the dynamos, resolve themselves, as we have seen, into two types, distinguished by the production of alternating and continuous currents in the armature. There are, however, certain functional differences between motors and dynamos, which require to be met in different ways, and particularly in the proportioning of the parts, and the relation of the field and armature systems. These need not be discussed in detail here.

As the dynamo machine became more and more efficient, it became evident that here was a means of producing electricity which could be used to drive a motor, as well as supply an electric lamp, and which would depend for economy not upon zinc, but upon coal. And thus the modern system of electro-motors, and the transmission of power thereto at a distance, came into existence: and of this the essentials are a heat engine — steam or gas — to drive a dynamo, which supplies the current to a second dynamo; and this last converts the energy of the electricity, so supplied, into mechanical motion and work.

We know that the revolution of the armature of a dynamo produces a current; and that in large dynamos, producing a very strong current, it is necessary to use powerful engines to turn the armature. But if the circuit in the armature is broken, no such power is required. It is only when the current is being yielded, that hard work must be done to rotate the armature; and we therefore say that this work has its equivalent in the electric current which flows and in the heat which is caused in the circuit, which is rendered visible by the incandescence of, for example, an electric lamp placed therein. Now, whether the armature of a dynamo be rotated directly by an engine, or whether it be rotated by a current sent into the machine, a new current will be produced. If the dynamo be turned by the engine, this current will of course be the only one in the circuit; but if there is already a current existing there, as when the dynamo is driven by electricity, then the new current will be in the opposite direction to the original one, and tend to diminish the latter. This makes complications; and the result, among other things, is a quantity of mathematical calculation which, if printed here, might perhaps make the non-professional reader shut up this book in despair.

It will suffice, therefore, to say briefly, that, when the speed of the electro-motor is increased, this back current is also increased. If the motor be loaded so as to do work by moving slowly against considerable forces, then the back current will be small, and only a portion of the energy of the current will be turned into useful work. If, on the other hand, it be run rapidly so as to make considerable back current, it will utilize a larger proportion of the energy of the direct current, but can only be run fast enough to do this if its load be very light. When a motor is desired to do its work at the quickest possible rate, it is best operated at such a speed that the supply current is reduced to half its strength; but when speed is not necessary, a greater economic efficiency is attainable by letting the machine do lighter work, and run faster, so that the back current is nearly equal to the original current, which is thereby reduced to a small fraction of its strength. A Siemens dynamo-electric machine used as a motor can attain an efficiency of over eighty-five per cent. A good dynamo can turn eighty-five per cent of the mechanical power it receives, into the energy of the electric current; and the electro-motor can convert back eighty-five per cent of the current energy (or seventy-two per cent of the original power) into work, losses in the conductor and from leakage being neglected.

The simplest form of electro-motor is that used on electric bells. This consists of an electro-magnet which moves a hammer backward and forward, alternately attracting and releasing it. In Fig. 82, E is the electro-magnet, and C the hammer. By touching the push-button P, which is also shown enlarged in section, the circuit from the battery L is completed, and a current flows along the line and around the coils of the electro-magnet, which attracts a small piece of soft iron attached to the lever S, which terminates in the hammer C. The lever is itself included in the circuit, the current entering it below and quitting it by a contact-breaker A, consisting of a spring tipped with platinum, resting against the platinum tip of a screw from which a return wire passes back to the battery. As soon as the lever *S* is attracted forward, the circuit is broken at *A* by the spring moving away from contact with the screw: hence the current stops, and the electro-magnet ceases to attract the armature. The lever and hammer therefore fall back again, establishing contact at *A*, whereupon the hammer is once more attracted forward, and so on.

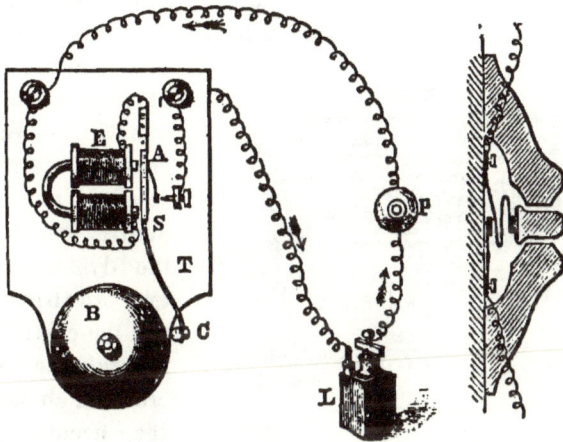

Fig. 82.

The most important modern application of electro-motors is to the driving of locomotives. The credit of the first successful electrical railway is due to Dr. Werner Siemens, who built in Berlin, in 1879, a narrow-gauge line, laid down in a circle some nine hundred yards in length. A train of three or four carriages was placed upon it; and on the first carriage a dynamo-electric machine was fixed to the axle of one pair of wheels, in such a manner as to rotate the wheels when the armature of the machine was rotated by the passage of a current through its coils.

The rails were laid upon wooden sleepers, which, even in wet weather, insulated the rails very well for this length of line. A third rail ran between the other two, and it was by this central conductor that the current was led from the generating-machine placed at one terminus of the line. The current was drawn from this rail to the armature of the machine on the locomotive, by means of a brush of copper wires ; and after traversing the coils of the armature, it was led to the axle of the driving-wheels, which was insulated from the body of the car, and thence by the driving-wheels to the outer rails, and by them back to the dynamo machine at the terminus. Fig. 83 represents a section through the locomotive, showing the dynamo-electric machine B, and the central rail N, with the metal brush for abducting the current.

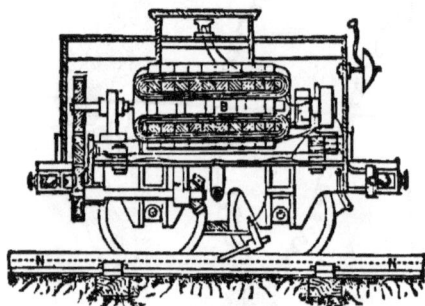

Fig. 83.

Between twenty and thirty persons could be accommodated on the train at a time, including the conductor, who rode on the first carriage ; and during the course of the summer no fewer than a hundred thousand were conveyed over the line at a speed of from fifteen to twenty miles an hour. Crowded trains left the stations every five or ten minutes, and a considerable sum was earned in this way for the benefit of charitable institutions. The locomotive was capable of exerting five horse-power ; and instead of being fitted with a steam valve like a locomotive to start or stop it, it was simply provided with a commutator for closing or opening the circuit of the current.

On the Siemens railway at the Paris exhibition of September, 1881, a distance of over sixteen hundred feet was traversed in a minute, which is at the rate of nearly twenty miles per hour.

In this country, electric railways have in many localities replaced ordinary street-railway systems depending on horses and dummy engines. At South Bend, Ind., for example, two twenty-horse-power dynamos are driven by a water-wheel, and supply current to one ten-horse-power and three five-horse-power motors. The track is laid with the ordinary flat rail, the rails being connected by copper plates. The other part of the circuit consists of a copper wire suspended above the track. From the under side of this wire hangs a carriage fastened to a flexible cable, passing to the inside of the car, where it is in connection with the switches, the motor, etc. When full current is turned on, the maximum speed of eight miles per hour is attained, this being the highest rate of travel allowable in the city limits. An electric railway was constructed in the fall of 1885 at the New-Orleans Exposition. Others are in successful operation in Baltimore, Minneapolis, Montgomery (Ala.); and there are probably few large cities in the country in which some system of electric railway has not been projected. At the date of writing (1886), experiments have for some time been in progress with the object of substituting electric engines for the steam-engines on the elevated-railway lines in the city of New York. On the Ninth-avenue road, arrangements have been made to employ the form of electric locomotive devised by Mr. Leo Daft. The total weight of the machine as constructed is $8\frac{3}{4}$ tons. The current is taken from the rails, which are insulated, and is supplied by dynamos situated at a main station. A third rail between the track rails is employed for the return current, and contact is made with this by means of a wheel which can be moved into or out of position. The maximum gradient of the road is one of a hundred and five feet to the mile. This has been surmounted with ease, with fairly well loaded trains; and an average speed of twenty miles per hour has been attained. The latest, as well as the most efficient electro-locomotive, is that devised by Mr. F. J. Sprague. This, also, at the present time, is being experimented upon on the elevated railways of New-York City. To describe the construction of Mr. Sprague's apparatus, would necessitate much technical detail not suited to these pages; but the practical results which he has attained, especially in control of speed, prevention of loss of power, and facility of stopping and starting, renders his motor a decided and very meritorious advance in electric propulsion.

It is impossible to fix a limit to the possible speed of electric locomotives ; but it is not improbable that eventually it will be found practicable to drive them at much higher velocities than the steam-locomotive has ever attained. The advantages of electricity over steam for railway propulsion are so great as to render the former almost an ideal prime motor. The locomotive itself is virtually done away with, for in many cases the electric motor can be placed under the car. As regards economy, it has recently been pointed out that "the evaporation of pounds of water to each pound of coal to make steam in locomotive-boilers does not average over $3\frac{1}{2}$ pounds of water, using the best grades of bituminous coal; while with stationary boilers, set to burn coal-screenings for fuel, an evaporation of nine pounds of water to one pound of fuel is made, and the reduction in cost of fuel is from one-third to one-half." The cost, therefore, of making the electric power, is already greatly less than that of generating steam-power in moving locomotives: and when electricity comes to be supplied, as it eventually will be, like gas and water, from great central generating stations, to be used for all purposes, the expense of its production will without doubt be still further lessened. Add to the above advantages, freedom from smoke and sparks, noiseless machinery and motion, and absolute control by the mere pressure of a finger, and one may predict with every certainty that the electric steed will replace the steam horse, as certainly as the latter did the horse of flesh and blood.

Electric power is already sold from central stations, in many places, just as steam-power is sold, with profit to both seller and buyer. The price at present is about the same as that for steam for small powers. In Boston, steam is generated from coal-screenings, to drive the engine which actuates the dynamos; and the power is transmitted all over the city, being used for running all kinds of machinery, including sewing-machines, ventilator-fans, printing-presses, elevators, etc.

It appears that ordinarily the loss in the process of conversion of power into electricity, and transmitting power from the dynamo to the receiver, amounts to from forty to fifty per cent. "Electrical transmission," says a recent writer, "has the unparalleled advantage of being superior to the obstacle presented by distance. Then, again, it operates its miracles in perfect silence and repose. No force appears in the wire, such as appears in shafting, in pipes with compressed air or water, in endless chains or belts; and in case of powerful currents, insulation is easy. The conductor can be bent or shifted in any way while transmitting many horse-power; provided, of course, its continuity be not interrupted. It can be carried round the sharpest corners, through the most private rooms, into places where no other transmitter or power could possibly be taken. There is nothing to burst or give away. In short, such a method of transmission is the acme of dynamical science."

Electro-motors have been ingeniously adapted to the driving of tricycles by Professors Ayrton and Perry. The motor is suspended beneath a platform under the seat, and is driven by several cells of storage-battery, which are supported on a second and lower platform. The machine has been driven at a speed of about six miles per hour.

Electric launches have also been constructed. One built by Messrs. Yarrow & Co., in 1883, measures forty feet in length by six feet beam, and is capable of carrying forty passengers. The motor is a Siemens machine, driven by a storage-battery; the weight of motor and batteries being about two and a quarter tons. The speed of the boat is about eight miles per hour. For the propulsion of ships' boats, electrical motors possess marked advantages over steam-engines; as an electric launch is much more easily swung from a ship's davits than a steam-launch, it has no fire to be put out in case of shipping seas, and the machinery will work under water.

The application of an electric motor to the guiding of a balloon has been made by M. Gaston Tissandier, with fairly successful results. The balloon used was lenticular in form. The motor was arranged in the car, and caused to rotate a large propelling-fan. The current was obtained from a number of bichromate-of-potash batteries. The motor was so arranged that its speed might be varied from sixty to a hundred and eighty revolutions per minute. With the high speed, the forward motion of the balloon under the influence of its propeller was plainly observable, and for a short period it maintained its place even against a moderate breeze. It was also found possible to swerve the balloon from the direction of the wind.

Telpherage is a name coined by the late Professor Fleeming Jenkin, to designate a system devised by him, by which the transmission of vehicles by electricity to a distance is effected independently of any control exercised from the vehicle. It is an aërial electrical railway, as at present projected, in which the track is either a single or double wire rope from which the carriages or skips are suspended. The line is divided into sections, each a hundred and twenty feet in length ; and each section is insulated from its neighbor. A train is made up of a locomotive and a series of skips held at uniform intervals apart by wooden poles extending from skip to skip. The skips hang below the line from V-wheels supported by arms which project out sideways so as to clear the supports at the posts : the motor or dynamo on the locomotive is also below the line. The entire train is a hundred and twenty feet in length, the same length as that of a section. A wire connects one pole of the motor with the leading-wheel of the train, and a second wire connects the other pole with the trailing-wheel : the other wheels are insulated from each other. Thus the train, wherever it stands, bridges a gap separating the insulated from the uninsulated section. The insulated sections are supplied with electricity from a dynamo driven by a stationary engine ; and the current passing from the insulated section to the uninsulated section, through the motor, drives the locomotive. This will be easily understood from the diagram Fig. 84. Here one pole of the dynamo is connected to the left-hand extremity of the conductor represented by the continuous line ; the other pole being connected to the

uninsulated line shown dotted. *M* and *N* represent two
trains.   When these are in the position shown, it will be
evident that a portion of the dynamo current will go
through each train as indicated by the arrows; and this
current passing through the motor in the locomotive sets
it in motion, and so propels the train.

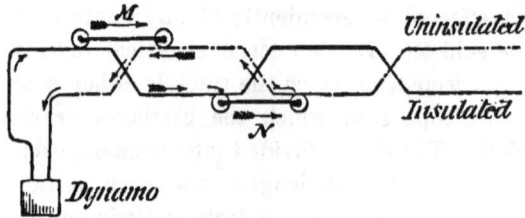

Fig. 84.

Another arrangement, called the series system, is illustrated in the diagram Fig. 85. Here there is but a single
wire, on which the trains are supported; this consisting of
a series of spans. The breaks between these spans are
normally kept closed by means of switches. Each switch
is opened automatically as soon as a train bridges it, so

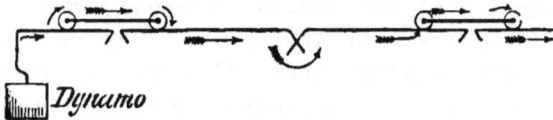

Fig. 85.

that the current is thus caused to pass through the train,
and so keep it in motion. When a train has passed over
a break, the switch is automatically closed, so that the
continuity of the circuit through the wire is preserved.

Telpherage is as yet in its infancy, and, in fact, has not
been tried on a sufficiently extensive scale to determine

even the most salient questions bearing upon its economical efficiency.   So far as can be foreseen, the invention

Fig. 88.

bids fair to be of great practical value.   Professor Jenkin
has pointed out that "wherever railways and canals do
not exist, telpher lines will provide the cheapest mode of

inland conveyance for all goods such as corn, coal, root-crops, herrings, hides, etc., which can be conveniently sub-divided into parcels of one, two, or three hundred weight. In new colonies, the lines will often be cheaper to make than roads, and will convey goods far more cheaply. In war they will give a ready means of sending supplies to the front. Moreover, wherever a telpher line exists, power is thereby laid on ; and this power may be used for other purposes than locomotion. A flexible wire attached to the line will serve to drive a one, two, or three horse engine, which may be used for any imaginable purpose, such as digging, mowing, threshing, or sawing.'' Tel-pher lines will also act as '' feeders of great value to the railways, extending into districts which could not support the cost even of the lightest railway.'' Fig. 86, from a photograph, represents Professor Jenkin's first line. The buckets, or skips, weighed about three hundred pounds each, the locomotive the same. Each skip carried as a useful load about two hundred and fifty pounds. The projected speed was five miles per hour, at which it was estimated about ninety-two and a half tons hourly of freight could be conveyed.

General Thayer, U.S.A., has devised a remarkable sys-tem of war balloons, which are designed to travel upon wires or light cables stretched across the country on ordi-nary poles. The balloon itself is in the shape of a cir-cular spindle, and supports a deck for the transport of troops, cannon, etc. The electricity is generated at the end of the line, and is conveyed along the wires to a motor on the deck of the balloon. The motor drives the wheels which impel the balloon along the cable. General Thayer states that such a road could be built at the rate of from three to four miles a day, at a cost of fifteen hundred dol-lars per mile, and the speed attained might be from sixty to seventy miles per hour. The wire could be run across country in a direct line, where it would be impossible to build a railway. Men and ammunition could thus be rapidly transported; and, as an army advances into an enemy's country, the balloon-way could be put up in its rear, and thus establish a line of communication with its base of supplies.

CHAPTER X.

ELECTROLYSIS. — ELECTRO-METALLURGY AND THE STORAGE-
BATTERY.

In the galvanic battery a chemical re-action takes place, and the result is the production of an electric current. If, conversely, we place in a decomposable liquid two conducting bodies, and thus enable a current of electricity to pass through the liquid, we shall find that the result is a chemical decomposition. This decomposition by means of the electric current is called electrolysis; the liquid decomposed is known as an electrolyte, and the two conducting bodies are termed electrodes. In a galvanic cell, a definite amount of chemical action evolves a current, and transfers a certain quantity of electricity through the circuit: so, conversely, a definite quantity of electricity, in passing through an electrolytic cell, will perform a definite amount of chemical work. An electrolytic cell is, therefore, the converse of a voltaic cell.

The discovery of the decomposing effects of the electric current was made by accident, and followed almost immediately after the invention of Volta's pile. Volta addressed a letter to Sir Joseph Banks, then President of the Royal Society, on March 20, 1800, wherein he announced the discovery of his pile. The first portion only of this letter, which described the construction of the apparatus, was sent on the above date; and the remainder

followed during the succeeding month of June. Until the
latter date, the whole missive was not published; but in
the meanwhile Sir Joseph Banks showed such parts as he
had received, to Mr. W. Nicholson and Mr. (afterwards
Sir) Anthony Carlisle. These two gentlemen at once constructed a pile composed of silver half-crown pieces, alternated with equal disks of copper, and cloth soaked in
a weak solution of common salt. It so happened, that a
drop of water was used to make good the contact of the
conducting wire with a plate to which the electricity was
to be transmitted. In noticing this, Carlisle observed a
disengagement of gas from the water; and Nicholson recognized the "odor of hydrogen" coming from it. They at
once took measures to determine the cause of this singular

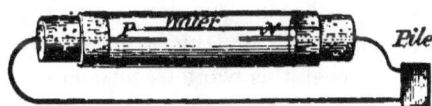

Fig. 87.

effect; and, using the first materials at hand, filled a piece
of glass tube with water, plugging both ends with cork,
and inserting through each cork a piece of brass wire, as
shown in Fig. 87. When the wires P and N were put in
communication with opposite ends of the pile, bubbles of
gas were evolved from the point of the wire by which the
current left the tube, and the end of the wire by which
the current entered became tarnished. The gas evolved
appeared on examination to be hydrogen; and the tarnish
was found to proceed from the oxidation of the entrance,
or positive, wire. In order to prevent this oxidation of
the material of the wire itself, another apparatus was
made, in which platinum wires were used. Then gas was
evolved from both wires; and this, ascending through the

water, was collected separately in two tubes. The contents of the tubes being examined, hydrogen was found in one, and oxygen in the other; the two gases being almost exactly in the proportions known to constitute water.

In this way the decomposing power of the electric current was established very shortly after the first knowledge of Volta's invention had reached England. Of course, experiments so remarkable attracted the attention of other investigators. Cruickshank decomposed a variety of compound substances, and found, that, as a consequence of decomposition, the acids and oxygen always collected around the positive wire, by which the current came in; and hydrogen, metals, and the alkalies, around the negative wire, by which the current went out. The pile as Volta had made it became manifestly inadequate to the production of the strong and uniform currents that were needed; and to meet this want Cruickshank devised his well-known trough battery, in which zinc and copper plates were fixed in vertical grooves, the liquid being interposed between the successive pairs of plates. Cruickshank's battery, or modifications of it, are still in common use.

Meanwhile, a young German chemist, Ritter of Jena, had also independently discovered the electro-decomposition of water and saline compounds; and, more than this, he had found out that this singular decomposing power could be transmitted through sulphuric acid, so that, if on both sides of the acid there were water, oxygen and hydrogen would still be evolved from the wires dipping in the water. It seemed, therefore, that one or the other of the elements of water must have passed through the sulphuric acid: for, clearly, if the water was decomposed at the positive wire, where only oxygen appeared, the hydrogen must somehow get across to the negative wire; while, if the decomposition occurred at the negative wire, then oxygen must also in some unexplained way cross over to the positive wire.

This was the singular phenomenon which attracted the notice of a scientific student who was then just commencing the labors which earned for him an imperishable name. Humphry Davy wondered whether, if the two wires were immersed each in a glass of pure water, the gases would be produced. He tried it: nothing happened. Then he put a finger of his right hand in one glass, and a finger of his left hand in the other. It was very extraordinary: then the gases appeared. Next he got three people to stand in a row, hand in hand, forming a chain between the glasses: still the gases appeared. It was a simple experiment, — the experiments of most great thinkers are simple, — but it demonstrated conclusively, that, if any material principle passed between the wires, it must have been transmitted through his body, or the bodies of all three people who formed the line of communication between the gases.

Then in October, 1800, began Davy's famous experiments which stand and will stand forever as the foundations of a great branch of electrical science. Beginning upon the voltaic pile itself, he found that the chemical changes in it were the cause of its electrical effects, and that the action in a cell is similar to the decomposition of water at the extreme wires of the pile; that a battery could be made of liquid elements with conducting-plates of identical material placed in them. And then, branching from the chemical to the calorific properties of the battery, he constructed a huge apparatus whereby he fused wire, and for the first time produced the electric arc between carbon points. Brilliant as Davy's discoveries then were, they were merely the prelude of others which startled the world.

When water was first decomposed, it was noted that at the positive electrode there were always present indications of an acid, while at the negative electrode an alkali appeared. There were not wanting philosophers who jumped to the conclusion that here were new things in water, not known in anybody's philosophy. One wanted to suppose an " electric acid," — a neat example of the art of explaining something which is not understood, by giving a name to it. Another insisted that the acid and alkali were " generated " out of the elements of the water by voltaic action ; thus anticipating the later claims to other singular things " generated " from water by the inventor of the so-called Keely motor. One peculiarly conscienceless individual announced that the most carefully distilled water nevertheless yielded " muriate of soda." Why " muriate of soda," he failed to explain ; and some people, anxious to know about this, who called at the address appended to his memoir, came back, and said that nobody of the author's name lived there. Altogether, although the fact of electro-decomposition had been established, the subject as a whole was in a state of confusion ; and it was to bring order out of this chaos, that Davy resumed his investigations into electro-chemistry.

The first thing he did was to explode thoroughly and elaborately the notion that any thing but hydrogen and oxygen could be got out of water ; provided the water was pure, and such disturbing causes as acids and alkalies in the vessels used were eliminated, — not in the vessels in the sense of contained in them, but in their substance, be it noted. And from this singular circumstance, that the current

was powerful enough to drag acids and alkalies out of
the very material of cups of agate and glass, grew the
idea that the same power might be brought to bear on
other bodies, and thus force from substances hitherto
considered simple and elementary, the secrets of their
complex composition.

Davy's first efforts were directed to potash. The alkali
liquefied by heat was placed on a platinum disk, which
was connected with the negative pole of a battery, while
a wire connected with the positive pole was applied to its
upper surface. At the upper surface there was a disengagement of gas; at the lower surface, small metallic
globules appeared, like mercury in appearance. Some of
these burned by contact
with air. The gas dis-
engaged at the positive
wire was oxygen ; and
the metal deposited was
the base of the alkali
afterwards called po-
tassium, thus for the

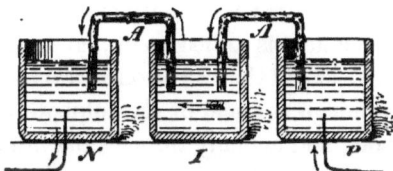

Fig. 88.

first time revealed. In like manner, from soda Davy produced the metal sodium ; and then from baryta, strontia,
lime, and magnesium, came barium, strontium, calcium,
and magnesium. Still more refractory materials were then
attacked ; and alumina, silica, zirconia. and glucinia
yielded silicium, aluminum, glucinium, and zirconium.

Davy not only found that the electric current was capable of decomposing compound bodies, but also of trans-
ferring — or, if the term may be permitted, of *decanting*
— their constituents from one vessel to another. Some
of the results of his experiments were most singular.
Three cups were arranged as shown in Fig. 88 ; the positive wire entering the cup *P*, and the negative wire enter-

ing the cup N. I is an intermediate cup, between which
and the cups P and N extend strips of asbestos, A, which
act as siphons. The current then passed from the positive
wire through the liquid in cup P, thence by the asbestos
through the liquid in cup I, by the asbestos again to the
liquid in cup N, and so out to the negative wire. The
negative cup N was filled with a solution of sulphate of
potash; the centre cup, with water in which litmus had
been infused; and the positive cup P contained simply
distilled water. When the current passed, the acid constituent of the sulphate of potash should appear at the
positive pole P; but, to get there, it obviously would
have to traverse the litmus solution in the middle cup I.
Now, litmus is a very delicate test for the presence of an
acid, inasmuch as, normally dark blue, it at once reddens
when acid is added to it; and hence the passage of the
acid should thus be at once revealed. But, strange to say,
although the acid of the sulphate went over to the positive
pole, and actually through the litmus solution, no redden-
ing of the latter followed. If the acid thus seemingly
lost its power, in transit, to affect vegetable solutions,
what would happen if a strong alkali were put in the
middle cup? Would the acid and alkali instantly rush
together by reason of their affinity, as they had done since
the beginning of the world? No: sulphuric acid went
directly through a solution of ammonia, without producing chemical change. Hydrochloric and nitric, strongest
of the acids, were driven through concentrated alkalies:
conversely, strong alkalies were passed through strong
acids. It seemed as if either alkali or acid, when in the
control of the current, was powerless until the current
had forced it to its destination. One exception appeared
to this rule: sulphuric acid could not be driven through
strontia or baryta, nor the latter through sulphuric acid;

precipitation occurred in the middle cup. The result of the affinity was, however, an insoluble substance ; and so it was determined, that, wherever the element transmitted forms, with the medium through which it passes, an insoluble compound, the passage is stopped. But that in other cases the transmission did go on, and the affinities of the substances were suspended, was evident from the fact, that, when the current was broken for a moment, combination of acid molecules with the alkali through which they were travelling instantly occurred.

In 1826 Nobili discovered, that when a current of electricity is passed into a solution of acetate of lead by means of a plate of platinum, and out of it by means of a platinum wire, rings of beautiful colors, caused by the formation of thin films of peroxide of lead, appeared on the platinum plate. These colors are very like those produced on steel in tempering, and on the surface of molten lead, which are due to a film of oxide overspreading the metal.

In another chapter we have alluded to the splendid discoveries in magneto-electricity, made by Faraday in 1831. Three years later he supplemented these with the investigations which established the laws of electro-chemistry. He found that the amount of chemical action in the cell is always proportional to the quantity of electricity passing through it ; and that the quantities of substances dissolved and set free by electrolysis are in definite proportions by weight, and these proportions are identical with the ordinary chemical equivalents of the substances. From the first law we know that a current of a certain strength will always liberate just so much hydrogen, for example, from water, and will cause the solution of just so much zinc in the cell whence the current is derived. To illustrate the second law : nine grains of water, for example, contain eight grains of oxygen and one grain of hydrogen; and hydrogen and oxygen always combine in these proportions to form water. Now, if we tear apart, so to speak, the constituents of water, we shall always find eight grains of oxygen at the positive electrode, and one grain of hydrogen at the negative electrode. Why this happens, is not definitely proved; but the generally accepted theory, that of Grothuss, is neatly illustrated in the accompanying engraving, Fig. 89, which represents the case of hydrochloric acid, each molecule of which is composed of one atom of hydrogen and one atom of chlorine. The plate *A* is the positive electrode, and the plate *B* the negative electrode. The oval objects are supposed to represent the molecules; the white half of each representing chlorine, and the dark half hydrogen. The row marked 1 shows the molecules distributed at random, as before the current passes. When the current is established, the molecules arrange themselves in innumerable chains in which every molecule has its constituent atoms pointing in a certain direction; for, as we see, all the chlorine atoms point to the positive plate *A*, and all the hydrogen atoms to the negative plate *B*. Now, if the current is strong enough, the chlorine half of the molecule next the positive plate is divorced from its wedlock with the hydrogen half. Atoms abhor celibacy. They are polygamous or polyandrous to the last degree; but single-blessedness they will have none of if they can help it. So, no sooner is the hydrogen atom off with the old love, before it is immediately on with the new; because

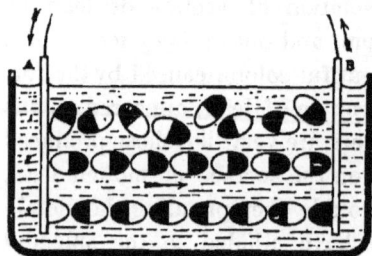

Fig. 89.

it promptly appropriates the chlorine partner of its next neighbor. The thus deserted hydrogen atom helps himself to *his* neighbor's consort in like manner; and so on through this singular chain, until at last there is a hydrogen atom left solitary and alone at the negative plate, matching the solitary chlorine atom at the positive plate, as in row 3. And so it looks as if all the chlorine atoms had somehow made their way to one plate, and all the hydrogen atoms to the other. Faraday called these apparently migrating atoms *ions ;* and gave the name *anode* to the positive plate, and *cathode* to the negative plate. Then the ions which went to the anode were termed *anions ;* and those which appeared at the cathode, *cathions.*

There was a grave and dignified professor once, who by dint of much persuasion was induced to attend a dancing-party. Among the complicated figures of the German, there was one in which the several couples interchanged partners until a single couple were left unmated. The professor, who had regarded the proceedings hitherto rather stoically, and with a somewhat bored expression, suddenly brightened, and emitted a peculiar pleased chuckle which the writer well knew from past experience was of the same character as that which always followed a neat bit of scientific demonstration, accompanied by a muttered '' Beautiful, ah, beautiful ! ''

'' Who, professor? '' was asked.

'' Who? Nobody. It's what they're doing.''

'' Oh, — the German figure. Yes, it is rather '' —

'' German figure? Oh, you mean Grothuss, of course. But now, doesn't that — doesn't this interchange of the women beautifully — beautifully illustrate his idea of the migration of the ions? Eh? ''

Two years after Faraday had made his discoveries, De la Rue observed the singular fact, that in a peculiar form of

Daniell's battery the copper plate became covered with a coating of metallic copper, which took the exact impress of the plate, even to the fine scratches upon it. In 1837 Dr. Golding Bird decomposed the chlorides of sodium, potassium, and ammonium, and deposited their respective metals on a negative pole of mercury, thus obtaining their amalgams.

It would have been almost a phenomenal occurrence if the discovery soon to be made, and which ultimately became of such great industrial importance, should have failed to have more than a single claimant; but the process of electrotyping differs from most other electrical discoveries in that all the claimants appeared at once, and did not come stringing along after the manner of their kind, for years after some one, bolder than the others, had announced his success. In 1839 Jacobi in St. Petersburg, Spencer in Liverpool, and Jordan in London, described independently a method of converting any line, however fine, engraved on copper, into a relief, by galvanic process, — by depositing copper upon the engraved object. Jacobi published his description in a newspaper; Jordan wrote a letter to the editor of "The Mechanics' Magazine;" and Spencer, last of all, read a paper on the subject before the Liverpool Polytechnic Society, — all in the same year. Their respective adherents argued about their respective priority of invention, quite steadily in the public prints, for the next three years, and intermittently contradicted one another for some time afterwards. Spencer wrote the best account of what he had done, — despite the fact that his opponents sneered at him for being only a carver and gilder, and not a professor, which to their minds logically disproved, of course, his pretensions, — and the general public somehow understood what he wrote about; for, as a recent writer remarks, " thousands of persons, of all classes of society, at once became fascinated by the new art." At about this time the Elkingtons of London began coating military and other metal ornaments with gold and silver, simply by immersing them in solutions of those metals. In 1840 John Wright, a surgeon of Birmingham, came to them with the news that he had succeeded in obtaining electrically a thick, firm, and white deposit of silver, upon articles treated in a liquid made by dissolving the cyanide of this metal in an alkaline cyanide. The Elkingtons saw the value of his discovery, and did what would have been impossible in this country, — embodied Wright's idea in their patent; not for the purpose of depriving Wright of his reward, but in order to perfect and complete the description of a process which proved to be the basis of all successful electroplating of gold and silver. Wright, in fact, profited well, for he was paid a royalty of one shilling an ounce for every ounce of silver deposited; and a handsome annuity was settled on his widow after his death.

The history of electro-chemistry from this point is that of technical details, out of place here; so that we pass at once to practical applications, and these are fourfold: first, electrotyping, or the copying of types, casts, or other objects, by deposits of metal; second, electroplating, or the covering or plating of objects of baser metal, with a thin film of another metal, usually gold or silver; third, the reduction of metals from solutions of their ores; and, fourth, the secondary or storage battery.

Electrotyping finds its widest utilization in the reproduction of engravings and pages set in type. A mould of the object, made in wax, lightly covered with plumbago so that a conducting surface may be present, is placed in a bath of saturated solution of sulphate of copper, and attached to the cathode, or pole at which the current leaves the bath. A plate of copper is attached to the anode, or wire at which the current enters. This plate is decomposed at the same rate as the copper is deposited from the solution, on the plumbago-covered surface of the mould; and in this way the strength of the solution is kept uniform. The copper, as it is deposited, covers every portion of the surface with a bright layer, usually starting from the suspending wire and extending itself gradually over the entire area. Generally the electrotyping operation takes about twenty-four hours; but for newspaper work this time is necessarily much shortened. It is not uncommon for pages of illustrated papers, especially if containing important engravings of recent events, to be electrotyped in eight, six, and even four hours.

When a good adherent film of copper has been deposited over the surface, the mould is removed. The wax is melted to liberate the electrotype, which is then backed with an alloy of lead, antimony, and tin. The plate thus produced is an absolutely exact reproduction of the original types or relief engraving from which the wax mould was made. It only remains to mount the plate upon a block of wood, type high, when it is ready to take its place in the form which is placed in the printing-press. Usually the woodcuts and types are set up and arranged in page form, and then the whole page is electrotyped. The pages before the reader have been thus prepared. When an electrotype is to be submitted to hard usage, — as when a great many impressions are to be taken from it, — it is sometimes coated with a pellicle of electrically deposited iron. Messrs. Christofle & Co. of Paris have recently made very beautiful electrotypes by the direct deposition of nickel in the mould, strengthened by a copper backing.

The electrotyping process has been used on a large scale for the reproduction of statues of even colossal dimensions. In such cases, instead of making moulds the plaster-of-Paris figure itself is sacrificed. The mode of operation is interesting.

After the figure is well saturated in linseed oil, it is covered with a film of black-lead, and then placed in a large cistern of sulphate-of-copper solution, which is allowed to precipitate its copper on the object until a coating is formed of about one-sixteenth of an inch in thickness. The object is then lifted from the bath, the copper envelope cut through at suitable places, the plaster figure broken away with great care, and the whole of it extracted. The outer surfaces of the copper forms (with wires attached) are now thoroughly varnished all over, to prevent any deposit being formed thereon ; the forms exposed to sulphuretted hydrogen, to prevent adhesion of the deposit ; and the parts are immersed in the depositing-vat again, which is filled with copper solution. A dissolving plate of pure electrotype copper is suspended within each portion, and a deposit of copper thus formed all over its interior, until a considerable thickness, varying from one-eighth to one-third of an inch, is deposited, which requires a period of three or four weeks. Each piece is now removed from the liquid, washed, and the outer shell torn off ; when all the parts of the figure remain nearly complete, and ready for fixing together. Some of the objects made by this process, by the Messrs. Elkington, are colossal. The statue of the Earl of Eglinton is thirteen and a half feet high, and weighs two tons ; and the vat in which it was formed is capable of holding 6,680 gallons of liquid. The Messrs. Christofle made a statue twenty-nine feet six inches high, and weighing about five and a half tons. About ten weeks were required to deposit the metal.

Electroplating is now practised with a great variety of metals. The ordinary arrangement of a silver-plating bath, to which a battery-cell supplies current, is represented

in Fig. 90.   Of late years, the nickel-plating of all sorts
of metal articles, from the parts of steam-engines down
to surgical instruments, has become a very important
branch of the industry, replacing to a great extent gold
and silver plating.   Nickel-plated articles take a fine pol-
ish, do not tarnish, and their coating is hard and lasting.
The solutions commonly used for nickel-plating were invented by Mr. Isaac Adams, and patented in this country in 1869.   They may be the double chloride of nickel
and ammonium, or the double sulphate of nickel and

Fig. 90.

ammonium; the bath being neutral, that is, neither acid
nor alkaline, upon which fact the success of the Adams
process greatly depends.   The cheapness of nickel, and
the rapidity with which it is deposited, — from fifteen minutes to an hour, when the dynamo is used to supply current, being sufficient time, — have resulted in nickel-plating
becoming an every-day process in many engineering work-
shops.

It can hardly be said, however, that nickel-plating is
anywhere carried on on the gigantic scale in which silver-
plating is practised, especially in Europe.   The house of

Christofle & Co. in Paris annually deposits more than thirteen thousand pounds of silver, and since its establishment in 1842 has used not less than a hundred and eighty-five tons of that metal.

Gold is usually deposited from the double cyanide of gold, and potassium. The metal is sometimes deposited in solid form upon moulds for the production of articles of jewellery having very complex or under-cut ornaments upon them. By the use of certain solutions, the gold-plating can be beautifully colored; and in this way the red gold, orange gold, etc., of fashionable jewellery, are produced. In gilding base metals, a film of copper or brass is generally first produced upon them. The insides of vessels are gilded by filling the vessel with the gold solution, suspending a gold anode in the liquid, and passing the current. Many very beautiful objects of art are made by incasing in gold, silver, and copper, for example, ferns, foliage, flowers, insects, and lizards. So also anatomical specimens, such as brains, have been thus treated; the electro-deposit preserving every minute wrinkle and fissure. An even more grim application has recently been proposed by a French chemist who advocates the coating of the bodies of the dead with impervious platings of gold, silver, or copper, as a means of preserving them. He even suggested making statues in this way. Copper has been deposited upon fabrics and upon glass, and is almost invariably applied to the carbons of arc lights.

The electrolytic refining of copper, for the purpose of obtaining the metal in a chemically pure state, is largely carried on in Europe. The Keith process of refining lead is utilized, we believe, in this country only. The precious metals are commonly separated in the electrolytic bath by combining them with copper to form an anode and then electrically depositing the copper, leaving the gold and silver as a residuum.

A curious application of electroplating is in the manufacture of the so-called compound telegraph-wire, which consists of a central wire of steel covered with a coating of copper. This coating is deposited upon the steel by galvanic action, while the wire is drawn continuously through a long trough containing the solution. A wire thus made is found to offer much less resistance to the current than an ordinary iron wire.

Up to within a few years, the use of electricity for actual work, such as lighting or driving motors, has been attended with a great drawback, almost as important as the high cost of generating the current; and that is, it has been necessary to make the electricity as it is needed. We can store water in a reservoir, and use it to drive a wheel at one time as well as another. We make gas during the day, and store it in huge gasometers from which a supply is drawn at night. But with electricity it is necessary to keep a constant current flowing through the conductor, equal to meeting all likely needs, whether it is actually utilized or not. Of course this involves continual expense, unremitting wear of machinery, and a great deal of additional apparatus ready to take the place of any thing which may break down or need repair. Inasmuch, also, as the hours of the night when lights are needed are few, it is necessary to have very powerful machinery, capable of supplying a great deal of electricity in a short time. The reader can easily imagine how much greater the cost of gas would be if all of it had to be made between the hours of 6 P.M. and midnight, instead of its being produced as it is, throughout the day. In fact, at the present time central stations for the supply of electricity from dynamos employ their capital fruitfully only about six hours in the twenty-four.

The question of how to store electricity so that we can generate it at one time, and use it at another, is therefore of very great moment. We know, however, that electricity is not a thing capable of storage, any more than it is a thing capable of being burned in a lamp. The water which in falling drives a wheel is not consumed: simply its energy is expended. If we go a step farther, and cause the wheel thus driven to wind up a spring, or lift a weight, we know that we can keep the spring wound up, or the weight in its lifted position, as long as we choose; and that when we release the spring, or drop the weight, then we can use the energy thus stored. So that we are not to conceive of the idea of pouring an electrical fluid into something, and keeping it there; but of causing the energy which exists in the form we know as electricity, to become stored, just as the energy of the water becomes stored in the wound-up spring or lifted weight. There is, therefore, no such thing as storage of electricity. What is really done is the changing of the electrical energy from the active condition to the potential condition, — from the state in which it may be doing work, to the state in which it is not doing work but is capable of so doing.

We have already found that if we plunge the ends of two wires leading from a galvanic cell into water, — or, better, dilute sulphuric acid, — bubbles of gas will appear upon the immersed wires, — hydrogen at the wire by which the current leaves, oxygen at the wire by which it enters. This experiment is usually shown by means of the apparatus shown in Fig. 91. This consists of a glass vessel (V) containing water, and also two glass test-tubes (AB) inverted over a pair of platinum plates projecting up from the bottom of the cell or vessel. These plates are connected by wires to the poles of the voltaic battery (C), as shown ; and therefore they act as electrodes, and pass the current from the battery through the water.   Now, as the water is decomposed, the hydrogen gas is found to collect on the cathode, by which the current is supposed to leave the water, while the oxygen collects on the anode, by which the current is believed to enter the water ; and as the gases are lighter than the water, they rise into the upper ends of the tubes.   The volume of hydrogen at the cathode is

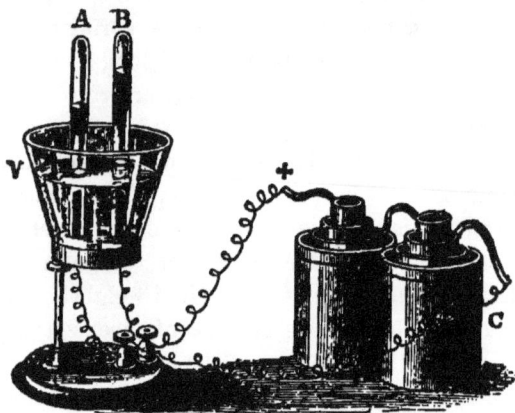

Fig. 91.

always twice the volume of oxygen at the anode, and this agrees with the known constitution of water.   Further, the quantity of water decomposed in a given time is proportional to the strength of the electric current ; and hence, if the tubes are graduated to show the volume of gases collected in them, the instrument becomes a *voltameter*, or current-measurer.   Faraday arranged the apparatus in the form shown in Fig. 92, so that the gas could easily be collected and measured.   Here two small platinum plates dip in the acidulated water, and are connected to wires which pass up through the cork of the bottle: binding-screws are attached to the upper ends of these wires, and a glass tube fixed into the cork serves to discharge the gas formed within. When the binding-screws are connected to the poles of a battery, the water in the bottle is decomposed, and the hydrogen and oxygen rise to the surface.

In this voltameter we have two plates and a liquid in a suitable vessel. If one of these plates were zinc, and the other copper, we know that the zinc would be attacked by the acidulated water, and the apparatus would at once be a galvanic cell capable of yielding its own current. But here the plates are both of the same material, immersed in one liquid; and hence one is not more attacked than the other, and the arrangement cannot act as a galvanic cell.

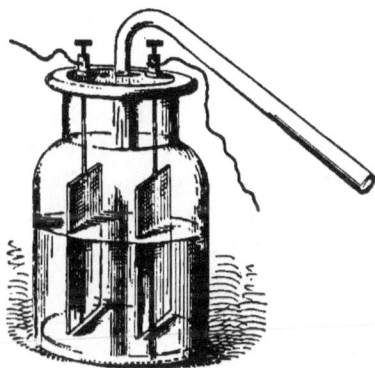

Fig. 92.

When, however, the electric current from another battery is sent into the voltameter, then its plates respectively yield, as we have seen, hydrogen and oxygen; and these gases, in fact, coat the plates. Now they have become different. Hydrogen and oxygen form a galvanic pair by themselves; and as soon as the voltameter is disconnected from its charging battery, and its wires brought into contact, a current is set up through that wire, which goes from the hydrogen to the oxygen within the liquid.

It will be remembered, that, in referring to the so-called polarization of the primary form of the galvanic battery,

we noted that after the hydrogen had formed on the unattacked element, a current occurred from the hydrogen
to the zinc, which ran opposite to and so greatly weakened
or destroyed the original current. In the voltameter there
is a like action, and the current yielded by the voltameter
is in the reverse direction to that of
the battery current which charged it.
Let us fix this with a diagram (Fig.
93). Here we have first the primary
cell, with its wires joined. The current goes in the liquid from zinc to
carbon, and thence back by the wire to
the zinc, the arrows showing the direction. Next, we connect the cell to the
voltameter (Fig. 94). Here the current goes from the carbon to one plate of the voltameter, and produces oxygen
thereon ; then through the liquid to the other voltameter
plate, where hydrogen is generated ; then back to the zinc,
and so through the cell to the carbon again. Now dis-
connect the voltame-
ter, and join its wires
(Fig. 95). Then the
current goes in the
liquid from the hy-
drogen to the oxy-
gen, and then by the
wire back to the hy-
drogen. Compare
the direction of this
current as indicated by the arrows, with the direction of
the current in the battery cell, similarly indicated, and it
will be seen that the currents move in opposite directions.

We have now accomplished a very important result.
That is, by the action of an electric current we have made

Battery
Fig. 93.

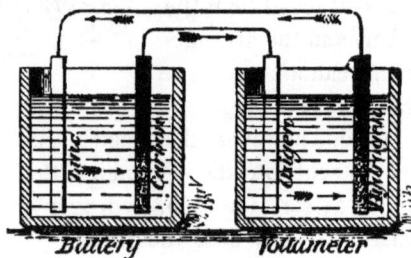

Battery   Voltameter
Fig. 94.

a contrivance into a galvanic cell which before was not one ; or, to put it in another way, we have led a current into something from which, after the source of supply is wholly disconnected, we can get a current out. This is electrical storage — the misuse of the term aside. It looks as if we had poured the electricity into the voltameter, just as we might pour in the liquid, and *afterwards* drawn out the one as we might the other.

The voltameter reversed as above described yields, however, only a momentary current; for very little of the gases stay on the plates, the greater portion mixing and rising as we have seen. The gases do not act on either plate, because the material of the latter, platinum, is not easily attacked.

The first secondary battery was devised by Ritter of Jena, very shortly after the invention of the voltaic pile. It had been found, that, if an oblong slip of wet paper have its extremities in contact with the poles of the pile, each half of the slip will be electrified ; and

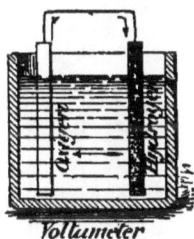
Voltameter
Fig. 96.

if it be removed from contact with the pile, by a rod of glass or other non-conductor, its electric state will continue. This was observed by Volta, and, according to Dr. Lardner (writing in 1841), " was the means of suggesting to Ritter the idea of his secondary pile ; which consisted of a series of disks of a single metal, alternated with cloth or card moistened in a liquid by which the metal would not be affected chemically. If such a pile have its extremities put in connection, by conducting substances, with the poles of an insulated voltaic pile, it will receive a charge of electricity in a manner similar to the band of wet paper, — one half taking a positive and the other a negative charge ; and, after its connection with the primary pile has been broken, it will retain the charge it has thus received. The secondary pile, while it retains its charge, produces the same physiological and chemical effects as the voltaic apparatus."

In 1859 M. Gaston Planté made a secondary cell based upon the principles above briefly sketched. Instead of plates of platinum he used plates of lead, rolled as shown in Fig. 96. The consequence was, that, when the current passed through these, the oxygen produced at one plate combined with the metal, and deposited lead oxide; the hydrogen as before remained free on the other plate. Thus he produced a cell in which, after the charging current was removed, were elements of lead and lead oxide. These being connected yielded a current, but, however, for a short time, because but very little of the oxide was produced, — a mere film on the surface. Planté thereupon devised his so-called "forming" process, which consisted in first charging his plates, then discharging, then charging again with the battery current reversed, and so on, increasing intervals of rest being left between the operations; until finally he produced, through the repeated oxidations and subsequent reductions of the oxidized material to a metallic state, very porous or spongy plates. These, by reason of their porosity, exposed a very large surface to the oxidizing action of the current, so that the result was as if he had charged a plate of great superficial area.

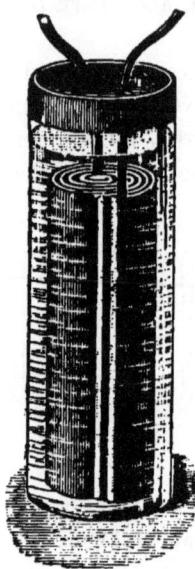

Fig. 96.

As we have already shown, when batteries are connected

in multiple arc, — that is, all the zinc plates together, and all the copper plates together, — then the plates of each kind act as one large plate, the surfaces of all being added together. Planté found that if he charged a number of secondary cells connected in this way, and, after charging, if he arranged his cells in series, — that is, the positive plate of one connected to the negative plate of the next, and so on, — he could obtain very powerful currents for short periods of time.

In 1880 M. Camille Faure covered Planté's lead plates with red lead, and then put them in little flannel jackets. The peculiarity of the red lead is, that, on sending a current through it, it is easily changed into spongy lead ; so that, instead of the "forming" operation taking weeks and months, it can be done in a few days or even hours. This discovery apparently removed the chief obstacle to Planté's cells becoming of commercial value ; and when it was announced, it was hailed as an extraordinary advance.

Fig. 97.

Since 1880 a great many patents have been obtained for secondary batteries, and they now exist in many forms. An example of the Faure type is Reynier's cell, which is represented in Fig. 97. In a glass jar are placed two spirals of rolled lead plate, against which the red lead is held by serge instead of the felt or flannel which Faure adopted. Mainly, however, the efforts of inventors have been directed to reducing the weight of the cells, and to devising new ways of holding the red lead on the plates. Brush packs his red lead or other active material in a frame of cast lead containing slots, cells, or openings. Sellon also makes a plate with receptacles for containing and holding the active material.

The storage-battery at the present time is simply a subject for further research and invention. No form of it exists in which grave defects are not present. The value and efficiency of many of the cells offered in the market have been over-estimated, and often greatly misunderstood. None are more eager to grasp at possible improvements than those who to-day most loudly vaunt the great merit of their own particular advertised contrivances; this not infrequently in the hope that the large amounts of capital already risked may by some stroke of good fortune be saved from loss.

The commonest defects of the storage-cell are "needling," "buckling," and "disintegration." Needling is the formation of the so-called "lead tree," — fine spiculæ of metal between the electrodes, which causes short circuiting and rapid waste of current. Buckling is the deformation or bending of the plates themselves, whereby one plate often makes contact with another, and short circuiting again follows. Disintegration and buckling also are usually due to chemical changes in the electrodes. The plates, disintegrating in time, drop to pieces. Besides these difficulties, certain solutions cause very high internal resistance in the cell; and there are a variety of other disadvantages.

One of the best forms of storage battery is that devised by Mr. Willard E. Case, in which he uses a neutral liquid, from which he deposits metal on one electrode while peroxidizing the other.

Mr. Case's investigations in the storage-battery have led him to the remarkable discovery that heat can be directly converted into electricity in the galvanic cell. He places in his cell an electrode of tin, an electrode of carbon, and a liquid which at ordinary temperature will not attack either electrode. Therefore no current is yielded. But as soon as the liquid is warmed, — and to do this the cell, which is hermetically sealed once for all, is merely put into hot water, — chlorine is set free from the liquid, and attacks the tin. Then the current starts, and continues until all the tin is converted into chloride. Now, if the cell be allowed to cool, the chlorine releases the tin, and returns to the liquid; and so the cell regains its original state. The chlorine, in fact, is a chemical pendulum, swinging from liquid to tin, and from tin to liquid, as often as the heat is applied and removed. Of course the cell lasts indefinitely; theoretically, forever. No material is used up in it. The temperature is never above that of boiling water. Its electro-motive force is about one-quarter volt.

In one sense this cell may be regarded as a heat-storage battery: it is really a wonderfully efficient heat-engine. It is not merely a most beautiful and ingenious illustration of the correlation and interconvertibility of the natural forces, but an advance apparently destined to be of the highest practical value.

Electrolysis has been applied to the rectification of alcohols, the improvement of wines, and to the deposition of aniline dyes.

CHAPTER XI.

THE ELECTRIC TELEGRAPH.

THE earliest suggestion of the electric telegraph appears in the *Prolusiones Academicæ* of Strada, an Italian Jesuit, who in 1617 spoke of "the instantaneous transmission of thoughts and words, between two individuals, over an indefinite space," caused by a species of loadstone, which possesses such virtue,· that, if two needles be touched with it, and then balanced on separate pivots, and the one turned in a particular direction, the other will sympathetically move parallel to it. These needles were to be poised and mounted on a dial with the letters of the alphabet around.

In "The Spectator" of 1712, Addison proposes the sending of love-letters in this way. In 1876, when the speaking telephone first appeared, and before many people had any conception of its extraordinary capabilities, "The New-York Tribune" suggested that its principal value might lie in the fact that lovers and diplomatists could thus secretly converse; and thus history repeated itself.

There was no lack of experiments upon electric telegraphs during the last century. All of them depended upon the idea of sending the charge of static or frictional electricity through one or more wires; for the galvanic battery had not yet been invented.

In 1729 Gray and Wheeler produced motion in light bodies at a distance of 666 feet. In 1747 Dr. Watson, in the presence of many scientific persons, transmitted electricity through twenty-eight hundred feet of wire and eight thousand feet of water, thus making use of the earth circuit. In the following year Franklin fired spirits on one side of the Schuylkill River, by the discharge from an electrical battery on the opposite bank.

Then followed a curious series of endeavors to adapt the results of the experiments of Watson and Franklin to every-day use. The first practicable form of electric telegraph was described in " The Scots Magazine " in 1753, in an anonymous communication over the initials C. M. The article was entitled " An Expeditious Method of conveying Intelligence." It was proposed to extend wires, equal in number to the letters of the alphabet, between two distant places ; support them at intervals on glass fixed to solid bodies ; let each wire terminate in a ball ; place beneath each ball a shred of paper on which the corresponding letter of the alphabet has been printed. Bring the farther end of the first wire into contact with an excited glass tube, and the paper A will instantly rise to the first ball. Thus the whole alphabet may be represented. Here, evidently, was the idea of complete insulation of the conducting wire, and at the distant end the production of a signal which should be either visible or audible'; for the inventor also proposed a series of bells, differing in tone from A to Z, instead of the paper.

Very little is known of the inventor. Sir David Brewster asserts that his name was Charles Morrison. It is frequently quoted as Charles Marshall. In fact, about the only definite information ever obtained was from a very old Scotch lady who remembered a " very clever man, of obscure position, ' who could make lichtnin' write an' speak, and who could licht a room wi' coal reek ' (i.e., coal smoke).'' That a great genius thus became lost to the world, can hardly be doubted ; for here was a man who had seen farther into the mysteries of electricity than Franklin himself. We can easily imagine his fate. Being ahead of his time, his neighbors — those typical neighbors of the inventor, who mend the adage to make the prophet not only without honor, but with positive dishonor, in his own country — called him a visionary and a madman. There is more true pathos in the many stories of the stout hearts thus broken, than in all the romantic vicissitudes of the Abelards and the Heloises since the Flood.

For several years following, little advance was made. Lomond in 1787 proposed a single wire and a pith-ball electrometer. Reizen in 1794 contrived a telegraph like Marshall's, but added letters of the alphabet cut out in pieces of tin-foil and rendered visible by sparks. Cavallo went back to the single-wire idea, and used sparks to designate the various signals, and an explosion of gas to alarm the operator.

Then came a lapse of some fifteen years, and meanwhile the voltaic pile was discovered. When the inventors came to apply this to telegraphy, they went to work in the same old way. Soemmering, in 1809, used as many wires as there were signals, but varied these by producing them by the decomposition of water. The battery not proving very successful, Mr. (afterwards Sir) Francis Ronalds abandoned it in favor of the more intense discharge of the Leyden-jar ; and arranged a pith-ball electrometer at the end of his line, wherewith he made his signals.

This was done in 1816. Seventy years had elapsed since Watson's experiment proving the possibility of transmitting the electrical discharge over long distances.

Yet the actual advance made toward a practicable and useful electric telegraph had been scarcely any thing. The discharge could be sent over one wire ; and repeated sparks, or movements of a pith-ball, would indicate signals — the weather permitting. It could be sent over twenty-six wires, and each wire might then make its own signal. The signals might be produced by the decomposition of water or salts, or by explosions, or illuminations of tin-foil letters. It is not surprising that the Lords of the Admiralty in 1813, after considering one of the many plans submitted to them, said that as the war was not over, and money scarce, they thought best not to carry it into effect.

Oersted's grand discovery came in 1819, and in 1820 Ampère devised the galvanometer. He was quick to see, that, if the current could deflect the needle at a short distance, there was a possibility of its doing the same at a long distance ; but he was unable, apparently, to break away from the multiple-wire idea. He, too, proposed the use of as many wires as letters or signals to be indicated. That happened in the same year that the electro-magnet was invented by Arago. Looking back on these proceedings now, it seems as if all these philosophers and inventors of Europe were groping through a labyrinth, one following the blind lead of the static charge, and another that of the multiple wire ; some rejecting the very means which would conduct them to a successful ending, in the belief that they were merely obstacles ; others clinging to obstacles, in the belief that they were clews. In 1820 the actual elements of the telegraph of to-day were in their grasp. They had the electro-magnet, the conducting wire, and the galvanic battery ; but no eyes to see what could be accomplished by these means. So far as they knew, no battery could send its current over a long line, and magnetize something at the other end.

The European philosophers kept on groping. At the end of five years, one of them reached an obstacle which he made up his mind was so entirely insurmountable, that it rendered the electric telegraph an impossibility for all future time. This was Mr. Peter Barlow, fellow of the Royal Society, who had encountered the question whether the lengthening of the conducting wire would produce any effect in diminishing the energy of the current transmitted, and had undertaken to resolve the problem. Here is his conclusion in his own words : —

" It had been said that the electric fluid from a common electrical battery had been transmitted through a wire four miles in length, without any sensible diminution of effect, and to every appearance instantaneously ; and if this should be found to be the case with the galvanic current, then no question could be entertained of the practicability and utility of the suggestion before adverted to. I was therefore induced to make the trial, but *I found such a considerable diminution with only two hundred feet of wire as at once to convince me of the impracticability of the scheme.*"

Barlow's conclusion would possess no especial interest now, other than that which would necessarily attach to the views of any eminent observer of the period, were it not for the singular fact, that the circumstance of its publication had probably more to do with the later successful realization of the electric telegraph, than any other occurrence in the history of the invention. The year following the announcement of Barlow's conclusions, a young graduate of the Albany (N.Y.) Academy — by name Joseph Henry — was appointed to the professorship of mathematics in that institution. Henry there began the series of scientific investigations which is now historic ; thus brilliantly opening a career which at its end found him easily the first among American scientists.

Up to that time, electro-magnets had been made with a single coil of naked wire wound spirally around the core, with large intervals between the strands. The core was insulated as a whole : the wire was not insulated at all. Professor Schweigger, who had previously invented the multiplying galvanometer, had covered his wires with silk. Henry followed this idea, and, instead of a single coil of wire, used several. He says, " These experiments conclusively proved that a great development of magnetism could be effected by a very small galvanic element ; and, also, that the power of the coil was materially increased by multiplying the number of wires, without increasing the length of each." He also found that he could obtain stronger results with the wires so wound that the pitch of one spiral should be the reverse of that of the spiral beneath it. And lastly he discovered that a magnet with a long fine-wire coil must be worked by a battery having high electro-motive force, composed of a large number of cells in series, when a distant effect was required ; and that the greatest dynamic effect close at hand is produced by a battery of a very few cells of large surface, combined with a coil or coils of short thick wire around the magnet.

"But, be this as it may," says Henry, after describing his discoveries as above very briefly outlined, "the fact that the magnetic action of a current from a trough is at least not sensibly diminished by passing through a long wire is directly applicable to Mr. Barlow's project of forming an electro-magnetic telegraph, and also of material consequence in the construction of the galvanic coil."

Barlow had said that the gentle current of the galvanic battery became so weakened, after traversing two hundred feet of wire, that it was idle to consider the possibility of making it pass over even a mile of conductor and then

affect a magnet.   Henry's reply was to point out that the
trouble lay in the way Barlow's magnet was made.   The
resistance of the line weakened the current.   Start, then,
with a strong current, — an " intensity current,"—Henry
said : let the line resistance weaken it, but make the magnet so that the diminished current will exercise its full
effect.   Instead of using one short coil, through which
the current can easily slip, and do nothing, make a coil of
many turns ; that increases the magnetic field : make it
of fine wire, and of higher resistance.   And then, to prove
the truth of his discovery, Henry put up the first electro-
magnetic telegraph ever constructed.   In the academy at
Albany, in 1831, he suspended 1,060 feet of bell-wire,
with a battery at one end and one of his magnets at the
other ; and he made that magnet attract and release its
armature.   The armature struck a bell, and so made the
signals.

Annihilating distance in this way was only one part of
Henry's discovery.   He had also found, that, to obtain
the greatest dynamic effect close at hand, the battery
should be composed of a very few cells of large surface,
combined with a coil or coils of short coarse wire around
the magnet, — conditions just the reverse of those necessary when the magnet was to be worked at a distance.
Now, he argued, suppose the magnet with the coarse short
coil, and the large-surface battery, be put at the receiving-
station ; and the current coming over the line be used
simply to make and break the circuit of that local battery.
That is a very small thing to do, — very different from making the tired current, so to speak, work a lot of signalling
or recording mechanism.   The local battery and magnet
then do the hard labor ; the current coming over the line
merely controls the force : or, in other words, instead of an
engine driven by power coming from a very long distance,

and wasted greatly on its way, we have one operated by power immediately at hand, but controlled from a point miles away. This is the principle of the telegraphic "relay." In 1835 Henry worked a telegraph-line in that way at Princeton. And thus the electro-magnetic telegraph was completely invented and demonstrated. There was nothing left to do, but to put up the posts, string the lines, and attach the instruments. The question asked thousands of years before by the prophet, "Canst thou send lightnings, that they may go, and say unto thee, Here we are?" Henry had answered in the affirmative. It remained for other men, following his example, to go and do likewise.

It is, as we have said, a common misfortune of inventors, to be ahead of the times in which they live; and this was Henry's experience. It is true that he contributed to the result himself, by refusing to patent his ideas, and so hiding his light under a bushel. But the fact none the less remains, that here was a discovery not merely of transcendent importance, but one which the world had been eagerly trying to make for years; and yet, when it was achieved, no one stood ready to put it to practical use. So little was it known or appreciated, that when on April 15, 1837, the Secretary of the Treasury, Hon. Levi Woodbury, sent out a circular letter proposing inquiries on the subject of a system of telegraphs for the United States, the Franklin Institute of Philadelphia, the leading scientific body of the land, could find nothing better to recommend than the semaphore, or mechanical telegraph. The report advocates the erection of forty stations between New York and Washington; each station being a building twenty-two feet square, with a quadrangular pyramidal roof on which the swinging arms of the semaphore were to be mounted. By moving the arms into different positions, numbers and letters were to be indicated, and the observer at one station would be enabled to recognize the signals made at the next station, some seven miles away, by means of a telescope. "In conclusion," says the report, "the committee would respectfully suggest to the Secretary of the Treasury to consider the propriety of causing two telegraphs to be erected, in which careful experiments may be made on all the points which bear upon the general questions submitted to him by the House of Representatives."

Meanwhile one electric telegraph had been erected in this country. This was based on the use of the static discharge. It was put up by Harrison Gray Dyer, on a race-course on Long Island; and it is a noteworthy fact, that he strung his wires on glass insulators upon trees and poles. The electrical discharge, after passing over the wire, acted upon litmus paper to produce a red mark. The difference in time between the sparks indicated different letters, arranged in an arbitrary alphabet; and the paper was moved by hand. This line was used in 1827–28.

It will be apparent, therefore, that, at the time the foregoing report was made by the Franklin Institute, both of the two known systems of electric telegraphy had been practically tested in this country; the static-discharge telegraph by Dyer, and the electro-magnetic telegraph by Henry. "In 1832," says Henry, "nothing remained to be discovered in order to reduce the proposition of the electro-magnetic telegraph to practice. I had shown that the attraction of the armature could be produced at any distance, and had designed the kind of a battery and coil around the magnet to be used for this purpose. I had also pointed out the fact of the applicability of my experiments to the electro-magnetic telegraph." Five years

after this, the learned scientists of the Franklin Institute
offered to the Government the services of their committee
to experiment, not upon electric telegraphs, but semaphores!

Among the replies forwarded to the Secretary of the
Treasury, in answer to his circular, were three letters
signed Samuel F. B. Morse, all advocating the establishment of an electro-magnetic telegraph. Morse was an
artist of some repute, but not in any sense an educated
electrician. In the latter part of the year 1832, while on
a homeward voyage from Europe, he conceived the idea
of an electric or electro-chemical telegraph, and devised a
system of signs for letters to be marked by the breaking
and closing of the electric circuit. Dr. C. T. Jackson of
Boston was a passenger on the same vessel; and, being
well versed in electricity, Morse went to him for information. It appears, however, that neither Morse nor Jackson at that time had conceived of any thing more than an
electro-chemical telegraph, in which the current might decompose chemical compounds so as to leave a permanent
mark. Morse's idea, from the beginning, seems to have
been principally to make the current record itself. In
1835 Morse was appointed to a professorship in the University of New York, and then he contrived the mechanical arrangement which formed the basis for his subsequent
inventions. This consisted, at the receiving-station, of a
strip of paper about half an inch in breadth, moved lengthwise over a roller by clock-work. Above the paper hung
a pendulum which vibrated across the paper, and carried
at its lower end a pencil. Normally, as the paper moved
along, the pencil traced a simple straight line. Near the
pendulum was an electro-magnet, the armature of which
was attached to the pendulum. The electro-magnet was
connected to the line wire. Whenever a current came

218 THE AGE OF ELECTRICITY.

over the wire, the magnet was energized, and caused to attract its armature, and so cause the pencil to move across the paper, so that zigzag lines were produced, which represented letters, numbers, etc.

Morse encountered the same trouble which all previous experimenters before him, Henry alone excepted, had met. His current was dissipated before it reached the end of the line. He then adopted the relay plan in the spring of 1837. On Nov. 28, 1837, Morse wrote to the Secretary: " We have procured several miles of wire, and I am happy to announce to you that our success has thus far been complete. At the distance of five miles, with a common Cruikshank's battery of eighty-seven plates (4 by 3½ inches each plate), the marking was as perfect on the register as in the first instance of half a mile. We have recently added five miles more, making in all ten miles, with the same result; and we have no doubt of its effecting a similar result at any distance."

In 1838 Morse took his apparatus to Washington, and exhibited it to Congress; but that body, despite the recommendations of its committees, took no action. Four years passed by, during which time Morse made appeal after appeal. He was at last successful.

He says, " My bill had indeed passed the House of Representatives, and it was on the calendar of the Senate; but the evening of the last day had commenced with more than one hundred bills to be considered and passed upon before mine could be reached. Wearied out with the anxiety of suspense, I consulted one of my senatorial friends. He thought the chance of reaching it to be so small, that he advised me to consider it as lost. In a state of mind which I must leave you to imagine, I returned to my lodgings to make preparations for returning home the next day. My funds were reduced to a fraction of a dollar.

In the morning, as I was about to sit down to breakfast, the servant announced that a young lady desired to see me in the parlor. It was the daughter of my excellent friend and college classmate, the Commissioner of Patents (Henry L. Ellsworth). She had called, she said, by her father's permission, and in the exuberance of her own joy, to announce to me the passage of my telegraph-bill at midnight, but a moment before the Senate's adjournment. This was the turning-point of the telegraph invention in America. As an appropriate acknowledgment for the young lady's sympathy and kindness, — a sympathy which only a woman can feel and express, — I promised that the first despatch by the first line of telegraph from Washington to Baltimore should be indited by her; to which she replied, ' Remember, now, I shall hold you to your word.' In about a year from that time, the line was completed ; and, every thing being prepared, I apprised my young friend of the fact. A note from her enclosed this despatch : ' What hath God wrought.' These were the first words that passed on the first completed line of electric wires in America."

Congress appropriated thirty thousand dollars for the construction of Morse's experimental line between Washington and Baltimore, a distance of forty miles. It was put in operation in the spring of 1844, and was shown without charge until April 1, 1845. Congress, during the session of 1844–45, made an appropriation of eight thousand dollars to keep it in operation during the year ; placing it, at the same time, under the supervision of the Postmaster-General. He fixed the first tariff of charges at one cent for every four characters made by or through the telegraph.

The object of imposing a tariff was to test the profitableness of the enterprise. The result of the experiment for the four days after April 1 was amusing. It was then very shortly after Polk's inauguration; and Washington was crowded with office-seekers, of whom large numbers came to stare at the telegraph as one of the sights of the capital. On the morning of April 1, a gentleman walked into the office, and directed that the operation of the contrivance be exhibited to him. The operator said he would be pleased to do so, at the regular charge of one cent per four characters, and it would therefore cost very little for the visitor to send his name to Baltimore, and have it telegraphed back, or make some other simple test. The applicant said that he did not propose to pay any thing; did not wish to send any message, but merely wanted to see the thing work. The operator remained firm. Then the gentleman got angry. He informed the operator that this was a new administration, and he had unlimited influence, and if the operator did not at once exhibit the machine, he would have him removed. The operator simply referred his visitor to the Postmaster-General, and the interview terminated.

This was as near as the new telegraph-office got to collecting any revenue for the first three days. On April 4 the same party returned, and renewed his demand, and finally said he had no money but a twenty-dollar bill and one cent. He was told that he could have a cent's worth of telegraphing, if that would answer, to which he agreed. Thereupon Washington sent Baltimore one signal which by a pre-arranged code meant, "What time is it?" and Baltimore sent back a single signal meaning "One o'clock." The charge for the two characters was half a cent; but the office-seeker laid down the whole cent, and departed satisfied.

This was the entire income of the Washington office for the first four days of April, 1845. On the 5th, twelve and a half cents were received. The 6th was Sunday. On the 7th, the receipts ran up to sixty cents; on the 8th, to $1.32; on the 9th, to $1.04. It is worthy of remark, that more business was done by the merchants over the line after the tariff was laid, than when the service was gratuitous.

When Morse began his petitions to Congress, several of Henry's friends, knowing what he had accomplished, urged that he present, not his claims, — for that idea he would not entertain, — but evidence of the fact that the principles of the electro-magnetic telegraph belonged to the science of the world. Shortly after this, Henry made the acquaintance of Morse, whom he describes as an "unassuming and prepossessing gentleman, with very little knowledge of the general principles of electricity, magnetism, or electro-magnetism." Morse made no claims to any thing but "his particular machine and process for applying known principles to telegraphic purposes;" and so, adds Henry, "instead of interfering with his application to Congress, I gave him a certificate in the form of a letter, stating my confidence in the practicability of the electro-magnetic telegraph, and my belief that the form proposed by himself was the best that had been published."

Morse obtained his first patent in June, 1840. Others were subsequently secured. Infringements of all sorts followed, and protracted suits, which resulted, however, in Morse's favor. As a consequence, Morse is popularly regarded as the inventor of the electro-magnetic telegraph. He has no right to the title, nor did he himself establish claim thereto. The true inventor was Joseph Henry. Neither is Morse entitled to the credit of having devised the mechanism of the telegraphic instrument attributed to him; nor of the dot-and-dash alphabet that bears his

name.   That was the work of Alfred Vail, who was employed by Morse to improve and develop the invention.
Vail produced the first so-called Morse instrument in the
fall of 1837, entirely of his own design, and without suggestion from Morse, and arranged it to emboss alphabetic
characters devised by himself.   Morse, in such late recognition as he made of what Vail had done, might well
have heeded the lesson in magnanimity given by Henry
to him.

The student who undertakes to glean the history of the
telegraph from English books will note with surprise very
little mention of Henry.   In fact, most English writers
claim that the true inventors of the electro-magnetic telegraph were Professors Cooke and Wheatstone of England.
This leads us to a brief review of what was going on in
Europe during the period between Henry's first discovery, and the successful operation of Morse's line in
this country.

In 1820 Ampère merely suggested the idea that a series
of needles could be deflected by currents coming over as
many wires ; eight years later, Trebouillet proposed a
single wire and an electroscope ; and finally in 1832–33
Schilling, a Russian counsellor of state, went back to the
multiple-wire idea.   In 1833–35 two German scientists
devised a needle telegraph in which a galvanometer-needle
was made to move by currents generated by a coil moved
to and fro on a magnet ; the transmitter being, in fact, a
small magneto-electric machine.

Meanwhile, in England, Barlow's conclusion that the
electro-magnet could not be worked over long distances
of wire became regarded as a fixed fact.   Cooke in 1837,
at the suggestion of Faraday, applied to Professor Wheatstone for some way of overcoming his " inability to make
the electro-magnet act at long distances."   Wheatstone

says that he at once told Mr. Cooke that this difficulty was insurmountable, and exhibited to him at Kings College experiments which supported the conclusion. This was not only after Henry's inventions were completed, but even after Morse had made his applications of them. But then, what could so distinguished a scientist as Wheatstone know of the work of a mere professor in an American college, still less of the ideas of an American portrait-painter? Besides, how could he be expected to know more about what American inventors and discoverers had done, than the Franklin Institute, which held its meetings not fifty miles from Henry's line, and which, nevertheless, solemnly advised the Government of the United States to experiment upon semaphores, and to pay $100,000 first cost, and $62,500 annual charges, for a series of them between New York and Washington?

After they had concluded that the thing could not be done, Wheatstone and Cooke, in 1837, applied for an English patent for it, — in which, among other devices, they describe five wires and five needles, two of which indicated the letters of the alphabet placed around, — and also a method of deflecting telegraphic magnetic needles by electro-magnets; these last being in horseshoe form, placed opposite one another, with the needle between their poles. The description of Wheatstone's first experiments, published in "Chambers' Journal" in 1870, is worth quoting: "In July, 1837, wires were laid down from Euston Square to Camden Town Stations, by the sanction of the North-western Railway; and Professor Wheatstone sent the first message to Mr. Cooke between the two stations. The professor says, 'Never did I feel such tumultuous sensation before, as when, all alone in the still room, I heard the needles click; and as I spelled the words, I felt all the magnitude of the invention now proved to be practical beyond cavil or dispute.' The form of telegraph now in use was substituted because of the economy of its construction, not more than two wires (sometimes only one) being required. Of course several persons claimed to have invented the telegraph before Professor Wheatstone. In the same month that the professor was working upon the North-western Railway, there was one in operation invented by Steinheil of Munich; but Wheatstone's patent had been taken out in the month before. An American named Morse claims to have invented it in 1832, but did not put it in operation till 1837. After this his system was generally adopted in the United States. It is a *recording* one."

It is a curious fact that the patent granted to Wheatstone and Cooke in this country, for their telegraph, is earlier in date by just ten days than the first patent obtained by Morse.

It is not possible, within the limits of the present work, to trace farther the history of the telegraph. Even at the early period of which we have been writing, it had resolved itself into two great types, depending upon the kind of signals given, — the visual or needle telegraph, the electric adaptation of the old semaphore which required the receiver to watch the oscillations of a needle ; and the recording telegraph, wherein the current was made to write its own message upon a slip of paper. The needle telegraph is not in use in the United States : it is essentially an English instrument, and is still largely employed in England upon the railways. Recording instruments of various forms are used in the United States ; but, in the majority of instances throughout the world, telegraph-signals are read by the clicking sound produced by the armature of the receiving magnet.

The amount of mechanical ingenuity expended in devising telegraphic apparatus has been and still is wonderful. To explain even the best-known systems in any detail, would require the dryest of descriptions of complicated mechanism, extended to the limits of a cyclopædia. We shall therefore endeavor to indicate what the telegraph can do, rather than how its machinery operates; resorting to explanation of the latter only where it may be indispensable to an understanding of the results achieved.

If we stretch a wire between the points *A* and *B*, and attach the ends of the wire to plates buried in the earth, then we have a circuit. If we place a battery in the wire,

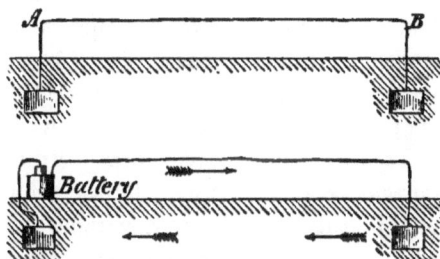

Fig. 98.

as in Fig. 98, then a current will pass from the battery, to and along the wire, in the direction of the arrow (for example), and thence to the distant earth plate. From this earth plate the current will apparently return by way of the earth, to the earth plate attached to the battery, and so back to the battery itself.

But how is it that a current sent, for example, over a thousand or more miles of wire, can find its way back through the earth to its source? About this there is a great deal of confusion. One writer regards the earth as a reservoir in which the positive electricity on the one side, and the negative on the other, are absorbed and lost. Another, considering the earth still as a reservoir, concludes that it offers no sensible resistance to the passage of a current. A third holds that the electricity is pumped into the earth at one point, and out of it at another; and so on through a variety of hypotheses, to attempt to reconcile which is simply bewildering.

According to Faraday's theory, the earth plays the part of a conductor, and becomes polarized by the passage of a current, the same way as any other part of the circuit. Recent experiments of Mr. Willoughby Smith go to substantiate this view. Mr. Smith says that " the current passes through the earth — or water, which amounts to the same thing — as through an ordinary conductor, in dispersed and curved lines. How far such curves extend, I am not prepared to speak positively; " but they probably " extend over the whole world, and what are termed the magnetic poles of the same are the immediate cause of the lines assuming the curved form. From whatever source a current emanates, it will diffuse itself over the whole mass of matter interposed, without in any way mixing or blending with a current or currents emanating from any other source or sources. The nearest analogy to this which I can think of is that the mind of each human being in this world of ours is constantly directing what are called lines of thought from its brain, or battery, far and wide, and those numberless lines of thought, so far as our own knowledge extends, never blend or become confused, but go and return each one to the source from which it emanates in precisely the same way as lines of electro-motive force when similarly manipulated. . . . Messages by electric signals have been sent and correctly received through a submarine cable two thousand miles in length, the earth being one-half of the circuit, by the aid of electricity generated by means of an ordinary gun-cap containing one drop of water; and, small though the current emanating from such a source naturally was, yet I believe it not only polarized the molecules of the copper conductor, but also in the same manner affected the whole earth through which it dispersed on its way from the outside of the gun-cap to its return to the water it contained."

The battery in Fig. 98, the wire, and the earth are in closed circuit; that is, there exists a path through which the current can continuously flow until the battery is exhausted. If, however, we should break the wire, and leave the ends separated, then we should have an open circuit over which no current passes or can. pass until we unite the separated ends once more. If we attach a lever, — or, as it is called, a key, — movable by the hand, to

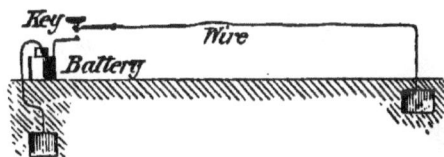

Fig. 99.

one part of the separated wire, as in Fig. 99, and arrange the key so that at will we can cause it to make contact with the other part of the wire, then, if we leave the key open, we have an open circuit; if we bring the key into contact with the opposite part of the wire, so that it bridges the interval between the two separated parts, then the effect is the same as if the wire were continuous, and we have a closed circuit.

We can therefore start with either an open circuit or a closed circuit. If we choose an open circuit, every time we move the key into contact with the opposite part of the wire, we let the current pass: if we prefer a closed circuit through which the current constantly travels, we can interrupt the current as often as we desire, simply by moving the key out of contact. And by making the periods of contact or the periods of interruption short or long, or more or less frequent, we can allow currents varying in duration and frequency to pass over the line.

At the opposite extremity of the line to that at which our key is placed, something is necessary to reveal the currents which come over; and for this purpose, as we have already explained, the electro-magnet is employed.

In Fig. 100, there is shown a closed circuit. Whenever we press down the key, the current which excites the magnet at the far end of the line is interrupted; and the magnet, which has attracted its armature to its pole, releases it. The armature is thus moved from one position

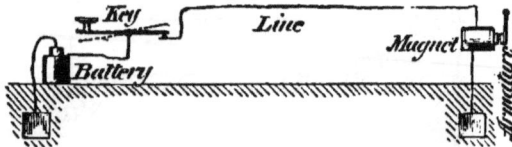

Fig. 100.

to another, and so held as long as the current remains broken, which is until we move the key into contact and back to its original position. Then the magnet attracts its armature back to its original place.

The consequence is, therefore, that the armature at the distant end of the line copies, so to speak, the movement of the key at the sending end. If the key is held down, and the circuit opened, for a certain period, the armature remains released and retracted for that period: if the key be held down only for an instant, the armature is instantly retracted and attracted. Consequently, in order to send signals, we have simply to manipulate the key very much as a key of a piano is touched when it is desired to produce a note of greater or less duration.

It will be remembered, that, in describing Morse's original apparatus, we stated that a pencil-point rested upon a slip of moving paper, and by the attraction of a magnet made sidewise zigzag marks thereon. Leaving out the idea of sidewise motion, suppose we move the point at intervals away from the paper, which keeps on travelling. Then we shall make broken lines, long or short, depending upon the length of the intervals of time during which we keep the pencil away from the paper. For example: suppose above a magnet, as shown in Fig. 101, we arrange an armature fastened to one end of a pivoted lever which carries a pencil at its opposite end.

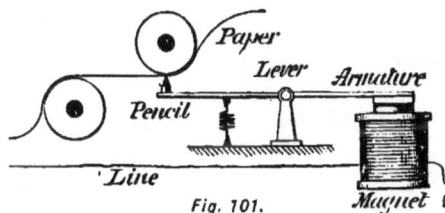

Fig. 101.

This pencil bears against the under side of a strip of paper, which is moved under a roller, by clock-work or any other suitable means. So long as the current comes over the line, the magnet will attract its armature, and keep the pencil-point pressed against the paper, on which a continuous line will be made. But if the current is broken, — which is done by manipulating the key at the sending end of the line, as already explained, — then the magnet will no longer attract its armature, and the pencil-point end of the lever will drop down, or be drawn down by a spring, so that the pencil will no longer mark. Now, we have only to agree upon an alphabet made up of short lines and long ones, arranged in a different way for each letter, to make the apparatus spell out words.

The shortest signal that can be made is, of course, a dot; and this at the sending end involves opening the circuit and closing it very quickly by a sudden movement of the key. The dot is usually taken as the standard; and with dots are combined dashes, which may be regarded as lines produced while the current is passing three times as long as is necessary to make a dot. The letter A may therefore be represented by a dot and a dash; E, by a single dot; F, by dot, dash, dot; and so on, through various combinations in which the spaces or intervals between the dots and dashes also are used to cause variations to produce a different symbol for each letter: so that any one knowing these symbols can read the message from the marked paper as easily as from a printed page.

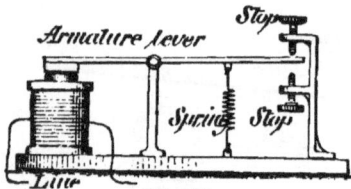

Fig. 102.

This is Morse's recording system, which he used on his first line, and for which Vail invented the alphabet of dots and dashes still employed all over the country.

Nowadays, however, telegraph-operators receive messages by sound; and the recording part of Morse's contrivance is little used. To this end the receiving magnet is arranged about as indicated in Fig. 102. Here the opposite end of the armature moves between fixed stops, and strikes them alternately, producing a sharp click. It is a great puzzle to many people, to understand how it is that a telegraph-operator sitting beside one of these little instruments, which appears to be rattling away with great rapidity, manages to comprehend what it says, apparently as well as if the instrument actually spoke to him. Of course long practice has as much to do with this skill, as it has in enabling any one to comprehend readily a foreign language. The lever, however, in striking its stops, produces two distinct sounds, according as it meets one or the other stop. When a dot is made, the lever strikes one stop, and instantly afterward the other: when a dash is signalled, there is a longer delay between the sounds. The two sounds are in themselves just alike; but the dot and dash, to a practised ear, are easily distinguishable, because there is a longer wait, or delay, between the clicks which begin and end a dash, than those which begin and end a dot. We say, to a practised ear, because to the ordinary organ there is no apparent difference. The average hearer can of course perceive that there is an irregularity about the clicks, and that they do not come at regular intervals like the beats of a clock-pendulum; but all the instruction ever given by written description never made a skilful telegraphic sound-reader, and probably never will. To learn to manipulate a key so as to send dots and dashes with fair speed, is not difficult; but to translate a bewildering succession of clicks, spelling out words at the rate of perhaps thirty a minute, simultaneously to write down the received message, and to do this with perhaps other instruments in the room clicking away at the same time, and perhaps unlimited conversation going on, and all this with the knowledge that a blunder may involve the company in an expensive lawsuit, is not an accomplishment easily acquired. Yet a skilful operator can send and receive forty-five words per minute.

When a telegraph-line is of considerable length, or for any other reason offers much resistance to the passage of the current, Henry's invention of the relay is employed; which is placed in the main line, and merely performs the duty of opening and closing the circuit of a local battery at the receiving station, which in turn operates the sounder already described. The diagram (Fig. 103) will render the relay arrangement easily understood. The current coming over the line excites the magnet marked "relay," which attracts its armature, and thus moves the latter into contact with a stop. The circuit of the local battery is thus established through the magnet of the sounder.

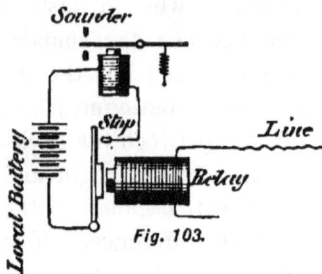

The closed-circuit system which is in almost universal use throughout the United States is shown in its simplest form in Fig. 104. At each key there is a circuit-closing lever whereby the line is kept closed, so that a current constantly traverses the line. This current goes from the main battery at New York, for example, through the circuit-closing lever, to the relay magnet which attracts its armature. In Fig. 104 the sounders and local batteries are not shown. But when this armature is attracted, it makes contact with a stop, and thus completes the circuit from the local battery through the sounder at New York. Hence, at the New-York end, both armatures stand normally attracted. After passing through the New-York relay, the current goes over the ninety miles or so of line to the Philadelphia relay, which attracts its armature, and establishes a local circuit through

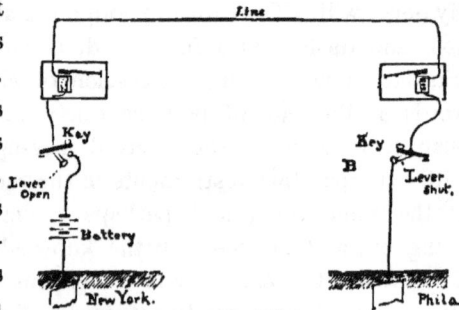

Fig. 103.

Fig. 104.

the sounder in Philadelphia. This is the normal condition of affairs.

Suppose now New York wants to send a despatch to Philadelphia. The first thing that the New-York operator does is to open his circuit-closing lever, when all of the armatures both at his and at the Philadelphia end will be released. Then he manipulates his key, making and breaking the current to form the desired signals ; and as he does so, all of the armatures at both ends of the line will respond, so that the Philadelphia receiver has merely to listen to the clicks of his sounder to receive the message. Meanwhile the New-York sender's instruments keep clicking too, which indicates to him that the message is reaching Philadelphia. If, however, his instruments should stop, he would know that the Philadelphia man had opened the circuit. Then he would close his own lever, and wait for a message from Philadelphia explaining the reason of the break, — such, for instance, as " message not understood," or something of that sort. The instruments at the Philadelphia end being the same as those at the New-York end, a message from Philadelphia to New York would of course be transmitted in the same way. It will be seen, however, that there is but one main-line battery, which is at the New-York end. In practice this battery is usually divided, half of it being placed at each terminal station. As many as forty intermediate stations are sometimes operated in this manner.

So far we have described simply a main line, the current of which establishes a new circuit at the receiving end, so that the work of recording the message, or of operating the sounder, is thrown upon a battery at that end. But suppose we have to telegraph over very long distances — say from Augusta, Me., to San Francisco, Cal. A single main-line battery might be wholly unable

234 THE AGE OF ELECTRICITY.

to send its current through so much resistance ; and if we
divided the line into short sections, it would be necessary
for the operator at each station to receive and understand
the message, and then repeat it to the next station. In
the early days of telegraphing, this was in fact done ; but
now it is automatically accomplished by a simple exten-
sion of the relay principle known as "repeating." Instead of there being simply a short local circuit in the
receiving station, which is controlled by the arriving current, the latter governs a circuit which extends, perhaps,
a long distance to another station. The current which
comes to station No. 2 closes contact in a circuit which
extends still farther to station No. 3, and so on from
station to station, until the sounder at the far-distant end
of the series of lines is operated ; just as if one could fire
a gun, and with the bullet strike the trigger of a distant
gun, the missile from which would fire a third gun, and so
on. So that, in practice, suppose a message to be sent from
Augusta, at which place the battery is located. When the
key is closed, a current goes over the line, and energizes
a magnet at New York, for example. This magnet then
closes the circuit, say, between New York and Chicago,
and in this circuit there is a new battery located at New
York. The current from New York closes at Chicago
the circuit between that city and San Francisco, and finally
San Francisco receives the message on its sounder in the
usual way. Repeaters are also often used for connecting
one or more branch lines with a main line, for the purpose
of transmitting press news, etc., simultaneously to different places. This enables all the stations in connection
to communicate with each other as readily as if they were
situated upon the same circuit.

The use of repeaters has aided many very wonderful
feats of rapid long-distance telegraphing. The news of

the Hanlan-Trickett rowing match in England, in 1881, travelled to Sydney, Australia, a distance of twelve thousand miles, in one hour and twenty minutes. The distance from Singapore to Sydney, 5,070 miles, was traversed in thirty-five seconds. There were fourteen repetitions of the message *en route.* But perhaps the most extraordinary direct long-distance telegraphing is that now possible between London and Calcutta, — seven thousand miles, — of which a writer in the London "Telegraphist" gives the following graphic account : —

"In the basement of an unpretentious building in Old Broad Street, we were shown the Morse printer in connection with the main line from London to Teheran. We were informed that we were through to Emden ; and with the same ease with which one 'wires' from the city to the West End, we asked a few questions of the telegraphist in the German town. When we had finished with Emden, we spoke with the same facility to the gentleman on duty at Odessa. This did not satisfy us, and in a few seconds we were through to the Persian capital (Teheran). There were no messages about, the time was favorable, and the employees of the various countries seemed anxious to give us an opportunity of testing the capacity of this wonderful line.

"T H N (Teheran) said, 'Call Kurrachee ;' and in less time than it takes to write these words, we gained the attention of the Indian town. The signals were good, and our speed must have equalled fifteen words a minute. The operator at Kurrachee, when he learnt that London was speaking to him, thought it would be a good opportunity to put us through to Agra ; and to our astonishment the signals did not fail, and we chatted pleasantly for a few minutes with Mr. Malcom Khan, the clerk on duty. To make this triumph of telegraphy complete, Agra switched us on to another line, and we soon were talking to a native telegraphist at the Indian Government cable station, Calcutta. At first the gentleman 'at the other end of the wire' could not believe that he was really in direct communication with the English capital, and he exclaimed in Morse language, 'Are you really London?' Truly this was a great achievement. Metallic communication without a break from London, to the telegraph-office in Calcutta! Seven thousand miles of wire! The signals were excellent, and the speed attained was not less than twelve, perhaps fourteen, words per minute."

One of the most paradoxical of all the applications of electricity is that which appears to solve that rather insoluble problem of how to make two locomotives pass each other while moving in opposite directions on a single track. This is the so-called duplex system of telegraphy, whereby two messages are transmitted over one wire simultaneously and in opposite directions.

To explain the duplex without resort to technicalities, is exceedingly difficult, chiefly because it is scarcely possible to suggest an analogy which meets all conditions. It should be remembered, that, in dealing with electricity, our ideas of lapse of time are very apt to lead us altogether astray; and we frequently consider occurrences as simultaneous, because they seem so to be to our senses, when in fact they are necessarily successive. So, in the case of the duplex, for all practical purposes two messages do travel in opposite directions on one and the same wire; but probably the signals in one direction alternate in inconceivably small periods of time with those coming from the opposite direction. To obtain any clear idea of the duplex, therefore, it is necessary to forget the apparent paradox, and simply to regard the apparatus as affording means whereby each of two widely separated operators may control an instrument at the end of the line distant from him. On such a line, at each end there is, of course, a sending key and a receiving instrument. But ordinarily, when two receivers are thus connected, a current sent upon the line affects both of them. Hence if A at one station, while telegraphing to B at the other, keeps his receiver clicking under his own signals, B at the other end, in sending to A, cannot exercise the necessary control over A's receiver; and in the same way, if B's receiver is constantly disturbed by B, it cannot correctly be governed by the signals sent by A. Therefore the main principle of the duplex is to arrange matters so that A's signals will affect, not A's receiver, but B's receiver; and conversely, so that A's receiver will respond only to B's signals, and B's receiver to A's signals.

There are several ways of doing this; but for these, the reader is referred to the technical treatises.

The diplex is a system by which two messages can be sent at once in the *same* direction; and is called "diplex" in contradistinction to the "duplex," where two messages are sent simultaneously in opposite directions. In the diplex, the two keys are of course at the sending station, and the two relays are at the receiving station. Key number one sends a weak current, while key number two sends a stronger current. The two relays are so arranged that one will respond to the strong current, and the other to the weak; when both currents are sent at once, both relays respond. It is this system, using both poles of the battery in connection with the so-called bridge duplex, which forms the so-called quadruplex of Edison. A description of the quadruplex would, however, be altogether too technical for these pages.

Multiple telegraphic systems have for their object the transmission of a large number of messages simultaneously over the same wire. The harmonic system is one of the

most ingenious of these, although it has never come into
extended practical use. It depends upon the principle of
acoustics, that two tuning-forks or tuned reeds will vibrate in
unison, and be set in vibration one by the other; whereas,
of two forks not in unison, the reverse is true. Suppose,
for example, half a dozen tuning-forks A, B, C, D, E, F,
be arranged conveniently together, and suppose three persons should strike three other tuning-forks respectively in
unison with A, B, and C of the series. Then the air-waves
produced by the three forks set in vibration would affect
only A, B, C; and these three forks would respond, the
others remaining silent. Now suppose the three persons
mentioned should strike their forks simultaneously, and in
a particular way; as, for instance, say that each person
should make the signals of a different telegraphic message in the Morse alphabet by taps on his fork. Clearly,
the result of all these taps sounding together would be a
confused jumble to the ear, but when the combined sounds
reached the three tuning-forks A, B, and C, they would
be disentangled. The tuning-fork A would be entirely
indifferent, audibly, to the vibrations affecting B and C,
and would not reproduce them, but would pick out and
respond only to those emanating from a fork in unison
with it. So also of forks B and C; and, consequently,
three messages made simultaneously might thus be transmitted through the air, and analyzed at the receiving
forks. In multiple harmonic telegraphy, these vibrations
are transmitted by the electric current, through a wire,
instead of by waves of condensation and rarefaction in
the air. If two tuned reeds be sounded together, then
the electrical impulses from each, moving at different
rates at the same moment, will traverse the wire simultaneously, and these will be disentangled by each of two
receiving reeds vibrating responsively under the impulse

of the transmitting reed in unison with it. In this manner two messages are sent simultaneously over a single wire, and received by sound separately from different reeds. And the same principle governs the sending of more messages by the aid of a greater number of reeds, and underlies the construction of the harmonic telegraphs of Gray and others.

One of the most recent inventions in multiple telegraphy is that of Mr. Delany. A great many varieties of telegraph-apparatus depend upon synchronism between the movements of certain devices in the transmitting apparatus, and certain other devices in the receiving apparatus. Two tuning-forks are said to be synchronous when they make the same number of vibrations in the same time, and have motions exactly similar. Mr. Delany has succeeded in keeping two bodies, separated by hundreds of miles, in synchronous rotation for periods of upward of seventy hours, without variation during that time of the one-thousandth part of a second. This is equivalent to two entirely independent bodies, separated from each other by hundreds of miles, starting together and passing through a distance of nearly one hundred miles without varying the one-hundredth part of an inch in that entire distance, or the one-thousandth part of a second during that entire time. The practical consequence is that circuits ranging in number from six to seventy-two, according to their capacity, have been obtained over a single wire, admitting of the possibility of the transmission of from six to seventy-two separate messages at practically the same time, either all in one direction or any portion of the whole number in opposite directions. Another extraordinary performance of Mr. Delany's apparatus was the automatic transmission of a single dot back and forth over the same wire between Boston and Providence, at practically the same instant of time, travelling over different circuits in rotation backward and forward for five minutes, during which time it travelled four hundred and fifty thousand miles. Mr. Delany's system is based on two main principles: first, that of synchronism, or the simultaneous motion of similar pieces of apparatus at two different places; and, second, that of distributing to several telegraphists the use of a wire for very short equal intervals of time, so that, practically, each operator has the line to himself during these periods.

Farther on, we shall see the great importance of synchronism in fac-simile telegraphy. But, in connection with the transmission of messages in the usual way, Mr. Delany's apparatus greatly increases the capacity of every wire, and probably at the present time allows of more messages being simultaneously transmitted over a given conductor, at the same time, than any other telegraphic system.

It is of course needless here to go into the minute details and very complex mechanism employed in multiple telegraphy: nor, in fact, shall we attempt, in the many forms of intricate devices which must find mention here, to do more than generally outline what they will accomplish. As we have seen, duplex, quadruplex, and other multiple telegraphic systems increase the capacity of wires, and expedite business through rendering it possible to send many messages at one time. There are many systems, however, which provide for very rapid transmission.

It will easily be understood, that, where telegraphic transmission depends upon the manipulation of a key by the human hand, a limit of speed is very soon reached. And not only this, but the human machine tires and makes errors; the signals lose legibility and clearness; and, in short, the various accidents and failures incident to all handiwork become manifest in greater or less degree. When, however, manipulation by the operator is replaced by the action of a machine, then not only great speed but precision within certain limits is obtained : and hence automatic instruments, both for the sending and receiving of telegraphic messages, have been invented and are in use.

Automatic telegraphy is largely employed in England, where it was first proposed in 1846 by Alexander Bain. He punched broad dots and dashes in paper ribbon, which was drawn with uniform velocity over a metal roller and beneath brushes of wire, which thus replaced the key ; for, whenever a hole occurred, a current was sent by the brushes coming in contact with the roller. The same idea is now applied to the musical instrument known as the mechanical orguinette, in which a strip of paper having apertures of various sizes is moved in front of the melodeon reeds so as to control the air supply to them, and hence the notes produced. Bain used as a recording instrument his chemical marker, wherein the current was received through a strip of paper moistened with a chemical solution which became decomposed on the passage of the current, so that the contact point in touching the paper caused dots and dashes of a bright blue color to appear.

The apparatus used throughout Great Britain is that invented by Professor Wheatstone. Its construction is too complicated for description here ; but, in general terms, it includes a punching-machine for producing the perforated strips of paper, a transmitting apparatus through which these strips are very rapidly passed, and a receiving device which marks on another strip dots and dashes in ink. The punching-machine will make the holes in three or even four strips at a time, and in the hands of an experienced operator will punch at the rate of forty words a minute. The disposition of holes in a strip when

thus prepared is shown in Fig. 105; the large openings
being for the message, and the centre row of small ones
serving to receive the teeth of a wheel which in turning
moves the strip along at uniform speed. When the paper
is thus prepared it is run through the transmitter, which is
permitted to operate to send a current whenever certain
moving rods can pass through the holes and establish a
contact, the currents being alternately positive and negative. If a succession of currents in reverse directions are
caused to pass upon the line, the receiver at the opposite
end will record a series of dots. To make a dash, one
reversal of the current is missed; and, in brief, the func-

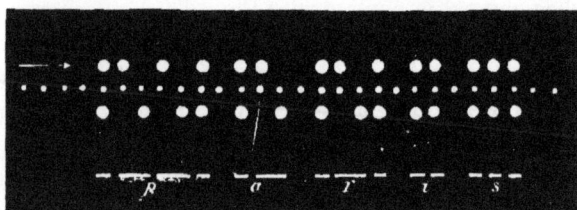

Fig. 105.

tion of the paper is so to regulate the motion of the transmitter as to produce reversal, or missing of reversal, of
the current at the proper moments, and thus to cause the
current to flow in such a way as to form dots and dashes.
The speed is determined by the rate at which the receiver
can receive; because the apparatus contains a controlling
electro-magnet which takes time to be magnetized and
demagnetized, and hence, if the current reverses too
quickly, the marks will run together instead of being
separate and distinct. The maximum useful speed is
about a hundred and thirty words per minute on a short
line. One strip of punched ribbon will do for any number
of circuits, so that from a central telegraph-station a
single strip disseminates news to many places.

With Edison's system of automatic transmission, a much greater speed than this has been obtained. The receiving apparatus here consists simply of a wire tipped with tellurium, which always rests on the moistened paper. The effect of the current is to decompose the water in the paper, and through the effect of the tellurium the contact point makes a dark mark. Mr. Edison in this way claims to have transmitted 3,150 words in a minute, on a line between New York and Washington.

We have now seen what can be done in the way of quick transmission. Next in importance is legibility at the receiving end; or, rather, the possibility of receiving messages, not in dots and dashes, but in ordinary characters. For this purpose type-printing and autograph systems are employed. The first printing telegraph actually used was that devised by Royal E. House of Vermont in 1846, — now obsolete. It was followed by Hughes's system, in which the principle of synchronism between the sending and receiving instruments entered materially into the success of its working. Hughes's apparatus is not used in this country. It has two type-wheels kept rotating synchronously together at each station by means of a train of gearing provided with a governor. Connected to the mechanism is a transmitting cylinder, arranged with and controlled by a keyboard having a key for each letter of the alphabet. A printing-lever, controlled by an electro-magnet placed in the main line, causes the printing of a letter upon a long fillet of paper while the type-wheel is rapidly moving. This movement is caused by the energizing of the controlling magnet by the transmission of a single wave of electricity from the distant station at the proper time. Simultaneously with the printing of a letter, the type-wheel, by the action of the printing-lever, is thrown slightly forward or backward, thus correcting at every impression any slight variation in the synchronous movement of the wheel.

The printed despatches on the long slips of paper now delivered by the Western Union Telegraph Company are transmitted by Mr. G. M. Phelps's electro-motor telegraph. In this system, the gearing of the Hughes apparatus is replaced by a simple but powerful electro-motor. As in the Hughes machinery, the transmitting device and type-wheel of the receiving instrument are caused to revolve synchronously under control of a governor, and each separate letter is printed by a single pulsation of the electric current, of a determinate and uniform length, transmitted at a determinate time ; but, unlike the Hughes apparatus, the motion of the type-wheel is arrested while each letter is being printed, and it is automatically released the instant the impression has been effected. By this means a very high speed of transmission has been attained.

There is one form of printing telegraph which is notable for the danger attending its use. It has probably, innocently, been the means of more injury to the human race than the most potent of electrical torpedoes, which it resembles occasionally in effect, — that is, metaphorically speaking. We allude to the stock exchange "ticker" when combined with a widely fluctuating market. For the benefit of those who have never watched the motions of the intricate little mechanism, — let us say, while waiting for the next quotation, — it may be explained, that there is usually a type-wheel rotated by a lever from an electro-magnet. The magnet is excited, and the lever worked, by pulsations over the wire. The lever turns the type-wheel step by step. Usually there are two type-wheels ; one printing the cabalistic letters which indicate the name of the stock, and the other the quotation in numbers. When a letter or number is to be printed, the proper wheel is brought into position, and then another magnet operates to bring the " tape " into contact with the type.

Despatches may be sent automatically, and received in printed characters, by several systems, of which Bonnelli's is an example. The message is set up in ordinary type, which are connected to the battery and earth. Over the face of the type passes a comb of fine points of wire, each point being connected to a separate line proceeding to the distant station, and the line wires there being connected to another and similar comb, which is moved over chemically prepared paper. When the comb at the sending end is rubbed over the raised parts of the characters, the comb at the receiving end receives a current which decomposes the chemicals in the paper, producing a mark similar to the character traversed. Little use has been made of systems of this character.

The autographic telegraph is one of the most ingenious of the various known systems. It is not used in this country, although recently the improvements in effecting synchronism have directed anew the attention of inventors to its possibilities. It transmits the handwriting of the sender, and also simple drawings. Its advantages at present appear to depend on whatever benefits may be derived from these capabilities ; thus it may be useful to send sketches and illustrations to newspapers, or to verify signatures, or to telegraph bank-checks in facsimile : but beyond this, it has not much promise. Its operation depends upon synchronism at both ends of the line. Casselli's apparatus, which is used in France, consists of two large pendulums kept swinging in unison by electro-magnets placed in the line wire. One pendulum transmits electric waves at certain intervals, which, acting upon the magnets, cause them to correct variations from exact unison of swing. The message for transmission is written upon metallic foil, with a non-conducting ink : this is laid upon a platen connected to the earth through a battery. A fine platinum wire connected to the line wire is recipro- cated from one end of the foil to the other ; the foil being advanced one-hundredth of an inch after each reciproca- tion, until the point has passed over the whole of the foil. The platinum point, when passing over the foil, allows the current from the battery to go to the line. At all points, however, where it passes over the non-conducting ink with which the message is written, the current is pre- vented from passing to line. At the distant station a similar point is reciprocated over a platen upon which is laid a sheet of chemically prepared paper: the passage of the circuit through the reciprocated point and moistened paper causes a blue mark to appear. If both pendulums are started at the same instant, the form of the metallic foil upon which the message is written will be reproduced upon the chemical paper by blue lines blending one into the other. But owing to the non-transmission of any cur- rent where the transmitting point passes over the non- conducting ink, no mark will appear ; hence the message would be inscribed in white characters on a blue ground, were it not for an ingenious little device which reverses the action, causing the characters to appear in blue. In Fig. 106 is represented a design as prepared and then trans- mitted in facsimile by Casselli's apparatus. In the more recent forms of writing telegraph, notably Cowper's, a different principle is employed ; the message, in fact, being transmitted by the act of writing it. The idea followed is, that every position of the point of a pen, as it forms a letter, can be determined by its distance from two fixed lines — say, the adjacent edges of the paper. Hence if these distances, so to speak, are transmitted by telegraph,

and recombined, so as to give a resultant motion to a duplicate pen, a duplicate copy of the original writing is produced. Cowper uses two separate circuits, one to transmit
the vertical, the other the horizontal, movements of his pen.

And now we come to the most wonderful of all telegraphs, — that which transmits messages from continent
to continent, for thousands of miles, under the depths of
the sea. "Does it not seem all but incredible to you,"
said Edward Everett in his oration at the opening of

Original.   Facsimile.
Fig. 106.

Dudley Observatory, "that intelligence should travel for
two thousand miles along those slender copper wires far
down in the all-but fathomless Atlantic, never before penetrated by aught pertaining to humanity, save when some
foundering vessel has plunged with her hapless company
to the eternal silence and darkness of the abyss? Does
it not seem, I say, all but a miracle of art, that the
thoughts of living men — the thoughts that we think up
here on the earth's surface, in the cheerful light of day —
about the markets and the exchanges, and the seasons,
and the elections and the treaties and the wars, and all the
fond nothings of daily life, should clothe themselves with

elemental sparks, and shoot with fiery speed in a moment, in the twinkling of an eye, from hemisphere to hemisphere, far down among the uncouth monsters that wallow in the nether seas, along the wreck-paved floor, through the oozy dungeons of the rayless deep; that the last intelligence of the crops, whose dancing tassels will in a few months be coquetting with the west wind on these boundless prairies, should go flashing along the slimy decks of old sunken galleons which have been rotting for ages; that messages of friendship and love, from warm living bosoms, should burn over the cold green bones of men and women whose hearts, once as warm as ours, burst as the eternal gulfs closed and roared over them, centuries ago!''

It is not definitely known who originated the idea of submarine telegraph-lines. The notion was often discussed long before it even approached successful realization. The first working-line was laid down by Professor Morse, between the Battery in New-York City and Governor's Island. This was in October, 1842. What Morse might have demonstrated with that line, can only be conjectured. It came to an untimely ending. The very next morning after it had been laid, some conscienceless mariners hauled up the wire on their anchor, and, probably realizing its advantages if devoted to splicing their standing rigging, cut off and confiscated as much of it as they conveniently could. In the same year Col. Samuel Colt, of revolver fame, put down a submarine line between Fire Island and Coney Island and New-York City, and, it is said, successfully operated it. In Europe the first submarine line was laid by Lieutenant Siemens, between Deutz and Cologne, across the Rhine, a distance of about half a mile; and on this wire gutta-percha was first used as an insulating covering. The first sea-line extended between Dover and Calais, a distance of twenty-four miles, and was laid in 1850.

The earliest suggestion of the possibility of a transatlantic cable appears to have been made by Gen. Horatio Hubbell and Mr. J. H. Sherburne of Philadelphia, who united in a memorial which was presented to the United-States Senate by Vice-President Dallas, and to the House of Representatives by Hon. J. R. Ingersoll, on Jan. 29, 1849. In this memorial the existence of the plateau or table-land between Newfoundland and Ireland is first announced to the world as the course over which the telegraph cable might be, and over which it finally was, successfully laid. The Senate was inclined to ignore the subject, and not even refer it to the limbo of a committee. But one senator, Mr. Jefferson Davis, finally moved its reference to the Committee on Commerce, remarking that "the world was not yet prepared for the project, but might be soon." Congress did not grant the memorialists' request for a vessel to make the necessary soundings ; but five years later Lieutenant Berryman conducted the surveys of the ocean bottom upon which Lieutenant Maury made the reports which determined the cable route over the plateau.

The first attempt to lay a transatlantic cable was made in August, 1857. After about 380 miles had been submerged, the engineer thought that there was not sufficient strain on the line, and ordered more applied. It was not properly done, and the cable snapped. In August, 1858, the work was successfully accomplished ; the cable extending from Valentia Bay, Ireland, to Trinity Bay, Newfoundland, a distance of 1,950 miles. Congratulatory messages were interchanged between the Queen and the President, and a few other despatches were sent during the ensuing fortnight ; and then the cable refused to work.

A defect in it was found, but all attempts to remedy it proved unsuccessful.

Of course, a good many people had important despatches coming over the cable, or expected to send them; and when it began to fail, there were innumerable messages sent to Trinity Bay to find out what the trouble was. The manager there, an electrician named De Sauty, usually sent back the most re-assuring replies, and continued quite roseate in his anticipations until the cable positively refused to transmit any thing more, and then he disappeared from public gaze. All this has been told in verse by that most charming of humorists, Dr. Oliver Wendell Holmes, in the following poem, which, as the Professor at the Breakfast Table, he declares to be his " only contribution to the great department of ocean-cable literature. As all the poets of this country will be engaged for the next six weeks in writing for the premium offered by the Crystal-Palace Company for the Burns Centenary (so called, according to our Benjamin Franklin, because there will be na'ry a cent for any of us), poetry will be very scarce and dear. Consumers may consequently be glad to take the present article, which by the aid of a Latin tutor and a professor of chemistry will be found intelligible to the educated classes."

DE SAUTY.[1]

AN ELECTRO-CHEMICAL ECLOGUE.

PROFESSOR.   BLUE-NOSE.

PROFESSOR.

Tell me, O Provincial! speak, Ceruleo-Nasal!
Lives there one De Sauty extant now among you,
Whispering Boanerges, son of silent thunder,
    Holding talk with nations?

[1] Reprinted by kind permission of Dr. Holmes.

Is there a De Sauty ambulant on Tellus
Bifid-cleft like mortals, dormient in night-cap,
Having sight, smell, hearing, food-receiving feature
    Three times daily patent?

Breathes there such a being, O Ceruleo-Nasal?
Or is he a *mythus*, — ancient word for "humbug," —
Such as Livy told about the wolf that wet-nursed
    Romulus and Remus?

Was he born of woman, this alleged De Sauty,
Or a living product of galvanic action
Like the *acarus* bred in Crosse's flint solution?
    Speak, thou Cyano-Rhinal!

BLUE-NOSE.

Many things thou askest, jackknife-bearing stranger,
Much-conjecturing mortal, pork-and-treacle waster,
Pretermit thy whittling, wheel thine ear-flap toward me.
    Thou shalt hear them answered.

When the charge galvanic tingled through the cable
At the polar focus of the wire electric,
Suddenly appeared a white-faced man among us:
    Called himself "DE SAUTY."

As the small opossum held in pouch maternal
Grasps the nutrient organ whence the term *mammalia*,
So the unknown stranger held the wire electric,
    Sucking in the current.

When the current strengthened, bloomed the pale-faced
    stranger, —
Took no drink nor victual, yet grew fat and rosy,
And from time to time in sharp articulation
    Said, "*All right!* DE SAUTY."

From the lonely station passed the utterance, spreading
Through the pines and hemlocks to the groves of steeples,
Till the land was filled with loud reverberations
    Of "*All right!* DE SAUTY."

When the current slackened, drooped the mystic stranger,
Faded, faded, faded, as the stream grew weaker,
Wasted to a shadow, with a hartshorn odor
    Of disintegration.

Drops of deliquescence glistened on his forehead,
Whitened round his feet the dust of efflorescence,
Till one Monday morning, when the flow suspended,
    There was no De Sauty;

Nothing but a cloud of elements organic, —
C, O, H, N, Ferrum, Chlor., Flu., Sil., Potassa,
Calc., Sod., Phosph., Mag., Sulphur, Mang. (?), Alumin. (?),
    Cuprum (?),
    Such as man is made of.

Born of stream galvanic, with it he had perished.
There is no De Sauty, now there is no current!
Give us a new cable, then again we'll hear him
    Cry *"All right!* De Sauty."

Shortly after the failure of the first Atlantic cable, other deep-sea cables became inoperative, and immense sums of money were lost. In 1865 the immense "Great Eastern" steamship, which had proved a veritable white elephant to its owners, was fitted for service to transport a new cable. After about half of this line had been laid, it broke, and the hapless promoters of the enterprise feared that some three million dollars had been added to the great aggregate of losses already incurred. Preparations were, however, at once made for another attempt during the following year. The managers of the enterprise, at the head of which was Mr. Cyrus W. Field, had indomitable faith in its practicability. A close watch was kept on the broken line, now resting on the ocean-bed. "Night and day," says an English journal of the time, "for a whole year an electrician was always on duty, watching the tiny ray of light through which signals are given ; and twice every day the whole length of wire — 1,240 miles — was tested for conduction and insulation. The object of observing the ray of light was of course not any expectation of a message, but simply to keep an accurate record of the condition of the wire. Sometimes, indeed, wild incoherent messages from the deep did come ; but these were merely the results of magnetic storms and earth-currents, which deflected the galvanometer rapidly, and spelt the most extraordinary words, and sometimes even sentences of nonsense, upon the graduated scale before the mirror. Suddenly, early one morning the observer noticed a peculiar flicker of the light which to his experienced eye showed that a message was on hand. In a few minutes afterward, the unsteady flickering was changed to coherency, and at once the cable began to speak, to transmit the appointed signals which indicated human purpose and method at the other end, instead of the hurried signs, broken speech, and inarticulate cries of the still illiterate Atlantic. After the long interval in which it had brought nothing but the moody and often delirious mutterings of the sea stammering over its alphabet in vain, the words ' Canning to Glass ' must have seemed like the first rational word uttered by a fever-patient when the ravings had ceased. The exact spot in the trackless ocean where that cable had parted had been found ; the slender wire had been picked up, although two miles down under the sea ; and from the great ship the signals were being sent."

Meanwhile the new cable, stronger, lighter, and more flexible than its predecessors, had been successfully carried across the Atlantic by the " Great Eastern," and was in working order. Then the ship went back, and, as already stated, picked up the broken end. How this wonderful feat of engineering was accomplished, Mr. Field thus graphically tells : —

"After landing the cable safely at Newfoundland, we had another task, — to return to mid-ocean, and recover that lost in the expedition of last year. This achievement has perhaps excited more surprise than the other. Many, even now 'don't understand it,' and every day I am asked how it was done. Well, it does seem rather difficult to fish for a jewel at the bottom of the ocean two and a half miles deep. But it is not so *very* difficult when you know how. It was the triumph of the highest nautical and engineering skill. We had four ships, and on board of them some of the best seamen in England, men who knew the ocean as a hunter knows every trail in the forest. There was Captain Moriarty, who was in the 'Agamemnon' in 1857–58. He was in the 'Great Eastern' last year, and saw the cable when it broke ; and he and Captain Anderson at once took their observations so exact that they could go right to the spot. After finding it, they marked the line of the cable by a row of buoys ; for fogs would come down, and shut out sun and stars so that no man could take an observation. These buoys were anchored a few miles apart. They were numbered, and each had a flagstaff on it so that it could be seen by day, and a lantern by night. Thus having taken our bearings, we stood off three or four miles, so as to come broadside on, and then, casting over the grapnel, drifted slowly down upon it, dragging the bottom of the ocean as we went. At first it was a little awkward to fish in such deep water ; but our men got used to it, and soon could cast a grapnel almost as straight as an old whaler throws a harpoon. Our fishing-line was of formidable size. It was made of rope, twisted with wires of steel, so as to bear a strain of thirty tons. It took about two hours for the

grapnel to reach the bottom, but we could tell when it
struck. I often went to the bow, and sat on the rope,
and could feel by the quiver that the grapnel was dragging
on the bottom two miles under us. But it was very slow
business. We had storms and calms and fogs and squalls.
Still we worked on day after day. Once, on the 17th of
August, we got the cable up, and had it in full sight for
five minutes, — a long, slimy monster, fresh from the ooze
of the ocean's bed ; but our men began to cheer so wildly
that it seemed to be frightened, and suddenly broke away,
and went down into the sea. This accident kept us at
work two weeks longer ; but finally, on the last night of
August, we caught it. We had cast the grapnel thirty
times. It was a little before midnight on Friday that we
hooked the cable, and it was a little after midnight Sunday
morning when we got it on board. What was the anxiety
of those twenty-six hours ! The strain on every man's
life was like the strain on the cable itself. When finally
it appeared, it was midnight : the lights of the ship and
in the boats around our bows, as they flashed in the faces
of the men, showed them eagerly watching for the cable
to appear in the water. At length it was brought to the
surface. All who were allowed to approach crowded to
see it. Yet not a word was spoken : only the voices of
the officers in command were heard giving orders. All
felt as if life and death hung on the issue. It was only
when it was brought over the bow and on the deck, that
men dared to breathe. Even then they hardly believed
their eyes. Some crept toward it to feel of it, to be sure
it was there. Then we carried it along to the electrician's
room, to see if our long-sought-for treasure was alive or
dead. A few minutes of suspense, and a flash told of
the lightning current set free. Then did the feeling long
pent up burst forth. Some turne away their heads, and

wept. Others broke into cheers, and the cry ran from
man to man, and was heard down in the engine-rooms,
deck below deck, and from the boats on the water and
the other ships, while rockets lighted up the darkness of
the sea. Then with thankful hearts we turned our faces
again to the west. But soon the wind rose, and for thirty-
six hours we were exposed to all the dangers of a storm
on the Atlantic. Yet in the very height and fury of the
gale, as I sat in the electrician's room, a flash of light
came up from the deep, which, having crossed to Ireland,
came back to me in mid-ocean, telling that those so dear
to me, whom I had left on the banks of the Hudson, were
well and following us with their wishes and their prayers.
This was like a whisper of God from the sea, bidding me
keep heart and hope. The 'Great Eastern' bore herself
proudly through the storm, as if she knew that the vital
cord which was to join two hemispheres hung at her stern ;
and so, on Saturday the 7th of September, we brought
our second cable safely to the shore."

As we all know, other cables have since been laid across
the Atlantic with comparative ease, by the aid of special
machinery and specially constructed vessels. The French
cable between St. Pierre and Duxbury, Mass., went into
operation in 1869 ; followed by the direct cable between
Ballinskilligs Bay, Ireland, and Rye, N.H., via Nova
Scotia, in 1875 ; and the Mackay-Bennett cable ten years
later.

The cable laid by the "Great Eastern" in 1865–66 is
represented in Fig. 107. The current is conducted by a
strand of copper wires ; the remainder of the cable serving
to secure insulation, and to protect it from abrasion, etc.

The transmission of telegraphic signals through a long
submarine cable is a very different matter from accomplishing the same thing over a land line of similar length ;

and it is therefore necessary to explain, in as simple terms as possible, some of the principal difficulties encountered, and how the cable is made to operate in spite of them.

In describing the invention of the Leyden-jar, in an earlier chapter, we noted the curious fact, that, while electricity cannot pass through an insulating substance such as glass or air, it can act across the same by induction. And in the Leyden-jar we have an illustration of this; for, when a plus charge of electricity is imparted to the inner coating, it acts inductively on the outer coating, attracting a minus charge into the face of the outer coating nearest the glass, and repelling a plus charge to the outside of the outer coating, and this through the hand

Fig. 107.

or wire to the earth. After the jar has acquired its full charge, it will, as we have already seen, retain it for a considerable period of time.

When a quantity of electricity flows through a line, in the form of a current, the first portion of the current is retained or accumulated upon the surface of the wire in the same way that a charge is retained and accumulated upon the surface of a Leyden-jar. The wire itself answers to one of the conducting coatings of the jar; the earth, or other wires connected to earth, to the other conducting coating; and the air, to the glass or separating di-electric. The quantity of electricity thus accumulated depends upon the length and surface of the wire, upon its proximity to the earth, and upon the insulating medium that separates it from the earth.   This power of retaining a charge is called the electro-static capacity of the circuit.

The effect of this accumulation is to hold back or prevent the appearance of the first portion of the current sent at the distant station ; and, furthermore, before a current in the reverse direction can be sent through the circuit, the whole of this charge upon the wire must be withdrawn or neutralized before a second charge of opposite sign can be accumulated upon it.   The result of this is to prolong the current flowing out at the distant end.

In submarine cables, the conducting wires are separated from the earth upon which the cable rests, and the water which surrounds it, simply by the insulating covering; and hence the whole cable becomes one huge Leyden-jar of much capacity.   The consequence is, that the current is retarded so much, that, unless the signals are sent very slowly, they will run together and be illegible.   The retardation upon an Atlantic cable is about four-tenths of a second.   Twenty dots per second can be firmly and clearly recorded on a short overground line, with little induction ; while on a long cable, not more than two dots per second can be received.

Besides the difficulties due to retardation, earth-currents varying in strength are set up in the cable, by reason of its connecting portions of the earth which happen to be of different potentials.   These were the cause of the strange signals which came from the broken cable of 1865 ; and at times they acquire such magnitude as to become "electric storms," interrupting the circuits to such an extent as greatly to hinder working, and sometimes endangering the safety of the cable itself.   It is necessary, therefore, in cable telegraphy, to counteract the ill effects of earth-currents, and also to reduce to the lowest possible point the retarding influence of induction ; and the ordinary apparatus used in telegraphing upon land lines becomes useless for this purpose.

Two new instruments, not necessary upon land lines, are therefore introduced ; the first being the condenser, which prevents induction, and sharpens the signals ; and the second being the mirror galvanometer, or siphon recorder, which indicates or records them.

The condenser is simply a modified form of Leyden-jar, of large surface, and constructed to have any desired capacity. It is usually made of alternate layers of paraffined paper or mica and tin-foil ; as indicated in Fig. 108, in which the dark lines $a\,a^1\,a^2, b\,b^1\,b^2$, represent tin-foil, and the shaded intermediate portions, the paraffined paper. The series $a\,a^1\,a^2$ of tin-foil sheets are con-

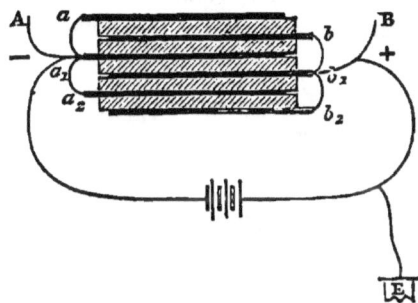

Fig. 108.

nected together, thus forming one of the coatings of the Leyden-jar ; and the alternating sheets $b\,b^1\,b^2$ are united to form the other coating. If we connect one pole of a battery to the sheets $a\,a^1\,a^2$, and the other pole to the sheets $b\,b^1\,b^2$, the condenser will be charged with a quantity of electricity depending upon the number of battery-cells used, upon the surface of the plates opposed to each other, and upon the number of plates in the respective sets. In this way condensers of any desired capacity can be made, having a charge varying from that accumulated upon one mile of overground wire up to that accumulated upon an Atlantic cable. The unit or standard of reference by which capacity is known is called the microfarad, and is equivalent to the charge contained by about three miles of cable.

The conventional mode of representing a condenser is by two parallel lines as a b, in Fig. 109, from which illustration the operation of the condenser, when applied to a telegraphic line, will easily be understood.

Let us suppose that A B is a cable crossing the Atlantic. At one end is an ordinary key and battery, and at the other a condenser having one set of its conducting plates connected to the cable, and the other set to a galvanometer which in turn is connected to earth. The circuit is evidently broken at the condenser, so that it is impossible

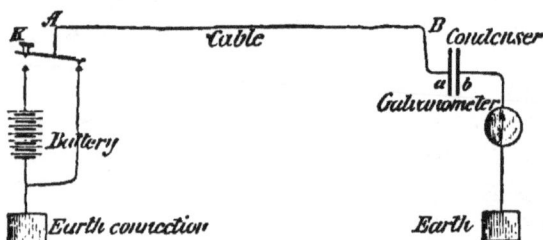

Fig. 109.

for the battery current to proceed directly to the galvanometer; but if we depress the key, a current flows from the battery into the cable to charge it. The plate a of the condenser, being thus charged in (say) positive electricity, attracts across the paraffined paper interposed between it and the opposite plate b, electricity of opposite name, and repels electricity of the same name, which apparently passes to earth through the galvanometer in the form of a short current or pulsation. When the key is returned to its normal position, the cable is discharged, the positive charge on b is released, and it flows to earth in the reverse direction through the galvanometer, in the form of a second current or pulsation. Thus, whenever we depress the key, we affect the galvanometer with a reversal.

By using galvanometers or other receiving apparatus of the most sensitive character, which are actuated by the first appearance of the current, cables are worked with the smallest electro-motive force; and generally by suitably determining the size of the condenser, the number of cells, and the delicacy of the galvanometer, we can transmit signals which give the maximum speed with

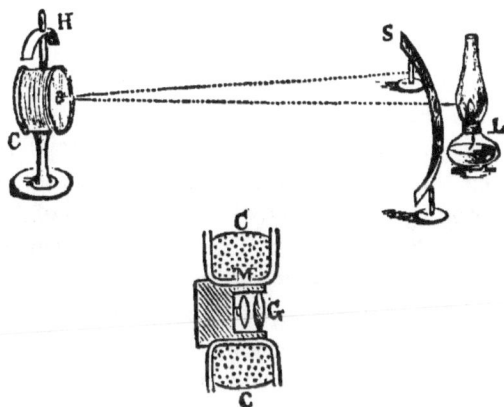

Fig. 110.

the minimum expenditure of power. In practice the condensers used have a capacity equal to that of about seventy miles of cable. From four to ten cells of one form of Daniell's battery furnish the current.

The receiving apparatus is either a mirror galvanometer or a siphon recorder, — both instruments of remarkable sensitiveness, devised by Sir William Thomson. The general arrangement of the mirror galvanometer is shown in Fig. 110, where *C* is a coil of fine insulated wire, surrounding a small magnetic needle hung by a silk fibre, and carrying a tiny mirror attached to it. The details are shown in the lower figure, where C C are sections through the coil. At M is the magnet-needle, carrying in front of it a small mirror. This needle is enclosed in a small chamber, glazed by a lens G, and inserted in the hollow of the coil C. A curved magnet H is supported over the coil to adjust the position of the smaller magnet in the chamber. Now a ray of light from a lamp L in front of the galvanometer is thrown upon the tiny mirror, and reflected back upon a white screen or scale S. The coil C is connected between the end of the conductor of the cable and the earth-plate, as in the land circuit; a condenser, however, being usually interposed between the cable and the galvanometer.

Then the signal currents in passing through the coil deflect the tiny magnet hung within it; and the mirror, being carried by the magnet, throws the beam of light off in a different direction. Positive, or " dot," currents are arranged to throw the spot of light toward the left side of the scale; and negative, or " dash," currents throw it to the right side. Thus the wandering of the spot of light on the screen, watchfully followed by the eye of the clerk, is interpreted by him as the message. Letter by letter he spells it out, and a fellow-clerk writes it down word for word.

Sometimes the fellow-clerk is a lady, — frequently perhaps now, since the fair sex has proven its ability to manage the key, — and this circumstance may account for the publication in a scientific journal, some years ago, of the following capital parody on Tennyson's " Bugle Song:" [1] —

[1] By Professor J. Clerk Maxwell.

A LECTURE ON THOMSON'S GALVANOMETER

Delivered to a Single Pupil, in an Alcove with Drawn Curtains.

The lamp-light falls on blackened walls,
  And streams through narrow perforations ;
The long beam trails o'er pasteboard scales,
  With slow decaying oscillations.
Flow, current, flow ! set the quick light spot flying !
Flow, current! answer, light spot ! flashing, quivering, dying.

Oh, look ! how queer ! how thin and clear,
  And thinner, clearer, sharper growing,
This gliding fire with central wire
  The fine degrees distinctly showing.
Swing, magnet, swing ! advancing and receding ;
Swing, magnet ! answer, dearest, what's your final reading ?

O love ! you fail to read the scale
  Correct to tenths of a division ;
To mirror heaven those eyes were given,
  And not for methods of precision.
Break, contact, break ! set the free light spot flying.
Break, contact ! rest thee, magnet ! swinging, creeping, dying.

This receiver, however, like the sounder, has the disadvantage of leaving no permanent record ; and Sir William Thomson has therefore introduced his siphon recorder on several long cables, — for instance, the Eastern Telegraph Company's lines to India, and the Anglo-American Company's cables across the Atlantic. The principle of its action is just the reverse of the mirror galvanometer. In that instrument, a tiny magnet moved within a fixed coil of wire ; in the siphon recorder, a light coil of wire moves between the poles of a powerful magnet. The signal currents pass through the suspended coil to earth ; and in doing so the coil turns to left or right, according as the currents are positive or negative. These movements of

the coil are communicated by a connecting thread to a
fine glass siphon, which is constantly spurting ink upon
a band of travelling paper; and hence the trace of the
ink on the paper follows and delineates the movements of
the coil. So fine is the bore of the siphon, that the ink
will not run unless it is electrified. A specimen of the
message it furnishes is given in Fig. 111, which represents
the alphabet.

That some day we shall be able to transmit pictures by
telegraph, is not without the bounds of reasonable possibility; not drawings or designs, such as can now be sent
by the autographic systems, but actual photographs, images
of things existing in front of the transmitting instrument,
so that a person in one place can see what is going on in

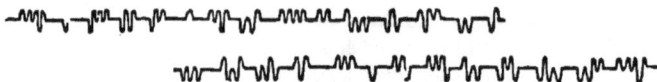

Fig. 111.

another. The first step in this direction has already been
accomplished by Mr. Shelford Bidwell, in his exceedingly
ingenious telephotograph, by means of which it is now
quite possible to transmit shadows or silhouettes. The
principle of Mr. Bidwell's apparatus is based upon the
fact that the resistance of crystalline selenium varies with
the intensity of the light falling upon it. Its operation
depends, as in the autographic telegraph, upon the synchronous movement of two cylinders at opposite ends of
the line, and will be easily followed by the aid of the
diagram, Fig. 112.

The transmitting instrument consists of a cylindrical
brass box, mounted upon but insulated from a metal spindle. The spindle is divided in the middle; and the halves,
while rigidly joined together, are insulated from each

other by a layer of wood. One of the ends of the spindle has a fine screw-thread cut on it; the other end is plain. The spindle is arranged to revolve in metal bearings, one of which is threaded so that when the spindle rotates it also has an endwise longitudinal movement like

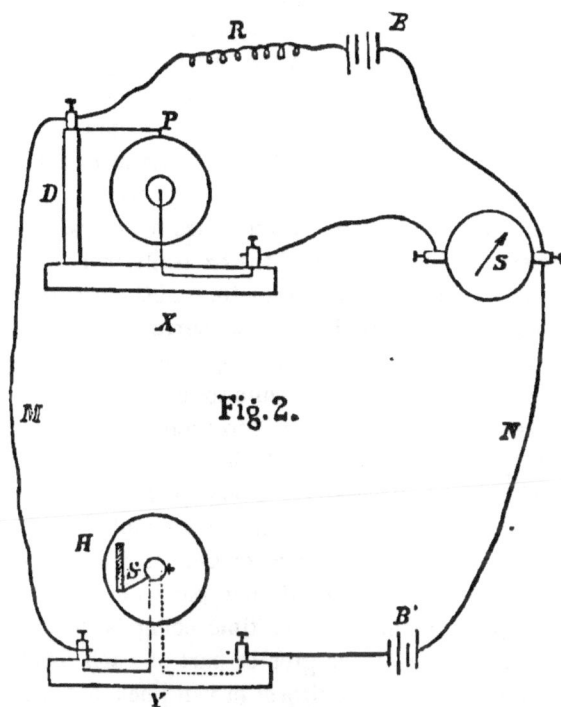

Fig. 112.

that of the cylinder of the phonograph. At a point midway between the ends of the brass box mounted on the spindle, a small hole is drilled; and behind this hole is fixed a selenium cell, the two terminals of which are connected respectively to the halves of the spindle, and the bearings of this last are connected electrically to binding-screws on the base of the instrument. In the engraving, Y represents the transmitter. The hole in the cylinder is at H, and at S is the selenium cell.

The receiving instrument shown at X (Fig. 112) contains another cylinder, similar to that of the transmitter, and mounted on a similar spindle, which, however, is not divided nor insulated from the cylinder. An upright pillar D, fixed midway between the two bearings, and slightly higher than the cylinder, carries an elastic brass arm with a platinum point P, which presses normally upon the surface of the cylinder. To the brass arm, a binding-screw is attached, and a second binding-screw in the stand is joined by a wire to one of the brass bearings.

In operation the cylinder of the transmitter Y is brought to its middle position, and a picture not more than two inches square is focussed upon its surface by means of a lens. The cylinder of the receiver is covered with paper soaked in a solution of potassium iodide.

The two cylinders are caused to rotate slowly and synchronously. The pin-hole at H, in the course of its spiral path, will cover successively every point of the picture focussed upon the cylinder; and the amount of light falling at any moment upon the selenium cell will be proportional to the illumination of that particular spot of the projected picture which for the time being is occupied by the pin-hole. During the greater part of each revolution, the point P will trace a uniform brown line; but when the hole happens to be passing over a bright part of the picture this line is enfeebled and broken. The spiral traced by the point is so close as to produce, at a little distance, the appearance of a uniformly colored surface; and the breaks in the continuity of the line constitute a picture which, if the instrument were perfect, would be a mono-chromatic counterpart of that projected upon the transmitter. Fig. 113 represents an image as projected by a magic-lantern upon the transmitter, and Fig. 114 the same reproduced by the receiver. A selenium cell whereby the

Fig. 113.

electrical resistance to the current is varied, is also used in connection with the photophone hereafter described.

Telegraphy is by no means confined to communication between fixed stations. It is now perfectly possible to

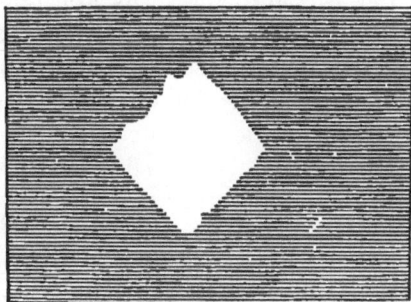

Fig. 114.

communicate with express-trains travelling at high speed, and it is not unlikely that some means will be found of maintaining telegraphic communication with ships at sea. Probably the earliest suggestion of transmitting a current to a moving vehicle was that made by Wright and Bain in 1842. These inventors proposed the ingenious plan of having a pilot-engine run some five miles ahead of the locomotive of a railway-train, and of establishing electrical communication between the two, so that in event of any accident, such as the derailment of the pilot-engine, the fact would be instantly known to the driver of the locomotive. The battery was to be carried on the locomotive; and circuit was made from the battery to an electro-magnet, and thence to a continuous conductor laid between the rails, along which contact-springs on the locomotive rubbed. The pilot-engine also carried springs held in contact with the central conductor; and the current thence passed to a governor on the pilot, which, while the engine was in motion, was driven by the wheels. So long as the pilot-engine was running all right, the governor kept the circuit closed; but if the engine stopped, the governor balls fell, opening the circuit, so de-energizing the electro-magnet on the following locomotive. The magnet was thus caused to release its armature, and thus to sound an alarm, and move a pointer on a dial to the word "Danger." A somewhat analogous system exists on several European railways, in which a contact brush or plate on the locomotive closes a circuit through the rails, so that the approach of the train is thus signalled to a station, or the driver is warned, by the sounding of an alarm, that a switch before him is not properly set. By the same means, the engine-whistle may also be blown, or the brakes automatically set in operation to stop the train.

Two systems of telegraphic apparatus have recently been devised for communicating with moving trains. Phelps's arrangement is based on the well-known fact that if two wires are extended parallel, near but not touching each other, and a current is sent through one, a momentary

current is excited in the other wire, opposite in direction to that flowing in the first. A telegraph-wire is arranged in the centre of the railway-track, and another wire is attached to the bottom of the railway-car, with which last-mentioned wire is connected a telegraph-sounder within the car. Whenever an electrical signal is sent through the track telegraph wire, it produces by induction a corresponding current in the wire attached to the car, and this current works the sounder, thus delivering the message. It matters not how fast the train may be moving, if the wire on the bottom of the car is brought within a short distance of the telegraph or track wire, any strong electric impulses, such as telegraph signals, that are passing along the track wire, will be taken up by induction by the car wire, and delivered by the sounder; and, *vice versa*, when the operator on the moving car operates the lever of his telegraph instrument, and sends electrical impulses or messages through the wire that hangs below the floor of the car, these impulses will be taken up by induction by the track wire, and conveyed to the sounding instrument of the railway-station. By this system communication has been successfully maintained with a train running forty miles per hour.

In another system devised by Edison and others, the induction takes place between the wires strung in the usual way on poles beside the track, and the metal roofs of the cars which are electrically connected together. An insulated wire runs from the roof of the telegraphing car, to a switch at the operator's desk; and by means of this switch the circuit may be completed through a receiving or a transmitting instrument. The receiver may either be an ordinary telephone, or a pair may be used and held to the ears somewhat after the manner of ear-muffs. After coming from the receiver, the wire is carried under the

car, and connected to a strip of copper which is pressed
against a copper cylinder on one of the axles by means of
a spring, thus giving a ground connection by the axle and
wheel. When, however, a message is to be transmitted,
the switch connects the roof to the secondary wire of an
induction coil, with the primary of which a battery, a
Morse key, and a vibrating circuit-breaker are in circuit.
When the current is established, the vibrator, which contains a metallic reed, is thrown into rapid movement; the
free end of the reed at each vibration striking against a
button, and so sharply making and breaking the circuit
into a great number of waves or pulsations. These pulsations in the primary coil induce currents of high potential in the secondary coil, which, so to speak, charge the
roof as if it were one plate of a condenser. The wires
on the poles thus become charged by induction, as the
opposite plate of a condenser is charged, through the intervening air; and as this charge is governed by the
manipulation of the Morse key, which throws the vibrator
into and out of action, dots and dashes of the Morse
alphabet can be signalled.

New applications of the telegraph are constantly being
invented. We are only at the very beginning of its utilization in the affairs of every-day life, and yet its developed
capabilities are bewildering. There is little exaggeration
in the statement that one can sit at home, and " steer a
torpedo boat in New-York harbor, or ring the bells in
Boston, or play the organ in St. Peter's, or explode a
mine in China, or write a letter on the desk of a correspondent in Constantinople," — and perhaps, in the
future, talk to a friend in Australia, and even see him
face to face.

From forty miles in 1844, the total length of telegraph-
wires in the United States has increased to 671,000 miles

in 1886 : enough to extend to the moon and back again, and then go nine times around the earth. Nearly two millions of miles of wire form an iron network over the globe ; and the great army of the telegraphers numbers over three hundred thousand souls.

CHAPTER XII.

THE SPEAKING TELEPHONE.

THE principle underlying all forms of apparatus for transmitting intelligence between distant points, by the aid of electricity, is to cause certain mechanical motions produced at one point to be imitated at the other. And these mechanical motions may range from the slow movement of a telegraph-key worked by the human hand, to the very rapid and complex vibrations of the air which the ear and brain translate into the sensation of sound. The motion of the telegraph-key is copied by the motion of the sounder armature, or that of the recording stylus; in autographic telegraphy, the movement of the point which traces the design is imitated by that of the point which reproduces the same; and the various synchronic systems have for their object the exact duplication at the separated stations of definite mechanical movements occurring at the same rate in the same time.

The simplest way of transmitting mechanical motion between distant points is by means of some solid body extending between them. The connecting-rod of an engine transmits movement from piston-rod to fly-wheel; by means of belts, we can cause one rotating shaft to move another at a considerable distance away; by pulling a cord or wire in one part of a house, we can ring a bell at another. In all of these instances, the whole of the communicating body — whether it be rod or belt or wire — moves simultaneously.

Motion, however, may also be transmitted by means of waves or pulsations in the communicating body, which then does not move as a whole. In such case, the movement is first imparted to the particles of the body nearest the source. These are set vibrating, or swinging to and fro; and in so travelling they communicate their motion to a succeeding set of particles, which in turn swing or vibrate; these, again, in turn actuate the particles next in advance; and so the vibration or wave travels from one end of the body to the other. This is called wave or vibratory motion. Light, for example, is propagated by motion of this kind, in an assumed luminiferous ether; heat, sound, and probably electricity, by wave-motions in the molecules of matter. We see this vibratory motion constantly at work in waves on water.

When any body vibrates in air or water, or any material substance, the air or other substance is set in motion, and the waves are propagated farther and farther from the impelling source, until finally their energy becomes exhausted. This movement of the air, on reaching the human ear, causes the sensation of sound, provided it is competent to affect the mechanism of hearing. It has been determined that the ear cannot perceive sounds when the number of vibrations is less than sixteen, or more than thirty-two thousand, per second; but the limits of hearing vary greatly. If the vibrating body be in the open air, the impulses spread equally on all sides around; sometimes having great mechanical force, as when an explosion of dynamite shatters walls even at a considerable distance. So also the air is competent to carry very minute vibrations; as, for instance, those which, as we shall see hereafter, cause the different quality of human voices. In order to prevent the diminution in intensity of the air-waves caused by the vibration of our vocal organs in speaking, due to their spreading in all directions, the speaking-tube is employed ; and this is the most common mode of carrying the voice between distant points. Here the column of air is enclosed in a pipe, and the pulsations are passed on from end to end, almost without loss, over short distances.

Solids such as wood, metal, the earth, and liquids such as water, are much better conductors of sound than air or other gases. A faint scratch of a pin on a long board is very easily heard through the board many feet away, even though it may not be audible through the air to the person making it. Savages often discover the proximity of enemies or of prey by applying an ear to the ground, and hearing the tread. The mutterings of earthquakes, due to subterranean explosions or upheavals, are heard through amazing distances of earth. The velocity of sound in air is about 1,120 feet per second ; in water, about four times, and in metals from four to sixteen times, as great.

The idea of transmitting sounds of the voice through solid conductors is known to date back to 1667. At that date Dr. Robert Hooke wrote : " It is not impossible to hear a whisper at a furlong's distance, it having already been done ; and perhaps the nature of the thing would not make it more impossible though that furlong should be ten times multiply'd. And though some famous authors have affirmed it impossible to hear through the thinnest plate of muscovy glass : yet I know a way by which it is easie enough to hear one speak through a wall a yard thick. It has not yet been thoroughly examin'd how far otacous-ticons may be improv'd nor what other wayes there may be of quick'ning our hearing or conveying sound through other bodies than the air : for that that is not the only medium I can assure the reader, that I have by the help of a distended wire propagated the sound to a very considerable distance in an instant or with as seemingly quick a motion as that of light, at least incomparably quicker than that which at the same time was propagated through the air, and this not only in a straight line or direct but in one bended at many angles."

In 1819 Sir Charles Wheatstone invented his magic lyre, and in 1831 exhibited it at the Polytechnic Institution in London. He called it the *telephone*, thus inventing the name. Performers on various instruments were placed in the basement of the building, and the sounds which they produced were conducted by solid rods through the principal hall, in which they were inaudible, to sounding-boards in a concert-room on an upper floor, where the music was heard by the audience precisely as if it were being performed there. It is related, that, shortly after Sir Charles Wheatstone had invented the above device, he invited a distinguished foreign musician — a noted performer on the violoncello — to dine with him. In order to surprise his guest, he suspended a violoncello in his entrance-hall, arranging in contact with it a concealed rod which communicated with a like instrument in another room. On the arrival of the visitor, he was left alone in the hall, and naturally his attention was at once attracted by the strains of music apparently coming from no visible source, yet clearly being produced in the same apartment. Finally he traced them to the instrument on the wall, examined it critically, could find no reason for them; and then as if struck with sudden terror, with a cry of dismay, the affrighted musician rushed out of the house. Nothing could convince him that the instrument was not bewitched, nor induce him to trust himself again in its proximity.

Meanwhile there had been known — probably since time

immemorial, for the Chinese are said to have used it ages ago — an apparatus called the "lover's telegraph," in which sounds of the voice were transmitted between distant points, over a stretched string or wire. The contrivance will easily be understood from Fig. 115, in which *A* and *B* are hollow cylinders, usually of tin, each having one end covered with a piece of membrane. The string is fastened at each extremity to the centres of the membranes, and is strained taut when the instrument is used. Words spoken into one cylinder are very clearly heard by a listener at the open end of the other. Just how and why this little device operates, is by no means clear.

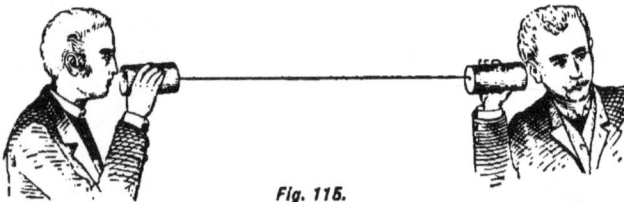

Fig. 115.

The membrane spoken to, however, vibrates correspondingly to the air-waves made by the speaker's voice; and probably the impulses passing over the string move the other membrane so that it copies the motions of the first, and thus becomes a body vibrating in a particular way, and competent in turn to make air-waves which the ear recognizes as speech, just as if the vocal organs of the original speaker had been transported to the distant end of the line. We say "probably," because it is by no means certain that this happens; and, in fact, there is a great deal to be discovered about the instrument. Whatever may be the true reason, it is certain that speech is very clearly transmitted and reproduced; and in its more improved modern forms the device now known as the acoustic telephone is much more efficient for short lines, where the wire can be suspended clear of other objects, than any telephone depending on electricity, which of course this does not.

In tracing the history of the telegraph, we have noted some of the early attempts made to produce sound-signals at the far end of the line. Prior to Morse's invention, it was difficult to record the operation of the current; and to rely on visual signals was to depend on the watchfulness of the receiving operator at all times. One inventor proposed explosions which would very effectually alarm the sleepiest attendant; another rang bells, and so on. For several years succeeding the introduction of Wheatstone's needle telegraph in England, this problem was widely studied. In 1837 Professor Page of Washington discovered that an electro-magnet when magnetized and demagnetized gives forth a sound; and when the current through its coil is rapidly established and broken, these sounds may succeed each other with sufficient velocity to produce a musical tone, — the pitch of which will depend upon the number of times the sound is produced per second. Page's discovery was made the basis of further investigations by Wertheim and others.

In 1854 M. Charles Bourseul published one of those curious speculations which have so often foreshadowed remarkable inventions. It is very frequently — sometimes too frequently — the case, that the imagination of the reader, after the event, causes him to detect in these prior records the recital of ideas never broached until long afterwards; just as one can find in Milton such lines as these : —

> "When with one virtuous touch
> The arch-chymic sun, so far from us remote,
> Produces with terrestrial humor mixed
> Here in the dark, so many precious things
> Of color glorious, and effect so rare," —

and thence argue that photography must have been known
in Milton's time. Bourseul, however, wrote much less
oracularly than is common in the circumstances. He
says, "I have, for example, asked myself whether speech
itself may not be transmitted by electricity; in a word,
if what is spoken in Vienna may not be heard in Paris.
The thing is practicable in this way. We know that
sounds are made by vibrations, and are adapted to the
ear by the same vibrations which are reproduced by the
intervening medium. But the intensity of the vibrations
diminishes very rapidly with the distance; so that it is,
even with the aid of speaking-tubes and trumpets, impossible to exceed somewhat narrow limits. Suppose that a
man speaks near a movable disk, sufficiently flexible to
lose none of the vibrations of the voice, *that this disk alternately makes and breaks the current from a battery: you
may have at a distance another disk which will simultaneously execute the same vibrations.* It is true that the
intensity of the sounds produced will be variable at the
point of departure at which the disk vibrates by means of
the voice, and constant at the point of arrival where it
vibrates by means of electricity; but it has been shown
that this does not change the sounds. It is, moreover,
evident that the sounds will be reproduced at the same
pitch. The present state of acoustic science does not
permit us to declare *a priori* if this will be precisely the
case with the human voice. The mode in which these
syllables are produced has not yet been sufficiently investigated. It is true that we know that some are uttered
by the teeth, others by the lips, and so on; but this is
all.

"However this may be, observe that the syllables can
only reproduce upon the sense of hearing the vibrations
of the intervening medium: *reproduce precisely these vi-*

brations, and you will reproduce precisely these syllables.
. . . It need not be said that numerous applications of
the highest importance will immediately arise from the
transmission of speech by electricity. Any one who is
not deaf and dumb may use this mode of transmission,
which would require no apparatus except *an electric battery, two vibrating disks, and a wire.*"

There can be no question as to the remarkable knowledge possessed by the writer, especially as indicated by the
words Italicized. Bourseul had undoubtedly realized the
fundamental principle, that, in order to reproduce sounds
in air at the distant end of a wire, the apparatus must be
competent to copy the vibrations which originally were
imposed on the sending apparatus by the voice. He
clearly saw, however, that his conception was by no means
adequate to the object.

Thus two ideas were well established before 1860 : first,
that it might be possible to cause an object to vibrate
by the voice, so as to make and break a current passing
upon a telegraph-line, causing in that current pulsations
corresponding in frequency with the vibrations due to the
sounds produced ; and, second, that when a current, rapidly interrupted, entered the coils of an electro-magnet,
the magnet would yield a sound which would be a musical
tone depending for its pitch upon the number of times the
current was interrupted per second.

But Bourseul, who proposed the making and breaking
of the current by the disk moved by the voice, apparently
knew nothing about reproducing the tone by the electro-
magnet ; and Page, who invented "galvanic music," knew
nothing about interrupting the current by voice-controlled
mechanism. And this brings us to the remarkable history
of Philipp Reis,—the man in whom his Fatherland persists
in recognizing the true inventor of the speaking telephone.

A tablet so inscribed marks the house in which he was born, and a like inscription is graven on the monument publicly reared in his honor.

Johann Philipp Reis was born at Gelnhaussen in the principality of Cassel, Germany, in 1834. His father, a master baker, gave him a good education, and finally apprenticed him to a color-manufacturer. A natural taste for scientific subjects led to his becoming in 1851 a member of the Physical Society of Frankfort, where he began the studies which subsequently led him to take up teaching as a profession. In 1858 Reis became a tutor in Garnier's Institution for Boys at Friedrichsdorf, and this was his position in life when he began his electrical experiments. The instrument which, in probable ignorance of Wheatstone's long-prior use of the name, he called "*das Telephon*," was devised in 1860 ; and he lectured on it publicly at various times between 1861 and 1864. Between those who misunderstood it entirely, and those who, like Poggendorf, refused even to publish Reis' memoir on the apparatus because the transmission of speech by electricity was regarded as too chimerical for serious consideration, the invention met with little or no appreciation. Various professors lectured upon it, and several instruments were sold to physical laboratories throughout the world ; but outside of Reis himself and a few intimate friends, it is doubtful if any one regarded the invention as more than a scientific curiosity — creditable, of course, to its originator, but by no means giving him any title to fame. Reis lived until 1874, but his labors upon his telephone appear to have ended ten years before his death. His opponents say, that, having failed to transmit speech by his apparatus, he perforce dropped it ; his friends, that he laid it aside partly from ill health, but mainly from a feeling of deep disappointment because of the lack of appreciation which it encountered among his brother scientists. It does not appear that he made any other inventions; and to his early decease may perhaps be attributed the fact that he rose to nothing higher than an humble tutorship. What with ill health, and the sense of many rebuffs preying upon him, his life, he says in his autobiographical notes, was one of "labor and sorrow;" yet there is little in Reis' history to support this conclusion, especially when contrasted with the records of the privations and hardships which have fallen to the lot of many of the world's greatest inventors. Reis does not appear ever to have suffered from poverty, nor to have depended in any sense upon the success of his invention for support. He was able to leave a useful trade, to prosecute studies which fitted him for his own chosen occupation, — teaching, — and equally able to secure a permanent position as a tutor, which afforded him not only leisure for the prosecution of his investigations, but congenial associates who have testified to their appreciation of his efforts. Contrast this with the long penury and want of Howe, of Whitney, of Henry Cort, and a host of others, and Reis' lot in life was comparatively enviable.

Reis, moreover, lacked that peculiarity of inventors, — persistence. It is enough to say, that, if he had the knowledge of the immense importance of his invention which is now ascribed to him, his failure to prosecute it for the last ten years of his life — between the ages of thirty and forty, when the enthusiasm of youth has hardly begun to be tempered with the conservatism which comes with later years — is simply phenomenal. Most inventors imbued with a great thought, like Stephen Gray, never relinquish it until death; and in the face of suffering and poverty, their devotion to their ideals too often results in sacrifices and self-denials far greater than those which,

when otherwise directed, have provoked the admiration
of the world, and made men heroes.

Reis devised several forms of telephonic instruments,
including many merely experimental, and substantially
embodied in more complete devices. His manipulative
skill was of a very low order. He had an actual poverty
of resource in adapting means to ends. He differed from
the generality of inventors, who construct means first, and
evolve theories afterwards.

In order to understand what Reis did, it is necessary to
recall a few salient facts relative to sound, to some of
which reference has already been made.

Sound, as we have seen, is due simply to wave-motion
or vibration of the air, or other material medium in which
the motion is propagated. The waves or vibrations may
differ in length, in frequency, or in shape. We can always
see on the ocean long waves and short waves, waves following each other rapidly or slowly, and waves smooth
and glassy, like the ground-swell, or broken up on their
surfaces into multitudinous smaller waves, as when the
wind blows strongly. The length of a sound-wave —
that is, the path over which the air-particles swing to and
fro — determines the loudness of the resulting sound ; the
frequency of the waves, the pitch of the sound, a higher
or lower note on the musical scale ; and the shape of the
wave governs the quality or *timbre* of the sound, upon
which depends the difference between the sound of a flute
and that of a violin, between the sweet note of the night-
ingale and the screech of a peacock, and between articulate speech and a groan or a howl or a moan.

We can thus form some notion of what a complex thing
an air-wave produced by speech is. We are constantly
raising and lowering our voices, and hence there are waves
of all conceivable lengths. We are also constantly using

different notes of the musical scale, and modulations of all sorts, even in talking ; and so the waves are set in motion by our vocal apparatus with all degrees of frequency. And, finally, we articulate, we use inflections ; our voice is rough or harsh, or sweet and melodious ; and so imposed on the air-waves are all sorts of ripples, smaller waves, which contort and change their shapes.

It is not difficult to conceive that the simple frequency of the waves of sound may set a disk free to be moved, — like a drum-head, — vibrating with like frequency ; so that, as Bourseul points out, we can cause that disk to make or break an electrical current as many times per second as there are air-vibrations in that time. But when the same disk is made, by the same waves, to vibrate over a long path or a short path, and even, at different periods of its motion, to travel slower or faster for infinitesimal intervals of time, corresponding to the little waves which articulation imposes on the large ones, how are we to modify the electric current by these motions? Merely making and breaking the current will simply cause it to set Page's needle, at the other end of a line, into vibration as many times per second as the current is made and broken per second ; and, if the " makes " and " breaks " are fast enough, the needle will sing in its own voice a note of corresponding pitch. There will be no variations in loudness, and the sound produced will not resemble the sound transmitted, except that both will be pitched on the same note. The needle will sound just the same when the same note is sung to the circuit-breaking disk by a Patti, or a steam-whistle, — just the same if the sound be produced by the most silvery-tongued of orators, or a hyena. Nothing but the pitch of the sound, nothing but the succession of vibrations making that pitch, will modify the current.

Reis, as we have said, knew all about these curious and complex characteristics of the sound-wave. He was a professor of physics, and it was his business to know them. Beyond this he knew of an ingenious little piece of apparatus called the phonautograph, which consisted of a cylinder, over one end of which was stretched a sheet of membrane; to the membrane a little stylus was fastened, the free end of which rested on a rotating cylinder covered with lamp-black. When any one talked into the phonautograph, the membrane diaphragm vibrated; and when the cylinder was turned, and at the same time moved lengthwise, the little stylus fastened to the membrane traced queer curves and sinuosities characteristic of the sounds produced: and so, in fact, in this way the sounds wrote down their own peculiarities.

Now we can see the problem which was before Reis. Bourseul had proposed to make the thing which under the influence of the current was to vibrate, and so reproduce the sounds at the receiving end, copy the movements of the thing vibrated by the voice at the sending end. Reis knew how complex the vibrations were, and equally knew that a stretched membrane would follow them, and could be set in motion by them. But how was the current to be controlled by the membrane, so that it in turn would govern something else far off at the other end of a wire, and make it copy the movements of that membrane? Let the reader think for a moment on the enormous difficulty involved. Not only must the current be modified in some way, to copy the frequency and amplitude (length) of the air-vibrations, but every little minor peculiarity of the vibrations superimposed on those vibrations, — these over-vibrations, these ripples on the large waves, often occurring at the rate of tens of thousands per second. Imagine a mechanism made by human hands capable of doing this!

Reis may be said to have exposed the tremendous obstacles which lay in the path of any one who should attempt to carry into practice Bourseul's theory; and for this he is entitled to lasting credit. Knowing what obstacles there are, is next best to knowing how to surmount them. But the first does not involve invention; the second does.

Reis began by carving a model of a human ear out of a piece of oak. Figs. 116 and 117 show it in edge and section.

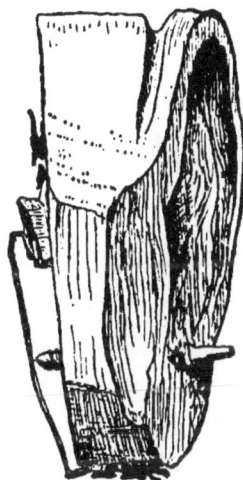

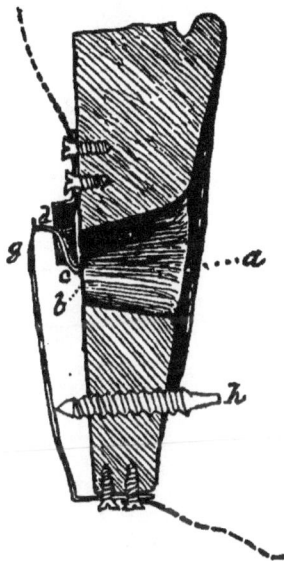

Fig. 116.   Fig. 117.

Through this he made a hole which he closed by a piece of thin membrane at *b* (Fig. 117), to imitate the drum of the natural ear. On the back he fastened a tin plate which served as a support for a little lever *c d*, pivoted to the plate at its middle, and resting at its lower end *c* against the membrane, and its upper end *d* against a strip of spring-metal *g* which was fastened by the two screws represented to the under edge of the ear. The screw *h* was intended to regulate the pressure of the spring *g* on the lever *d*. One wire from the battery went to the spring g; and the cur-

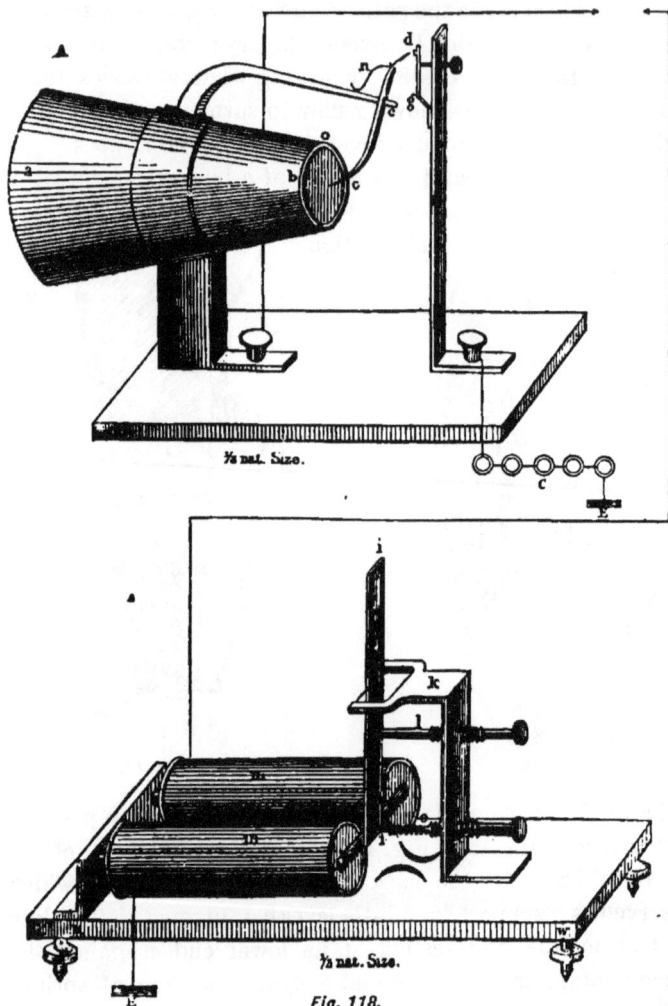

⅓ nat. Size.

⅓ nat. Size.

Fig. 118.

rent was conducted, therefore, through that spring, through
the little lever $c\ d$, then to the tin supporting plate, and

then to the line. This is a transmitting instrument into which speech is to be uttered. This instrument, in its most improved form, is represented in Fig. 118 ; and it is hardly necessary to point out how slight the modification that was effected. Instead of the carved ear, there is a tube *a*, closed as before with a membrane *b*. On the tube is a support *e*, which carries a little pivoted lever *c* as before, one end resting against the membrane, the other against a spring *d* which can be adjusted to the lever. The current goes from the battery to the spring, so to

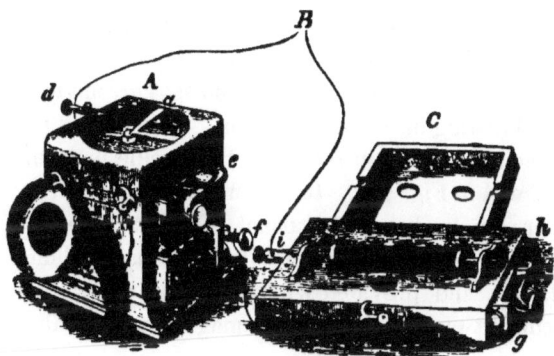

Fig. 119.

the lever, to the metal tube and its support, and so to line.

Reis' last form of transmitter is represented in Fig. 119. It is simply a box *A*, into the side of which passes a speaking-tube. In the lid of the box is a round hole, in which is arranged as before a membrane diaphragm. On this diaphragm is fastened a flat bit of platinum, which is electrically connected to a binding-post by a strip of copper. Above the platinum rests a point of the same metal, which was fastened at the apex of a loose angular piece of metal. The angle piece is supported at the end of one leg *b* by a sort of pivot; and at the end of its other leg *a* it has a point dipping into a little cup of mercury. This mercury cup is connected by a wire to the binding-screw *f*, in the engraving, so that the current from the battery might be said to enter at the screw *f*, thence go to the little tripod or angle piece; and as the point at the apex of this rests by gravity simply on the scrap of platinum fastened on the diaphragm, the current proceeds to the platinum, and so by the copper strip to the screw *d*, hence to line.

Reis made two receiving instruments, one of which is shown in Fig. 119 in connection with the transmitter just described. It is simply and purely Page's needle, which is seen passing through two supports, surrounded by its coil, and resting on a sounding-box. Reis' other receiver, which he abandoned in favor of the needle instrument, is represented in Fig. 118. It was modified from a telegraph-sounder; *m m* being the usual electro-magnets, before which was suspended an armature *i*, loosely hung in a standard *k*, and provided with adjusting screws *l* and *o*. The current passed through the magnet coils in the usual way.

The reader has now before him substantially all that Reis did. The instruments represented in Fig. 119 were those manufactured for the market, and they found their way to the United States. They were exhibited in New York in 1869, 1870, and 1871.

But how do these instruments work? And how, if at all, do they transmit speech? And, if they transmit speech, why did the world not have the speaking telephone twelve or fifteen years earlier than it did? It has cost already several hundred thousand dollars just to talk about those questions, and the end of the expense is not yet — in this country, at least. However existing controversies may be decided, three irreconcilable views of Reis' instruments will always be taken ; and these are : —

First, That Reis merely combined Bourseul's contact-breaking disk and wire with Page's singing needle ; using the voice to make the disk vibrate, and so make and break the circuit correspondingly with the frequency of the vibrations. This doctrine denies the possibility of Reis' apparatus ever having transmitted speech, or ever having been able to do so, because an electrical current now interrupted and now established must during the periods of interruption cease altogether. Hence the necessary vibrations are constantly being dropped out, and can never be reproduced at the receiver, because never existing on the line ; while those that do affect the current simply cause the needle to sing in its own voice, depending, as we have already explained, upon the rapidity or frequency of the closing of the circuit.

Second, That Reis' instruments, even if they do make and break the circuit in the manner described, will nevertheless transmit speech by virtue of the making and breaking. This is absurd ; and although it has been gravely advanced, and innumerable specious contrivances devised to establish its truth, all that these show is that speech can be transmitted through certain things different from Reis' apparatus even *despite* occasional interruptions in the circuit, — just as an occasional pressure on the windpipe may stop speech from time to time, and yet the speaker manage to make himself understood.

Third, That Reis' contact points above noted never broke circuit at all, but were always held together by the weight of the superimposed angle piece in Fig. 119, or the spring in Fig. 118. When this is the case, Reis' transmitter if carefully used will transmit spoken words.

If Reis' transmitter was not capable of transmitting

speech, it is of course immaterial whether his receiver could reproduce speech or not. He never could have known whether it was or was not operative for the purpose. If, however, Reis' transmitter could and did transmit speech, then it is very important to know whether his receiving instrument would reproduce speech, for a like reason. It will suffice here to say, that, with a fully operative transmitter, either of Reis' receivers can be made to reproduce the speech sent.

At the time that this work is written (1886), a contest of unexampled bitterness, into which even the Government of the United States has been drawn as a party, rages over the question who invented the art of transmitting articulate speech by electricity, and the speaking telephone. It is scarcely possible to make even the simplest statements without risking acrimonious contradiction from some quarter or other: even to doubt, is often to invite instant condemnation. In the recital which follows, it has been the endeavor to state facts, without partisan color.

The multiple harmonic telegraph of Mr. Elisha Gray, which has already been described in the chapter on telegraphy, was widely exhibited throughout the United States in the years 1875 and early in 1876, under the name of the "telephone." During this period, and for some time before, Mr. Gray had been studying the problem of articulate transmission. It is alleged, that, as early as 1874, he invented an apparatus which is a complete speaking telephone; but it appears that he did not construct it, nor in any wise test it, until some years afterwards. At the time Gray was lecturing upon his harmonic telegraph, — or musical telephone, as it was then commonly called, — and prosecuting his other researches, Mr. Alexander Graham Bell, then a teacher of a system of visible speech

to the deaf and dumb in a public institution in Boston.
was likewise at work upon telegraphic inventions. For
several years, beginning in 1870, Mr. Bell was studying
multiple telegraphic transmission by musical tones. He
devised various forms of apparatus for that purpose, and,
among other things, a receiving instrument which is represented in Fig. 120. This consists simply of an electro-
magnet placed vertically, over the poles of which extends
a thin bar of steel clamped to a support. This contrivance was contrived for use with a device for mechanically interrupting the current, the latter consisting in a
steel reed kept in continuous vibration by an electro-
magnet and a local
battery. The reed in
vibrating made and
broke the current to
the line ; and this cur-
rent, passing to the
electro-magnet in the
receiving apparatus,

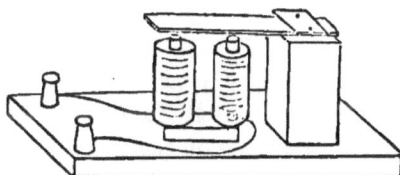

Fig. 120.

caused that magnet to attract and release the elastic
steel bar before it. If the normal rate of vibration of
the transmitting reed was the same as that of the receiving reed, then the latter would vibrate strongly, and
yield a note of the same pitch as that of the transmitting
reed ; but if the normal rates of vibration of the two reeds
were different, then the receiver would keep silent. The
principle of this is fully explained on page 238, in reference to Gray's harmonic telegraph.

During 1874 Mr. Bell did a great deal of thinking about
transmitting speech by electricity, and a little work on his
harmonic telegraph ; and this state of affairs continued
until the summer of 1875. On the second day of June
of that year, while experimenting with his multiple tele-

graph apparatus, Mr. Bell made an accidental discovery
which, he says, "convinced me in a moment that the
speaking telephone I had devised in the summer of 1874
would *if constructed* prove a practically operative instrument." The Italics are ours. Mr. Bell had arranged in
his workshop three experimental telegraph-stations, at one
of which were several of his circuit-breaking transmitting
reeds, and at each of the others an equal number of receivers, of the form represented in Fig. 120. Thus there
were three transmitters tuned to notes of different pitch,
as A, B, and C, at one station ; and at each of the other
stations, three receivers tuned to the same notes, A, B, C.
When transmitter A was in operation, only the reeds A
at the two distant stations should respond ; and so, for
transmitters B and C, only the reeds B and C should
correspondingly vibrate. While the experiment was in
progress, Mr. Bell's assistant, Mr. Watson, finding that
one of the reeds of the receivers at the station where he
was located adhered to the pole of the magnet, forcibly
plucked it away. At the same moment Mr. Bell, at the
other receiving station, noticed a motion in the reed of
the receiver, which corresponded to the receiver whose
reed had been plucked. "At all events," he says, "the
reed of the receiver at station 2 vibrated at a time when
no vibration was expected, so that the fact of its vibration immediately attracted my attention. I therefore kept
Mr. Watson plucking the reed at station 3 while I made
various changes at stations 1 and 2. These changes
proved that the vibration I had observed had indeed been
caused by the plucking of the reed at station 3, even when
there was no battery upon the circuit at the time. To
make the matter perfectly sure, we separated the receivers
B of stations 2 and 3, and connected them upon a circuit
by themselves, as shown in Fig. 5 of my March 7, 1876,

patent, but without any battery in the circuit. [The figure here referred to by Professor Bell is represented in Fig. 121. *E E* are the two receivers, each having an electromagnet, in front of the pole of which is arranged a spring armature or reed *A*. The reed is fastened at one end at *h*.] Upon plucking the reed of one of the receivers, the reed of the other was thrown into very considerable vibration. The vibrations produced by the plucking were still more intense when a battery was included in the circuit. A number of experiments were made to prove that the considerable amplitude of movement noticed was not caused by any vibrations mechanically conducted along the wire from one instrument to the other, but that the vibration of the

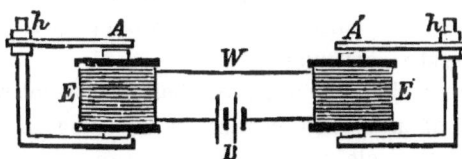

Fig. 121.

one receiving reed was due to electrical undulations caused by the vibration of the other receiving reed. *The discovery therefore that was made on the 2d of June, 1875, was that the vibrations caused in the armature of a receiving instrument, by electrical undulations occasioned by the vibration of the armature of another instrument in the same circuit as the first, would be of very considerable force.* As I have already explained, I had had the idea since the summer of 1874, that vibrations produced in this way would be of very slight amplitude, and that they might not prove sufficiently violent to produce audible effects that would prove practically useful either for the purpose of the reproduction of articulate speech, or for the purposes of multiple telegraphy. The experiments described above convinced me that this was a mistake. The vibrations produced in tuned reeds were so great in amplitude that I felt sure that they were even sufficiently great to be mechanically utilized in any system of multiple telegraphy. Even when the reeds of the two instruments connected in circuit (Fig. 124), (but without a battery), were not in tune with one another, — that is, did not have the same normal rate of vibration, — the feeble forced vibrations electrically produced in the one by the mechanical plucking of the other, though barely sufficient to produce a visible motion, were quite sufficient to cause a very perceptible sound."

The reader has now before him Mr. Bell's own description, not exactly of how he invented the speaking telephone, but how he became convinced that a speaking telephone which he had in his mind would prove "a practically operative instrument."

So far he had simply observed that the current produced in the coil of an electro-magnet, by vibrating an armature in front of the pole of that electro-magnet, was stronger than he had believed ; that is, it was strong enough, after passing over a telegraph-line, to set another armature, in front of another electro-magnet, vibrating audibly.

Mr. Bell's next step was to try whether he could move the armature — the reed — of the sending instrument by the air-waves produced by the voice, instead of mechanically by the finger. Just as Reis had done before him, and the inventor of the phonautograph before Reis, he made a hollow tube, and covered one end with a piece of membrane. He fastened his vibrating reed to the centre of that membrane. The apparatus as Mr. Bell says he made it is represented in Fig. 122. The electro-magnet is placed above the membrane diaphragm ; the armature fastened to the centre of the membrane. In order to leave the armature free to follow the membrane, the former was hinged to its support. Mr. Bell supposed that when some one talked to the diaphragm of this instrument, the magnet being connected to a line of wire, another person listening at a similar instrument also connected to the line would hear what was said. Unfortunately, when he caused the instruments to be made, they would not operate. He says he " knew from theory that the articulation was there ; " but there is obviously a wide difference between knowing of the presence of a thing by theory, and producing it.

This was the condition of affairs when Professor Bell obtained his celebrated patent which has since been judicially con- strued to cover the whole art of transmit- ting speech by electri- city. Like Reis, he had formulated theories in his own mind, and had made apparatus which he hoped would practi- cally realize them. But

Fig. 122.

neither Reis so far as the world knew, nor Bell so far as he knew, had ever successfully transmitted one word by electricity, at the respective times when death ended the labors of the one, and when the monopoly of a great public need fell into the hands of the other.

By the summer of 1876 Mr. Bell had considerably modified the form of his apparatus ; and at the Centennial Exposition he exhibited it before various distinguished persons, and succeeded in transmitting a few simple and easily recognizable words and phrases.

During the following year Mr. Bell applied himself assiduously to the improvement of his apparatus, and finally by June, 1877, brought it to the familiar form in which it has remained ever since. Our engraving (Fig. 123) shows it split in two lengthwise. The outer casing is of hard rubber. Through the middle runs a bar magnet, on the end of which is the wire coil. The ends of the coil

Fig. 123.

are connected by wires running through the case to two binding-posts, to which the circuit connections are fastened. Between the cover and case proper is clamped the diaphragm of thin sheet-iron which is disposed as close to the end of the magnet as possible without touching it.

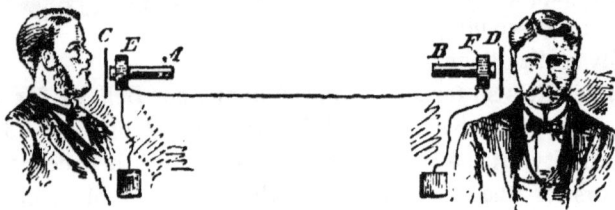

Fig. 124.

Finally, in the cover there is a recess which serves to converge the sounds uttered into the instrument toward the central sound aperture. This is known as a magneto telephone, and may be used both as a transmitter and a receiver, — that is, it may be employed at both ends of a line as shown in Fig. 124, which is simply a diagram of the important parts ; *A* and *B* being two permanent magnets, *C* and *D* being diaphragms respectively in front of each, and *E* and *F* being the coils.   One end of each coil may be connected to ground, and the other ends connected to line.   When permanent magnets are used, the transmitting instrument produces its own current: when a battery is placed in circuit, the telephone current is, as already stated, superposed on the main current.   The first telephone lines commercially employed had magneto telephones for both transmitters and receivers, but at the present time in this country the magneto telephone is used solely as a receiver.

It is a matter of history, that Mr. Bell has been the recipient of great honors, not merely as the inventor of the electric speaking telephone, but of the art of telephony, — of transmitting and receiving articulate speech by the aid of the electrical current.   And it is also well known, that, under Mr. Bell's earliest patent bearing date March 7, 1876, a gigantic corporation has asserted an inflexible control in the United States over every telephone line.   This control mainly is based on the famous fifth claim of Mr. Bell's patent, which is as follows : —

"The method and apparatus for transmitting vocal or other sounds telegraphically, as herein described, by causing electrical undulations similar in form to the vibrations of the air accompanying the said vocal or other sounds, substantially as set forth."

We have already alluded incidentally to the undulatory current in contradistinction to the intermittent or interrupted current.   The so-called undulatory-current theory is that which is most commonly accepted to explain the action of the telephone.   It involves the idea that only an unbroken current, variable in strength, can be modified by all the characteristics of a sound-wave ; that such a current will be undulatory in form, and that its undulations will copy or correspond to all the undulations of the sound-waves affecting the transmitting telephone, however minute, and, after passing over a wire, will cause in the receiving instrument the reproduction of the original sounds in all their characteristics. This is substantially the undulatory-current theory.

There are two principal ways in which an electric current is subjected to the influence of the voice. One, we have already seen, involves an armature in the form of a thin plate, which is vibrated by the sound-waves due to

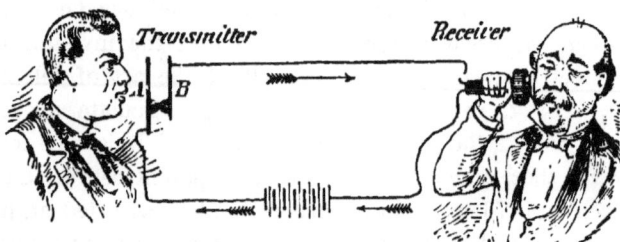

Fig. 125.

speech in front of the pole of an electro-magnet, as represented in Fig. 124. The other method depends simply on interposing in a closed circuit, two pieces of conducting material in loose but constant contact as represented in Fig. 125. One of these pieces, *A*, may be attached to the plate vibrated by the speaker's voice, and the other piece, *B*, may be held in constant contact with the first by a spring, for example. The battery current passes from one piece to the other, then to the line, and to a magneto receiving instrument. When speech is uttered before the diaphragm, the vibrations of the plate communicate themselves to the loose joint, and create variations in the resistance offered by this joint to the current. The result is, that the current is modified by the diaphragm vibrations, just as it is when the diaphragm is moved before the pole of a magnet; only, in the one case a current already flowing is more or less diminished in strength, and in the other it is more or less increased in strength. To illustrate: Suppose there is attached to a bucket of water a flexible pipe, as in Fig. 126, through which the water can freely flow. Then, by compressing the pipe in the hand, the escape of the water can be more or less prevented, while some flow always continues. The contact pieces *A*, *B*, in Fig. 125, when governed by the diaphragm, act like the hand in Fig. 126. Again, suppose the case of a railway-train, which can be made to move faster while constantly

Fig. 126.

running, by turning on more or less steam to the engine: that represents the conditions of the magneto telephone. So also, while running at a given speed, the train can be more or less checked by the brakes; that represents the conditions of the resistance telephone. In both cases, the train keeps on moving, but its speed is varied.

The reader will doubtless notice at once the similarity between the resistance form of telephone represented in Fig. 125, and Reis' transmitter represented in Fig. 118. The whole controversy as to Reis hinges simply on the question whether Reis did or did not maintain his loose contact pieces in *constant* contact. If he did, he had a resistance telephone, using an unbroken current, which will transmit speech: if he did not, he had simply a.

circuit-breaker, causing a broken current, which will not transmit speech.

Leaving the Reis question aside, however, it is a singular fact, that the first articulate speech obtained by Mr. Bell was transmitted not only after his patent had been obtained, but with an apparatus which Mr. Bell had never before made, or even described so that any one else could make it. In fact, the first words sent by Mr. Bell were not transmitted by the magneto telephone at all, but by a very imperfect form of resistance instrument, the construction of which was first described, not by Mr. Bell, but by Mr. Elisha Gray. It consisted of a membrane vibrated by the voice, and carrying a wire which dipped in water. A battery current was conducted to the water, passed to the wire, and so to the line. When the membrane was vibrated, it moved the wire up and down in the water, and so altered the length of the non-submerged portion of the wire, thus varying its resistance to the passage of the current. For practical purposes this apparatus is of no value, but it will always be of great historical interest for the reasons above stated.

In May, 1878, Professor D. A. Hughes announced his discovery of the microphone, so called because it rendered audible very minute sounds ; and this discovery was, that, if two pieces of conducting material be supported in very delicate contact, then the resistance offered by the joint to a current passing through it will be modified by very faint sounds, and the current, correspondingly affected, caused to reproduce them in a receiving telephone. This is of course the principle of the resistance telephone, which, in fact, is now commonly known as the microphone. Hughes made his microphone in the form represented in Fig. 128, in which A is a stick of hard carbon pointed at its ends, and held between two supports of like material projecting from an upright board. The battery current was led, as indicated by the wires, to one support through the carbon, and out through the other support; and a receiving telephone was connected in the circuit. A great many stories about hearing flies' footsteps, etc., were published when this apparatus first appeared, which were more fantastic than accurate. It is true that some faint sounds can at times be recognized; but as a general rule, true of all over-delicate microphonic contacts, the breaks

Fig. 127.

in continuity of the circuit caused by vibrations being strong enough to actually separate the parts of the loose joint, result simply in explosive cracks and snaps in the receiver, which practically obliterate all other sounds. In the resistance telephone, — the transmitter of the present day, — the chief problem has always been the devising of mechanical means of holding the contact pieces together so delicately that they will be under control of the minutest speech vibrations, and yet not so lightly that the grosser vibrations — as when words are loudly spoken — can throw them apart.

Shortly after the announcement by Hughes of his microphone, Mr. T. A. Edison laid claim to the discovery, asserting that he had some time prior found out that " semi-conductors " — whatever they may be, including carbon, however — vary their resistance with pressure. Mr. Edison at various times has contrived telephones in which a block of carbon, for example, is pressed against a diaphragm. It has been conclusively demonstrated by many investigators, that the pressure, greater or less, on carbon, has nothing to do with variations of resistance offered by that material to a current. Mr. Edison's instruments for a short time were commercially used in this country.

Of the various claimants to the invention of the telephone, none has presented a more remarkable history than Daniel Drawbaugh. Mr. Drawbaugh is one of those universal geniuses capable of turning his hand to any mechanical work, and of doing it well. He has always resided in an out-of-the-way little hamlet called Eberly's Mills, near Harrisburg, Penn. As an electrician, he is self taught. Between the years 1867 and 1876, he claims to have invented and actually used every type of telephone now known. He began with a transmitter made out of a jelly-tumbler, in which he used powdered carbon to vary the resistance correspondingly to the motion of a diaphragm vibrated by the voice ; and a receiver contrived from a mustard-can, but in other respects nearly identical with the first telephones made by Professor Bell. From these devices as starting-points, onward, he has constructed a series of telephones, more and more specialized in construction, until finally the instruments which he claims to have had at the time when Professor Bell made his earliest experiments approach closely in efficiency to the best forms of the present day. Mr. Drawbaugh has produced a large number of his telephones, and many witnesses to prove that he had them at the times he fixes. His claims are at this writing before the courts for adjudication. If they are ultimately sustained, there can be no question but that Mr. Drawbaugh's position as an electrical discoverer will be wholly unrivalled. Within the last four years, he has invented over thirty new telephones.

At the date of this work (1886), over a thousand patents in the United States alone have been granted for various forms of telephones, and devices thereunto appertaining. The great majority of instruments differ merely in unessential details. With the resistance transmitters, changes on means for holding the two contact pieces together have been rung to such an extent that it seems that every conceivable contrivance for the purpose must have been suggested. Magneto telephones are not used commercially as transmitters; for the modifications they produce in the current are feeble compared with those caused by the resistance instrument. They are, however, commonly employed as receivers; and, as has been already stated, the form which they now have has undergone no material change for some nine years. An immense amount of ingenuity has also been expended in devising telephone circuits and systems so as to allow of intercommunication between exchanges and subscribers.

The form of transmitting telephone in common use throughout the United States is that known as the Blake transmitter, a sectional view of which is given in Fig. 128. The contact pieces are here a platinum point which is supported on a light spring c, and a button of carbon, h, held in a heavy mass or anvil e, which is supported by a spring d. Both springs c and d are held in a plate F, which is itself sustained by a spring plate g upon a bracket

B'. The platinum point rests against the diaphragm, and also against the carbon button ; these parts being held in light contact by the several springs. On the lower part of the plate *F* is an inclined plane against which bears the point of an adjusting-screw *G*. The current from the battery is conducted through the primary wire of the induction coil *I*, thence through the contact pieces, and so back to battery. The secondary wire of the induction coil communicates with the line. The Blake transmitter is by no means the best, or even one of the best, of the carbon transmitters.

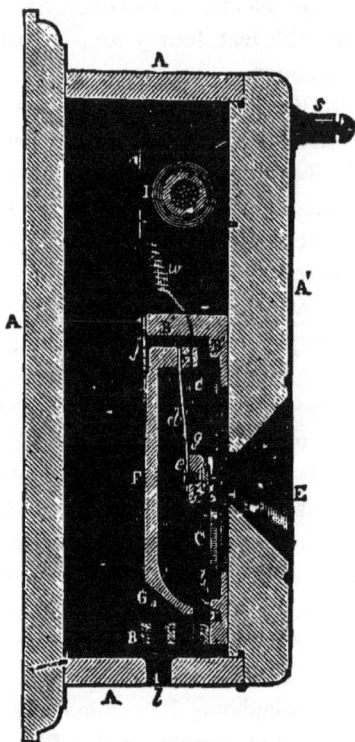

Various forms of transmitters have been devised, in which springs for holding the carbon contact pieces together are omitted, and the action of gravity substituted. One of the simplest instruments of this kind was devised by Mr. Daniel Drawbaugh in 1881, and is illustrated in Fig. 129. To the rear side of a diaphragm *A* is attached a little prism *B* of hard carbon ; and a similar prism *C* is secured to the back-board of the instrument. These prisms do not touch each other, but resting upon their inclined faces is a cylinder *D*, also of carbon. The

Fig. 128.

battery current passes through the three pieces of carbon, which remain always in proper adjustment simply by the weight of the carbon cylinder. This instrument has been adopted by the United States Signal Service, and has been officially pronounced of special efficiency for military purposes in the field, etc.

For producing loud sounds in the receiving instrument, the transmitters which use blocks or buttons of carbon are far inferior to those employing carbon in comminuted form. The usual construction of these instruments is represented in Fig. 130, in which A is a diaphragm of metal, B a fixed plate of metal, and C a mass of pulverized coke placed between the two. The current passes

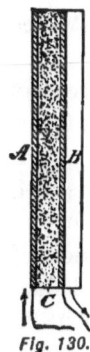

Fig. 129.

from the diaphragm through the coke, to the back plate, and so out. This telephone operates by reason of the immense number of contacts occurring between the particles of carbon. It is necessary simply to cause the air-vibrations due to the voice to jar or shake the mass. Fig. 131 represents a pulverized-carbon transmitter constructed by the author, in its full working size. It consists simply of a cylindrical box of hard rubber, lined within with a ring of brass, A, to which one of the conducting wires is fastened. A disk of brass B is firmly attached to

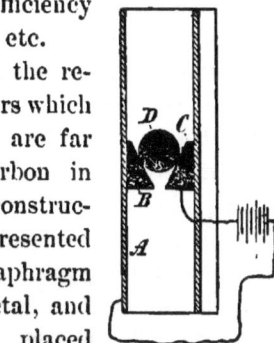

Fig. 130.

Fig. 131.

one of the inner faces, so as not to touch the ring A. The space in the box is loosely filled with comminuted coke, and then the cover is permanently fastened in place. In external appearance the instrument is nothing but a button from which the connecting wires extend. This contrivance transmits speech clearly when held in the fingers close to the mouth. Just why conducting bodies in loose but constant contact will cause a variation in the resistance to, and so render an electrical current capable of copying, speech vibrations, is not definitely known. Any pieces of conducting material will so operate, — even silver, the best of electrical conductors. The results, however, are much better when the contact pieces are of carbon, or other material of comparatively low conductivity. It appears probable that the true cause of the effect is variations in the infinitesimally thin air film existing between the parts of the joint.

With all telephone transmitters, at the present time, induction coils are used ; the contact pieces and battery being connected in the primary circuit, and the secondary wire of the coil to line. The principal object is to increase the electro-motive force of the modified current so that it may overcome the resistance due to long lines, and thus enable speech to be transmitted over greater distances than if the direct battery current were used.

As we have stated, the ingenuity of telephone inventors has chiefly been directed to the production of new forms of transmitters ; and some of these are remarkable as scientific curiosities. Professor Blake has transmitted speech by the earth's magnetism, by arranging a diaphragm before a rod of soft iron, the latter being held in the position of the dipping needle, and thus becoming a magnet by induction from the earth. Mr. Bell has devised a telephone in which the vibrations of the diaphragm produce a rubbing contact between pieces of glass and silk, so that, as he claims, the instrument "may be made to transmit articulate speech by means of frictional electricity generated by the voice itself." Another curious transmitter devised by Mr. Bell consists of a toy balloon about six inches in diameter, made of thin rubber and coated with plumbago. This is held between two fixed plates, and the current passes over the conducting envelope. The expansion and contraction of the body of confined air in the balloon is said to modify the resistance of the plumbago coating. Neither of the above instruments is of much practical utility.

The great majority of telephone transmitters vary simply in the arrangement of their contact pieces. In some, multiple contacts are used, ranging from two or more pairs of carbons held together by springs, and all governed by the same diaphragm, up to a dozen or more pairs. The carbons in some instruments are held together by gravity, and in others by hydraulic pressure. In some forms of apparatus, the carbon is pulverized: in others it takes the shape of balls like shot.

In telephone receivers, but little change has been effected since they have come into public use. In lieu of one magnet, several are sometimes employed. The metal diaphragm which forms the armature is in many forms polarized by a metallic connection with the magnet. The only part in the telephone receiver absolutely necessary to the reproduction of the sound is the coil. The diaphragm may be omitted, and sound will be heard from both coil and magnet. If the magnet is left out, the coil alone will speak, though the sound in such case will be much weaker. A simple platinum wire .001 inch in diameter and six inches long, stretched between a pillar and a diaphragm, will expand and contract under the influence of the current, and so reproduce speech.

Mr. Edison has invented a so-called electro-chemical telephone-receiver, in which there is a cylinder composed mainly of chalk, against which rests a platinum strip which is also secured to a diaphragm. The circuit passes through cylinder and strip, and the cylinder is rotated at uniform speed. The friction between cylinder and strip causes the diaphragm to be drawn inward, — that is, toward the cylinder, — so that the diaphragm is thus brought to a certain position. When a current passes through the instrument, the friction of strip and cylinder is reduced, and the diaphragm flies back by its own elasticity. As the variation in friction corresponds to the variations in the strength of the current coming to the instrument, the diaphragm is thus caused to vibrate so as to reproduce speech sent from the other end of a line. This apparatus produces loud sounds, but has not come into any practical use.

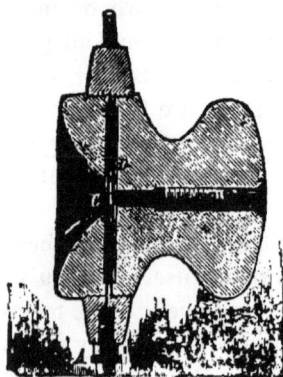

One of the most ingenious of the telephones is Professor Dolbear's condenser receiver, which is represented in Fig. 132. This consists simply of two metallic disks C, D, supported in the case of the instrument so as to be very close together, but not in contact. One disk is pressed upon by a screw at its middle, and is thus prevented from vibrating; the other is free to vibrate. One of these disks is connected to line, the other to earth. The line wire at the transmitting end is connected to the secondary wire of an induction coil, in the primary circuit of which a transmitter is included. As the varying currents flow into and out of this condenser, the two disks attract one another more or less strongly; and thereby vibrations are set up which correspond to the vibrations of the original sounds.

Fig. 132.

There is no instrument which employs such delicate forces, performs such intricate motions, or requires greater accuracy in construction, than the telephone. The total path of the vibrating air-particle is perhaps one millionth of an inch; its period (half vibration) is as short as $\frac{1}{400}$ of a second in many instances. Within this small limit of time and space, lie packed all the variations which distinguish from each other all words of all languages. The minuteness of these distinctions escapes computation and statement; and yet the telephone acts by taking note of them and reproducing them. The electrical force available in the magneto instruments has been reckoned at $\frac{1}{100000}$ of that due to a single cell of battery; and it is variations of more or less within this maximum limit which give rise to the speech heard at the receiver.

It has been estimated that currents of a ten-millionth of an ampère will give audible sounds. With delicately adjusted transmitters, especially those using pulverized carbon, it is not at all necessary to place the instrument near the mouth in speaking. It may simply be placed against some part of the body, preferably near the chest. With the little button transmitter above described, speech can be transmitted clearly when the instrument is pressed against the head, the throat, and the chest. The best results are obtained when the apparatus is placed directly over the breast-bone.

Wherever a conductor carrying a current is in proximity to another conductor forming a closed circuit, the current in the first conductor induces a current moving in opposite direction in the second conductor. These induced currents are often produced upon telephone lines by telegraph currents in neighboring wires, or stray currents in the air or earth; and the result is that the telephone current may be so retarded or modified that it no longer represents the speech vibrations imposed upon it. A great many devices have been suggested to get rid of this induction. A return metallic conductor — double wire — has been found the most efficacious so long as the insulation is good ; but the expense of two wires on each circuit renders this plan impracticable for ordinary uses. Cables have been suggested, provided with envelopes of metal connected to earth for the purpose of leading to ground the currents induced on them ; but these contrivances generally act just the opposite from that which is expected of them, the ground connection apparently leading currents from earth to the line instead of the reverse direction. Wherever a telephone-line approximates a telegraph-line, the Morse signals can be plainly heard in the telephone receiver ; and where a Wheatstone automatic instrument is at work, or, as in the case of electric-lighting wires, where a dynamo is supplying the current, the roars and whirs heard in the telephone completely obliterate all other sounds.

The distance over which a telephone-line will receive induced currents from another conductor is astonishing. In the early days of the telephone, Professor Blake, by connecting a receiver to a railroad-track, heard distinctly the Morse signals traversing the wires on the poles more than forty feet distant.

Telephoning over submarine cables is impracticable for long distances, owing to the effects of induction and retardation. Tests on artificial lines representing the Atlantic cable show that probably the maximum distance over which speech can be distinguished does not exceed a hundred and fifty miles. Conversation has, however, been successfully maintained between Brussels, Belgium, and Dover, England, through sixty miles of cable and two hundred miles of air line. So also speech has been transmitted between Holyhead and Dublin. In every submarine cable, before a signal can be made at the receiving end, the whole cable must be charged up with electricity; and if there be not sufficient electricity sent in for this purpose, practically no signal appears at the distant end. With telephone currents on long cables, the whole of the electricity is, as it were, swallowed up; that is, none appears at the distant end, or, if it does appear, it is rolled up in one continuous wave, bereft of those rapid variations that reproduce sonorous vibrations.

A telephone circuit when in connection with the earth gives distinct evidence of every visible flash of lightning, however far off the thunder-storm may be. No difference in time has been observed between seeing the flash and hearing the sound. If the instrument be connected to the gas and water systems of a house, distinct evidence of the flash can be heard, and even cracklings attributed to an aurora have been distinguished in this way. Earth-currents — those which naturally flow in the earth's crust — can often be clearly recognized.

Professor Bell has proposed to utilize the inductive influence of one circuit upon another to enable vessels at sea to communicate by telephone without the need of intervening wires. A conducting wire, say, a mile in length, is trailed over the stern of a vessel, and supplied with electricity from a dynamo on board. Circuit is made from the dynamo through the wire, and so back by the water. It is supposed that a conductor thus arranged will induce currents upon a similar conductor trailing behind the other vessel, whenever the two come in inductive proximity, so that speech can thus be transmitted. It is not at all improbable that ultimately, through the telephone, means will be found of warning vessels of the approach of other ships, and the direction in which they are moving; and possibly, by some thermo-electric arrangement, the proximity of icebergs will also be indicated.

Theoretically it is difficult to assign any distance over which speech may not be telephonically transmitted. Conversation has easily been maintained through an artificial resistance equal to that of a telegraph-line girdling the world ; but between talking through artificial resistances, and actual wires, there is a very great difference. So long as the effects of induction and leakage cannot be neutralized, the possible distance of telephoning must depend on accidental conditions. Sometimes it is utterly impossible to get speech over a line a few miles in length. Cases have been found where a line first passing over water and then over earth, or extending over rock and then gravel, would refuse to transmit until taken down and carried around the shore of the water-course or away from the varying soil. Speech has, however, been excellently transmitted between Chicago and New York, Washington and New York, and Boston and New York, on the regular telegraph-lines.

Telephoning without wires is already a possibility, and promises extraordinary results in the near future. Telephones have been fixed upon a wire passing from the ground floor to the top floor of a large building, the gas-pipes being used as a return, and the Morse signals sent from a telegraph-office two hundred and fifty yards away have been distinctly read ; in fact, if the gas and water systems be used, it is impossible to exclude telegraphic signals from the telephone circuit. There are several cases on record of telephone circuits miles away from any telegraphic wires, but in a line with the earth terminals, picking up telegraphic signals. When an electric-light system uses the earth, it is stoppage to all telephonic communication in its neighborhood. The whole telephonic communi-

cation of Manchester, England, was one day broken down
from this cause; and in the city of London the effect was
at one time so strong as not only to destroy telephonic
communication, but to ring the bells. A telephone circuit
using the earth for return acts as a switch to the earth,
picking up the currents that are passing, in proportion to
the relative resistances of the earth and the wire. Speech
has been transmitted across water-courses, by the aid of
large metal plates wholly submerged; the water apparently
closing the circuit between the plates.

Mr. Van Rysselberghe, a Belgian electrician, has succeeded in transmitting telegraphic and telephonic messages
over the same wire; an apparently impossible feat in view
of the constant breaking of the circuit by the telegraph
instruments, tending not only to render the current intermittent, and thus unable to receive all the sound-vibrations,
but also to produce in the receiving instrument loud explosive noises which effectually drown articulation. Mr.
Van Rysselberghe has succeeded in talking between Paris
and Brussels, over a wire nearly two hundred miles long,
which was used at the same time for ordinary telegraphing. His principle is to retard the telegraphic currents,
so as to modify their rise and fall, by means of condensers
and electro-magnets. The difficulty with this plan is that
it retards telegraphy; and it is doubtful whether the disadvantages due to this reason will not more than compen-
sate for any advantages gained by the invention.

The practical applications which have been made of the
telephone to various purposes are legion. One of the
most interesting features of the Paris Electrical Exhibition
of 1881 was a room fitted up with some eighty telephone
receivers which connected with an assemblage of microphone transmitters arranged around the front of the stage
of the Grand Opera. Listeners in the receiving-room

could hear the music with perfect distinctness; and as
each person was provided with two receivers communicating with transmitters placed at opposite parts of the stage,
by remarking the difference in loudness of the sound at
either ear he could thus in a measure follow the movements of the singer about the stage.   In Brooklyn, telephone transmitters have been arranged near the pulpits
of several popular preachers, so that members of the
congregation unable to attend may listen to the sermon
in their own dwellings.

Two very beautiful applications of the telephone have
been made by Professor Hughes.   These are respectively

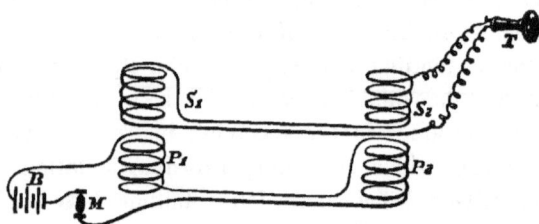

Fig. 133.

known as the induction balance and the sonometer.   The
induction balance is illustrated by diagram in Fig. 133.
The current from a small battery B, connected with a microphone M, passes through two coils of wire $P_1 P_2$, wound on
bobbins fixed on a suitable stand.   Above each of these
primary coils are placed two secondary coils $S_1 S_2$, of wire
of the same size and of exactly equal numbers of turns of
wire.   The secondary coils are joined to a telephone T, and
are wound in opposite directions.   The result of this arrangement is that whenever a current either begins or stops flowing in the primary coil P_1 it induces a current in S_1, and P_2
in S_2.   As S_1 and S_2 are wound in opposite directions, the
two currents thus induced in the secondary wire neutralize

one another; and, if they are of equal strength, balance one another so exactly that no sound is heard in the telephone. But a perfect balance cannot be obtained unless the resistances and the co-efficients of mutual induction and self-induction are alike. If a flat piece of silver or copper (such as a coin) be introduced between S_1 and P_1 there will be less induction in S_1 than in S_2, for part of the inductive action in P_1 is now spent in setting up currents in the mass of the metal, and a sound will again be heard in the telephone. But balance can be restored by moving S_2 farther away from P_2 until the induction in S_2 is reduced to equality with S_1, when the sounds in the telephone again cease. It is possible by this means to test the relative conductivity of different metals which are introduced into the coils, and even to detect a counterfeit coin. The induction balance has also been applied in surgery, to detect the presence of a bullet in a wound; for a lump of metal may disturb the induction when some inches distant from the coils. Its first trial as a bullet finder was in the case of President Garfield; but unfortunately the instrument then proved of little avail, as it was deceived by the presence of metallic springs in the bed.

The sonometer is a special form of balance for examining either the loudness of sounds, or the capacity of any ear for distinguishing sounds. It involves an ingenious arrangement of induction coils upon a graduated rod, which furnishes a scale of sensitiveness of hearing.

Dr. Boudet has succeeded in recording automatically speech reproduced by a telephone receiver, by removing the diaphragm and substituting a delicate armature carrying a stylus which made tracings on smoked paper. Some similarities between the sinuous lines traced have been detected, but there is evidently much to be discovered before we shall be able to read the telephone's writing.

The telephone has been used to hear the mutterings of earthquakes, and of volcanoes before eruption. It has served as a means of communication from earth to balloons, and from vessel to vessel at sea. It allows watchmen on the surface to listen to the operation of the pumps in deep mines, and to communicate with the miners. Buried in the earth, it has proven an efficient means of detecting subterranean springs, the gurgle of which is plainly heard. So also it has been proposed to place microphones on the picket-lines of armies in the field, or along roads or around camps, to reveal the movements of the enemy. It is employed to reveal the bodily sounds, such as heart-murmurs and the throbbing of the pulse.

In 1873 Mr. Willoughby Smith, while experimenting with the metal selenium as a means of measuring large resistances to electric currents, discovered that the material itself was very sensitive to the action of light, which apparently manifested itself by causing changes in the resistance of the selenium. One of the first practical applications of this discovery was the construction, by Dr. William Siemens, of a so-called artificial eye, in which a selenium plate was arranged to serve as a retina, upon which a lens converged the light. In front of the lens were arranged two sliding screens, which answered to lids; and these were controlled by an electro-magnet in circuit with the selenium, with which also a galvanometer was connected. Whenever the lids were opened, the light falling through the lens upon the piece of selenium caused a variation in the resistance offered by the latter to the electrical current passing through it, so that any changes in the intensity of the light were shown by the movement of the galvanometer needle. The electro-magnet, however, was adjusted to control the lids automatically, so that, as Dr. Siemens described it, here was " an artificial eye, sensitive to light and to differences in color, which gives signs of fatigue when it is submitted to the prolonged action of light, which regains its strength after resting with closed lids,'' and which closes its lids automatically on the occurrence of a vivid flash.

Shortly after the telephone came into use, Mr. Smith connected a piece of selenium with the instrument, and then for the first time actually heard a ray of sunlight fall upon the bar. Others had conceived of the same idea, and were working at it; but Professor Bell, in conjunction with Mr. Sumner Tainter, was probably the first to per-

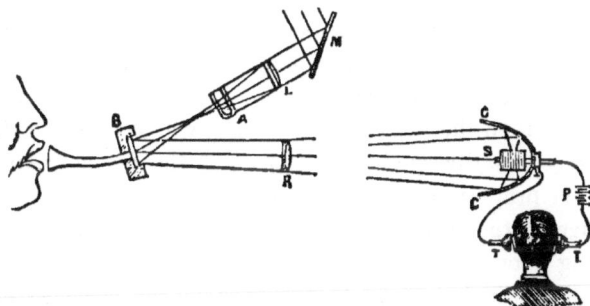

Fig. 134.

fect an apparatus to transmit speech by a ray of light, and to realize what Professor Bell called '' the extraordinary sensation of hearing a beam of sunlight laugh, cough, and sing, and talk with articulate words.'' This apparatus is called the photophone. It is operated by the voice of the speaker to produce variations in a parallel beam of light, corresponding to the variations in the air produced by the voice.

The simplest form of apparatus consists of a plane mirror of flexible material, such as silvered mica or microscopic glass. Against the back of this mirror, the speaker's voice is directed, a speaking-tube being used as represented in the diagram, Fig. 134. In this engraving *B* is the transmitter upon which the mirror *M* reflects a beam of light, which passes through a lens *L*, and then through a vessel *A* of alum-water, which serves to cut off the heat-rays. The beam reflected from the mirror *M* passes through a lens *R*, and then travels over the intervening space to a parabolic mirror *C*, by which it is reflected and concentrated upon the selenium cell *S*. This cell is included in circuit with a battery *P* and a pair of telephones *T T*.

When speech is uttered into the speaking-tube behind the transmitter, the silvered disk is alternately bulged out and in, and in this way it becomes more or less concave or convex; the degree of change in its form depending upon the variations in the sound. When the disk is most convex, then the ray reflected from it will be most widely scattered or diverged, and hence, of the whole beam, a smaller proportion will be received by the mirror *C*. Consequently the amount or fraction of the beam of light falling upon the mirror *C* depends upon the curvature of the disk, which in turn is governed by the speech-vibrations. Now, the more light falls upon the mirror *C*, the greater the quantity converged upon the selenium, and hence the greater the conductivity of this last to the battery current passing through it. In fine, therefore, the resistance of the selenium becomes modified, through the medium of the varying light, correspondingly to the sound-vibrations of speech; the current affected by passing through that resistance is correspondingly modified; and hence the original sounds are reproduced in the telephone.

Of course here is the transmission of articulate speech without wires of any sort, and simply by the agency of a beam of light. Over how great an interval this can be done, is not yet definitely determined : the longest distance up to the present time is two hundred and thirty-three yards.

The musical or direct photophone produces sounds from intermittent beams of light. The beam is received on a mirror, and by means of a lens brought to a focus upon a disk pierced with numerous holes arranged in a circle. The disk is rapidly rotated, — from one to five or six hundred times per second, — and the light passing through the holes, and thus rapidly interrupted, is converged by a lens upon a disk of ebonite from which extends a tube conveying the sounds to the ear. Disks of all substances apparently vibrate under the interrupted beam, producing very distinct musical sounds. By cutting off the light at any moment, by an opaque screen worked by a telegraph-key, Morse signals can be easily sent. Sounds have thus been transmitted for distances of a mile and somewhat over.

What improvements the future will bring to the speaking telephone, can hardly be conjectured. In the way of loud-talking receivers, much has already been accomplished of which the public knows little. Ordinary receiving telephones can be made to talk loud enough to be easily heard throughout a good-sized room, and at a distance of thirty or forty feet from the instrument. Transmitters are already sufficiently sensitive to speech to satisfy all practical needs. A good instrument should easily transmit speech uttered twenty feet away from it. The ordinary commercial instruments will not do this, simply because they are very inferior types. The great need is means for neutralizing the effects of induction, leakage, retardation, and other accidental conditions incident to all lines. When that is accomplished, there should be no more difficulty in talking between New York and

San Francisco than from room to room in the same building.

In May, 1886, Mr. Sumner Tainter patented a curious combination of phonograph and telephone, which is, in fact, an electrical phonograph. The phonograph, as hitherto known, is an apparatus for *mechanically* recording and reproducing sounds, including spoken words. Although it is very frequently described in electrical works, it is not in any sense an electrical instrument. The ordinary form of phonograph, as devised by Mr. T. A. Edison, is represented in Fig. 135. When the cylinder *A* is revolved on its own axis, it also moves laterally; and,

Fig. 135.

while it is thus moving, the operator talks or sings into the mouthpiece *B*, on the rear side of which is a thin plate or diaphragm, which carries a needle-point. The plate is thus thrown into vibration; and the needle-point is so caused to make an indented furrow spirally around a sheet of soft tin-foil which smoothly envelops the cylinder. Under a magnifying-glass this furrow looks like a series of very minute dots; but it is the handwriting of the sound.

After the foil is indented as described, the cylinder is brought back to its original position, and the needle-point is placed at the beginning of the line of dots. Then the cylinder is revolved as before ; but now the needle-point runs over and into the elevations and depressions made in the foil, and thus the thin plate carrying the point is set into vibrations which reproduce the original sounds.

In some forms of mechanical phonograph, in place of the revolving cylinder *A* a rotating flat circular disk is used, on the face of which a spiral line of indentations is produced in the manner already described. Mr. Tainter uses such a disk, which he covers

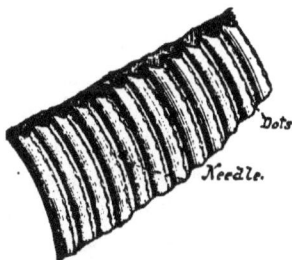

Fig. 136.

with wax in which he produces his indentations. From this wax-covered disk he makes an electrotype facsimile ; and then using his electrotype as a pattern to guide an automatically operating cutting-tool, he reproduces all the dots or indentations upon the crest of a spiral ridge which is formed on the face of a disk of iron or other magnetic material. A portion of the face of this iron disk is shown in Fig. 136. The disk thus prepared is called a "magnetic record ;" and it is mounted upon a shaft, as shown in edge view in Fig. 137, by which it is revolved between the poles of a horse-shoe magnet. One pole of this magnet is quite close to the rear

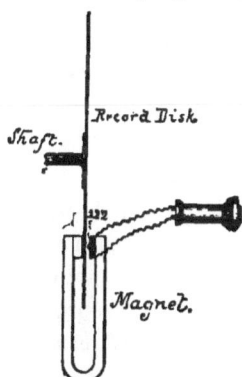

Fig. 137.

side of the disk ; the other pole carries a needle, the point of which is placed very near to the indented ridge on the disk, but *does not touch it.* In the mechanical phonograph, it will be remembered, the needle actually follows

the line of dots. Here the needle is entirely separated
from the indentations. Hence, because the needle is attached to one pole of the magnet, and the disk is very
close to the other pole, both needle and plate become magnetized by induction ; and as they are at opposite poles of
the magnet, and,. besides, are very close together, a very
strong magnetic field exists between them. Finally,
around the needle is a coil of wire, the ends of which
are connected to a receiving telephone of the usual form.

The reader will have no difficulty here in recognizing all
the parts of a magneto-electric machine in which the magnet (disk) revolves in front of the core (needle), and so
induces a current in the coil surrounding the core. Now,
while a perfectly smooth circular plate magnet might be
revolved in the way shown, in front of a coil, without
causing any current in the latter, here we have a plate
magnet on which there is a continuous line of elevations and depressions which successively pass before the
needle-point. Of course the surface of the magnet at
the bottom of a depression is farther from the point than
is the surface at the top of an elevation. Hence, as the
magnet revolves, the distance of its surface from the needle-point is constantly changing, and therefore changes are
produced in the magnetic field around the needle-point ;
and hence currents are set up in the coil of which the needle is the core, and in a telephone connected with the
coil. In this way the telephone is made to reproduce
the sounds which in the beginning caused the indentations
in the waxed plate.

The most striking feature of the apparatus lies in the
fact that here is apparently simply an iron disk revolving
quite slowly, and not in contact with any thing. A little
coil of wire is fastened near to it, and a telephone is in
circuit with that wire. The indented foil of the mechani-

cal phonograph, being rubbed by the needle, soon wears
out; and, indeed, after three or four repetitions of the
sound, the articulation becomes very much blurred if not
altogether indistinct. But this iron disk will last forever.
There is no frictional contact to wear it out. It is far
more durable as a record than even the printed page ; and,
like the latter, it may by electrotyping be infinitely re-
duplicated. Who knows but that the books of the future
will be made in this way? Imagine the author dictating
his thoughts to the slowly revolving waxed plate, and finally sending them to the world in the form of an iron
plate. And then the reader — or, rather, the hearer —
simply goes to the collection of plates which forms his
library, selects his volume, fastens it on the shaft driven
by a little electro-motor, touches the button which starts
the machine, puts his telephone to his ear, and listens to
the author's words read by the author, and so given the
meaning which the author intended. And further, by perhaps a little stretch of fancy, think how any one of the
noted novelists who nowadays delight the public by read-
ings of their own romances, might, so to speak, expand
himself. He might, for example, discourse each of his
novels before a separate plate. When a lecture-committee
invites him to the platform, — in lieu of a disagreeable
railroad-journey taken by himself, he merely forwards the
plate of the desired novel, by express. It is the plate
which comes on the platform, and not the reader —
although, no doubt, a life-sized photograph of the author
could be exhibited to add to the illusion. As it is as
easy to connect a hundred telephones as one, to the coil,
there the audience might sit, — there a score of audiences
might sit, in as many different towns all over the land, —
each person listening through his own telephone, while
the dignified functionary who usually introduces lecturers

might also turn the plate by a foot-treadle, regulate the current, and acknowledge the applause.

In fact, it would not even be necessary for an audience to gather. The plate would probably be sent directly to the central office of the local telephone exchange; and the subscribers would stay at home, and hear the lecture or reading over the lines.

Of course, noted singers might also have their plates, and the plates at least would never be indisposed and unable to sing. And, as for congressmen, to them the invention might prove indeed a boon; for a powerful oration duly impressed on a magnetic record plate could technically be delivered in Congress through the medium of a machine which would revolve the disk at say twenty thousand revolutions a minute; and then be re-delivered before one's constituents with all the emphasis to be got out of one revolution in five minutes.

Fanciful speculation, however, aside, Mr. Tainter's invention is of much ingenuity; and, while it is difficult to predict many practical every-day applications for it, that it will prove stimulative and suggestive to further research in the same field, is certainly to be expected.

CHAPTER XIII.

THE INDUCTION COIL, AND POWERFUL ELECTRIC DISCHARGES.

ALTHOUGH machines for the production of static or frictional electricity have been made the subject of many ingenious improvements within recent years, they have found little practical application out of the laboratory or lecture-room. Wherever discharges of high potential electricity are required, the same can be much more conveniently and certainly obtained through the agency of the induction coil. Two classes of static electrical machines are, however, recognized, — those in which a plate or cylinder of glass is constantly excited by friction, and as constantly discharged into a reservoir of force ; and those in which the electric is excited by friction at the commencement of the operation, but is not itself discharged. A small initial charge is given, for example, to a piece of ebonite ; and a revolving glass disk is thus caused to receive a succession of charges which are transferred to a condenser or conductor, which in turn re-acts upon the original charge, and gradually raises it to a high tension.

The first type of machine, depending entirely upon friction, has become nearly obsolete, because of its defects and the labor of working it. The second type, known as induction machines, produces equal effects with only a fraction of the mechanical work. The latest and best forms of this apparatus are those devised respectively by Voss and Wimshurst.

Where very powerful electrical discharges are now required, they are produced by means of the inductorium,
or induction coil. In explaining the phenomena of induction, and Faraday's great discoveries relating thereto, we
noted that whenever a conductor through which a current
was passing was moved into proximity to another conductor forming a closed circuit, an induced current was
caused in the second conductor ; and that this happened
whether the first conductor was moved into proximity to
the second, or the second into proximity to the first; and
this was illustrated in Fig. 43. Now, it is not at all
necessary to move either conductor in order to induce a
current by one in the other. The two conductors—as, for
example, the two coils in Fig. 43, may be rigidly fixed in
a stationary position, and the current itself moved into or
out of one of them ; that is, by establishing it or interrupting it. By this arrangement one conductor is always
in the magnetic field of force of the other ; and when we
make or break the current, we simply produce the field of
force or cause it to disappear. Every time we " make "
the circuit in the so-called primary conductor or coil, we
induce in the other, or secondary conductor or coil, a
momentary current in the opposite direction ; and at every
break of the primary current, a powerful secondary current in the same direction is caused.

In the induction coil, there are two coils of wire. The
primary coil is made of larger wire, so that it may carry
strong currents, and produce a powerful magnetic field at
the centre. It has few turns, so as to keep the resistance
low, and to prevent the inductive action of the turns of the
coil on each other. Within this coil is an iron core, which,
becoming itself magnetized by the current passing through
the primary coil which immediately surrounds it, increases
the number of lines of force passing through the coils.

This core is usually made of a bundle of straight fine wires. Finally, wound around the outside of the primary coil is the secondary coil, which is made of very thin wire in an immense number of turns. All of the wire is very carefully insulated, so that the currents traverse its entire length. Every time the current is established or broken in the turns of the primary coil, a momentary current is induced in the turns of the secondary coil; and the combined inductive effect of the turns of the primary coil, upon the immense number of turns of the secondary coil, occurring instantaneously, results in a current, or rather a discharge, of enormous electro-motive force.

Fig. 138.

In order to produce the necessary rapid interruptions of the current in the primary coil, an automatic circuit-breaker is provided. This may be simply a vibrating armature of an electro-magnet, alternately energized and de-energized, which armature in vibrating alternately makes and breaks the primary circuit. This arrangement is used in comparatively small induction coils, such as the one illustrated in Fig. 138; but in larger machines, such as represented in Fig. 139, Foucault's interrupter is used. This consists in an arm of brass *L*, which dips a platinum wire into a cup of mercury *M*, from which it withdraws the point, so breaking circuit in consequence of its other end being attracted to the core of the coil whenever the coil is magnetized. When the coil is demagnetized the arm is drawn out by a spring, so breaking the circuit.

As has been above stated, whenever a current is passed through a conductor, it acts inductively upon itself, producing a current which is known as the extra current. When the circuit is established, this extra current moves against the main current, diminishes its force, and prevents it rising to its full value. When the circuit is

Fig. 139.

broken, the extra current moves with the main current, and increases the strength of the latter just at the moment when it ceases altogether. The extra current in the primary coil of an inductorium would materially interfere with its efficiency. To prevent this, it is usual to connect in the circuit of the primary coil a small condenser, made of alternate layers of tin-foil and paraffined paper, into which the current flows when the circuit is broken. The effect of the condenser is first to make the break of the circuit more sudden by preventing the spark of the extra

Fig. 140.

current from leaping across the interrupter, and, second, to accumulate the electricity of this self-induced extra current in order that when circuit is again made, the current shall attain its full strength gradually instead of suddenly, thereby causing the inductive action in the secondary circuit at " make " to be comparatively feeble.

In the arrangement shown in Fig. 139, the battery is connected to the binding posts b, b', in circuit with which are a commutator at C, the primary wire of the coil which is secured to the posts f, f, and also the interrupter or break L, M. The condenser is disposed in the base of the instrument, and connects with the posts f, f. So that the battery current flows normally through the primary coil, is broken at the interrupter, and the extra current due to the breaks enters and is diffused in the condenser. The ends of the secondary coil connect with the upper ends of the glass posts at A, B, and between the terminals of this coil the discharge or spark is produced.

The most powerful induction coil in existence is that constructed by Apps for the late Mr. Spottiswoode. The secondary wire is 280 miles in length, and contains 341,850 turns. With thirty Grove cells this apparatus is competent to yield a spark forty-two inches long between the terminals of the secondary coil. These terminals are placed above the coil, in the same position as the terminals $A\ B$ in the much smaller coil represented in Fig. 139. The sparks produced by such a machine as this are veritable flashes of lightning, accompanied by reports, which represent the thunder in miniature. In order to produce a spark forty-two inches in length from a galvanic battery only, it has been calculated that from sixty thousand to a hundred thousand cells of the most favorable construction would be required.

Fig. 140 represents the great Spottiswoode coil. The

discharge occurs between the disk and the small ball shown immediately in front of the cylinder, and usually appears as a zigzag line of bluish-white light accompanied by both a crackling and a hissing sound. When the points are brought within some two or three inches of each other, the discharge appears as a mass of yellow flame from a half to three-quarters of an inch thick. The twenty-eight-inch spark will perforate a piece of glass three inches in thickness, and it is calculated that a glass block twice as thick could be penetrated by the forty-two-inch spark.

When a high-tension discharge of electricity is sent through rarefied air or through a vacuum, the appearance of the spark greatly changes. In rarefied air, the light assumes a red glow, and a beautiful green radiance is produced when a part of the glass is colored with uranium.

Induction coils, of course on a small scale, are used in medical electric apparatus. Their most important practical employment is in connection with the telephone transmitter, wherein the coil renders the working current from the battery of greater force, and so enables speech to be transmitted over longer distances. The huge coils above described have proved of great assistance in the study of the behavior of the electrical current in rarefied media; and a very elaborate series of investigations was made by Mr. Spottiswoode, by the aid of his coil, into the nature of the peculiar striæ or stratifications into which the electric discharge separates when passed through narrow tubes. When the exhaustion of a so-called vacuum tube is carried considerably beyond the point which gives the best striæ and luminous effects, a new set of phenomena is produced; the residual gas in the tube developing so many new and curious properties that Mr. William Crookes, F.R.S., has asserted that the gas may in fact be regarded as matter in a fourth or ultra-gaseous state. To the known conditions of matter, — solid, liquid, and gaseous, — he thus adds one which he terms " radiant."

Probably the most important application of static or frictional electricity to industrial use is the electric middlings-purifier devised by Messrs. Smith and Osborne. This consists of a series of hard rubber rolls electrified by the friction of hair, silk, wool, or other suitable material; under which rolls the middlings pass slowly to a shallow receiver, the latter being rapidly shaken so as to bring the bran to the top. The light particles of bran leap to the rolls, and cling thereto until brushed into a shallow gutter placed in front of each roll. Meantime the heavy and electrically rejected middlings descend by gravity, and pass through the bolts in the order of their fineness. Travelling brushes constantly sweep the bran from the gutters, into the bran-receiver on the side of the purifier. In this receiver is a spiral conveyer. By the time the last line of rolls is reached, the material has been successively diminished by the abstraction of the bran and the screening out of the several grades of middlings, until only a trifling quantity of heavy refuse (if there be any) is left to pass over the tail of the purifier into the spout provided for it. The bran which adheres to the rolls is brushed off when it reaches the sheepskin cushion, which lightly touches the top of the roll to electrify the hard rubber.

The curious suggestion has been made, that perhaps the lightning can be made to produce artificial diamonds through the volatilization of carbon confined in an immensely strong vessel. It was proposed to place such a vessel, containing some form of carbon, in the circuit of a lightning-rod, so that the current would necessarily pass through the carbon in going to earth ; the idea being, that after volatilization the carbon would perhaps crystallize into the diamond. This seems rather more fantastic than practicable.

The discharge of statical electric machines has been found very efficacious in causing the deposition of smoke ; the particles forming flakes, and rapidly sinking. Rooms filled with dense smoke have thus been rapidly cleared. A useful application of this discovery has been made in effecting the condensation of volatilized lead, for which purpose long passages, some two miles in length, are ordinarily required.

Whether the actual lightning discharge will be utilized, remains yet to be seen. Many years ago Mr. Andrew Crosse erected insulating supports throughout his grounds, and on these stretched three thousand feet of exploring wire, by means of which the electricity of the air could be conveyed into the house and there examined. When connection was made with the inner coating of his great Leyden-battery of fifty jars, exposing 146 square feet of coated surface, remarkable effects were obtained. Iron wire $\frac{1}{270}$ of an inch thick and thirty feet in length was fused into red-hot balls ; strips of metal laid on glass, and placed in circuit, were on discharge of battery instantly dissipated, leaving only metallic streaks.

CHAPTER XIV.

THE APPLICATIONS OF ELECTRICITY TO MEDICINE, WAR, RAILWAYS, TIME, MUSIC, ETC.

THE utilizations of electricity reveal the most singular contrasts. It is a vigilant and sleepless sentinel : it guards the signals which protect the swift-rushing express ; it warns us of the inroad of thieves or the outbreak of fire in our dwellings, the leak in the vessel, or the low water in the steam-boiler. On the other hand, it is a most treacherous foe : it drives and explodes the deadly torpedo, which, all concealed under water, steals noiselessly upon the fated ship : it fires the hidden mine beneath the very feet of the unsuspecting battalion ; and from its inert, harmless-seeming wires, the merest casual touch may bring forth instant death, swift as the greater lightning. In the hands of the physician, the curative effects of the electric current render it a potent ally for the relief of human suffering : yet its destructive certainty will in time render it the instrument of execution of the last penalty of the law.

It annihilates time and space in the telegraph ; yet it may govern the one in hundreds of clocks simultaneously, and measure the other as it is traversed by the railway-train or the steamship. It will impel the locomotive ; and, equally, it will control the brake which stops its motion. It will deposit the flakes of the smoke-cloud ; or fire the charge which hurls aloft whole acres of rock, and opens

great rivers to navigation. It will light up the inner cavities of the living body, so that the eye of the surgeon
may explore them; or illuminate the eternal darkness of
the depths of the great sea, so that the retina of the camera may see and record their mysteries. It will indicate
for us the heat of the steel-furnace, or that of the far
distant stars. In one form it will tear asunder the atoms
of water; in another, cause them to re-unite. It will set
type, and drive the printing-press; operate the intricate
pattern-mechanism, and move the loom. It is already in
use to control the warmth of the hatching egg: it has been
proposed to use the current to cremate the bodies of the
dead. It will protect a freezing-chamber from too high
a temperature, or a vineyard from the effects of frost. It
will make engravings and etchings, and then reproduce
its work *ad infinitum.* It will aid in dyeing and in bleach-
ing. It will reveal the approach of the earthquake or the
rumblings of the volcano, or the almost imperceptible
sounds of the human heart. It will steer a ship, and indicate her course. It will give to new wine the flavor of
the oldest vintages. It will ring the chimes in the steeple,
or the bells in the kitchen. It will turn on the gas in our
dwellings, light it for us, and turn it off. It will record
the votes which change the destiny of a great nation, or
set down the music of the last popular melody. It will
talk in our voices, hundreds of miles away. It will forge
in San Francisco the signature we make in New York.
From the great organ it will evoke all its majestic har-
monies, and yet set free the tumult of whole broadsides
of those

"Mortal engines whose rude throats
The immortal Jove's dread clamors counterfeit."

Where in the history of all magic are there wonders
greater than these?

And we can do no more than suggest their vast multiplicity. To attempt to compile even a mere list of the various applications of electricity to specific purposes, might well prove a hopeless task ; for, if fairly comprehensive to-day, to-morrow might find it behind the times. There is no exaggeration in the statement : the record of the hundreds of patents issuing weekly from the Patent Office of this country will amply substantiate it, and the files of the many technical periodicals will furnish superabundant proof. Since the first pages of this work were written, a few months ago, Professor Hughes has announced the results of his discoveries in the nature and character of electrical conductors, which, if not likely to engage popular attention, are fairly revolutionary of former ideas, and, in point of scientific interest and economic importance, can hardly be over-estimated. So also, since then, the first announcement has come of the possibility of the direct conversion of heat into electricity in the galvanic cell, using no temperature above that of boiling water, — a discovery great in its potency of future benefits, for it may mark the beginning of the end of the reign of steam.

The medical use of electricity — electro-therapeutics — belongs to the domain of the specialist physician. In the hands of the skilful practitioner, electricity as a curative agent often proves of incontestable value. A discussion of even the elementary principles of this branch of the science would be out of place in these pages ; so that we restrict ourselves simply to some of the more curious and salient facts attending the influence of electricity in and upon the animal economy. It is now believed that the production of electricity is constant in all the living tissues. Electrical currents occur in the muscles and nerves, and between different surfaces of the body. All of the bodily organs yield electrical currents when they are divided.

It is well known that electricity can be tasted. A copper coin and a silver coin, placed respectively above and below the tongue, will produce a sharp acrid flavor very easily recognized. An ingenious telegrapher once succeeded in receiving messages sent to a wrecked railroad-train in this way. After the accident, which occurred at a long distance from any station, the telegraph-wires beside the road were cut, and a message easily sent by alternately making and breaking contact of one end of the wire with the other. There was, of course, no receiving instrument available; but the ingenious operator simply placed the ends in his mouth, and — as the story goes — managed to read the signals sent him, simply by the recurrence of the acrid galvanic taste.

It further appears that the current is capable at least of stimulating the senses of smell, hearing, and sight. Ritter discovered that a feeble current transmitted through the eyeball produces the sensation as of a bright flash of light. Curiously enough, on the other hand, it has been proved that when a frog's eye is exposed to light, a current is produced in the optic nerve. A strong current causes in some people the perception of blue and green colors flowing between the forehead and the hand. Volta and Ritter heard musical sounds when a current was passed through the ears; and Humboldt found a sensation to be produced in the organs of smell when a current was passed from the nostril to the soft palate.

Quite an effective battery has been made from frogs' thighs, and it has been determined that the electro-motive force of a current from a frog's muscle equals about $\frac{1}{8}$ of a volt. When properly prepared, the legs of a frog constitute a galvanometer which will reveal excessively delicate induction currents barely recognizable by the most sensitive instruments. The effect of electrical currents on newly killed animals is very remarkable. A grasshopper has thus been made to emit its chirp ; fishes, sheep, oxen, and rabbits undergo spasmodic muscular contractions. Strong currents applied to the bodies of executed criminals have produced contortions of the most horrible character, and evoked motions of the members and organs almost identical with those of life. The power of contracting under the influence of the current appears to be a distinguishing property of protoplasm wherever it occurs. The amœba, the most structureless of organisms, suffers contractions ; and the sensitive-plant, and the Dionæa or Venus's fly-trap, both close when electrified. In the living human body, the contraction of muscles produces currents. These Dubois-Reymond obtained from his own muscles by dipping the tips of his fore-fingers into two cups of salt water communicating with the galvanometer terminals. A sudden contraction of the muscles of either arm produced a current from the contracted toward the uncontracted muscles.

"It appears," says Dr. Golding Bird, "that we are constantly generating this agent, and that *quoad* the supply of electric matter in man far exceeds the torpedo or the electric eel, and is only prevented from emitting a benumbing shock whenever he extends his hand to greet his neighbor, from the absence of special organs for increasing its tension. . . . Some, indeed, have gone the dangerous length of regarding electricity as the principle of life itself, and have dared to place it on a level with the divine essence, which, emanating from the Creator, constitutes what, for want of a better name, we call vitality. These pretensions have been given to this agent from its effects when made to traverse the muscles of recently killed animals, but more particularly when conveyed along the spinal nerves of a recently executed malefactor. This, in the hands of Dr. Ure in his celebrated experiment upon the murderer Clydesdale, worked on the dead but yet warm corpse a horrible caricature of life: by calling into violent contractions the muscles of the face, all the expressions of rage, hatred, despair, and horror, were depicted upon the features, producing so revolting a scene that many spectators fainted at the sight. But this experiment, striking as it was, merely afforded an additional proof of the susceptibility of the muscles to the stimulus of the electric current; and, when divested of its dramatic interest, becomes not more remarkable than the first experiment of Galvani on the leg of a frog."

The natural currents of the body will readily affect the telephone, the making and breaking of a muscular current being plainly perceptible in the instrument. M. Boudet of Paris has even used the telephone as a means of *hearing* the workings of the muscles in certain paralytic and nervous ailments; while the resistance telephone, or microphone, has proved to be a stethoscope capable of revealing murmurs in the circulation which cannot be detected by the ordinary instrument.

There are always a vast number of so-called electrical appliances in the market, in the shape of " electric " brushes, " electric " garments, " electric " belts, etc. Whatever curative value lies in these things resides mostly in the imagination of the user. Many of them are wholly incapable of producing any electrical effect whatever upon the body. It is a safe rule, never to attempt the use of electricity remedially, save under the advice of a regular physician; for, in certain bodily ailments, the current wrongly employed may be productive of great and lasting injury.

Some of the delusions about the curative effects of electricity have been very singular and amusing; and perhaps the first of them furnishes as good an instance as any of the extraordinary credulity with which they have been received, not only by the general public, but often by men really learned in science. In the year 1747 Signior Johannes Francisco Pivati, a "person of eminence" in Venice, propounded the remarkable theory, that if odorous substances were confined in a glass vessel, and the vessel electrically excited, the odors "and other medicinal virtues" would transfuse through the glass, and permeate the person holding the vessel; and from the person so permeated, all manner of diseases, like exorcised spirits, would at once depart, while the individual himself would be delightfully perfumed. In this absurdity even so eminent a philosopher as Winkler of Leipsic firmly believed; and then, not content with merely believing, he proceeded to improve upon Pivati's stories in a way that must have disheartened any one who had hitherto believed in him. He said that he had not only perfumed a whole company with cinnamon; but that by merely connecting a globe filled with balsam, by means of a long chain extending from the globe to his patient, the latter's "nose was filled with a sweet smell, and after sleeping in a house a considerable distance from the room where the experiment was tried, he rose very 'chearful' in the morning, and found a more pleasant taste than ordinary in his tea." Think of the transmission of perfumes by telegraph! The Royal Society sent to Winkler for tubes, and invited him to repeat some of his alleged wonderful results. But he found it inexpedient to try. Benjamin Franklin dealt the finishing stroke to the humbug, by a series of experiments which clearly demonstrated the entire " improbability of mixing the effluvia or virtue of medicines with the electric fluid."

Frequently during the last century, and even occasionally nowadays, persons have been brought before the public as possessed of wonderful inherent electrical properties. Sometimes they merely transmit disagreeable shocks to individuals who approach them ; and at others, they content themselves with performing extraordinary feats of strength, which are attributed to " electricity " somewhere in or about the performer. There was Angélique Cotton of Finisterre, France, who in 1846 is said to have thrown down powerful men, and to have taken chairs away from the strongest athletes. The chronicle says that her neighbors had her exorcised without avail, and that she was " most electric after dinner." At the present time electric boys flourish chiefly in dime-museums, where the deception is quite neatly done. A strong battery usually communicates with the metal plate on which the boy stands, and with a similar metal plate on the other side of a railing before which the visitor must place himself in observing the phenomenon. When the visitor touches the boy, circuit is made through the bodies of boy and visitor, and *both* receive a shock. The boy is used to it, and bears the infliction stoically : the visitor, who is just as electric as the show itself, experiences a spasmodic contraction, and departs much gratified. Some visitors have been thoughtless enough to present their knuckles to the lobes of the ears or the ends of the noses of electric boys, with the result of causing to the phenomenon much bodily misery, not to mention some interference with the orderly and peaceful progress of the entertainment.

Very powerful electric currents will cause death as instantaneous as, and in all respects similar to, that due to the lightning stroke. Several fatal accidents have occurred through workmen, engaged in adjusting electric lights, grasping the ends of wires leading to the dynamos ;

and there have been many instances where people having incautiously touched the brushes of dynamos in motion have been instantly killed. Professor Tyndall once, while lecturing, accidentally received the discharge of a large battery of Leyden-jars; which, he says, first caused a complete obliteration of consciousness, and then the curious sensation of a floating body to which the several members were one by one attached, until he finally recognized that he was all there, and resumed his normal condition. No permanently injurious effects followed.

It appears to be demonstrated, that death by the electric shock is painless, for the reason that the nerves do not have time to convey the sense of the injury to the brain before life is extinct. The substitution of the electrical shock for the present inefficient and demoralizing mode of enforcing the death-penalty, is strongly advocated; and there is little reason to doubt that in time it will be effected. A bill to this end was introduced in the New-York Legislature in 1886. With electric-light conductors conveying deadly currents throughout the streets, it would be a very easy matter to carry branches of these to the usual place of execution, and despatch the criminal instantly, certainly, and painlessly, by the mere touch of a button. It is said that a current of a strength of one-tenth ampère is as much as any one can safely allow to traverse his body in the period of one second; and this strength will depend upon the bodily resistance, which varies between six thousand and fifteen thousand ohms, depending materially upon the condition of the skin, whether moist or dry.

There has been one application of electricity to slaughtering purposes, not only proposed but patented. On March 30, 1852, a United-States patent was granted to Dr. Albert Sonnenburg and Philipp Rechten, of Bremen, Germany, for an electric whaling-apparatus, which is not without ingenuity, however impracticable it doubtless is. The whale is harpooned in the usual way, but to the iron is connected a stout metallic cable leading to a hand magneto machine in the whale-boat. The bottom of the boat is well coppered. As soon as the harpoon has struck, the pole is withdrawn so that the head of the harpoon, together with the metallic conductor, remains in the animal. "The machine," say the inventors, " is now set in motion ; the electric current through the metallic conductor and the head of the whale-iron circulates in the body of the fish or animal, and returns from the same through the salt water to the copper bottom of the boat, and thence by means of a short metallic conductor to the machine. The fish or animal receives about eight tremendous strokes at each turning of the machine handle." The inventors fail to explain what inducement is offered to the crew of the boat, to make them relinquish their oars, and turn a crank, during the rather critical moments when their craft is moored to a wild whale.

Several species of creatures inhabiting the water have the power of producing electric discharges by certain portions of their organism. The best known of these are the torpedo, the gymnotus, and the silurus, found in the Nile and the Niger. The raia torpedo, or electric ray, of which there are three species inhabiting the Mediterranean and the Atlantic, is provided with an electric organ on the back of its head. This organ consists of laminæ composed of polygonal cells to the number of eight hundred or a thousand, or more, supplied with four large bundles of nerve-fibres : the under surface of the fish is negative, and the upper positive. In the gymnotus electricus, or Surinam eel, the electric organ goes the whole length of the body, along both sides. It is able to give a most terrible shock, and is a formidable antagonist when it has attained its full length of from five to six feet. Humboldt gives an interesting account of the combats between the electric eels and the wild horses, driven by the natives into the swamps inhabited by the gymnotus. Prof. S. P. Thompson has called attention to the curious point that the Arabian name for the torpedo, *ra-ad*, signifies lightning.

Electrical apparatus for aiding medical diagnosis, or for surgical purposes, exists in many ingenious forms. The so-called dental engines, for actuating the burrs and other implements used in operations on the teeth, are now driven by small electric motors. A still smaller engine is concealed in the handle of the plugger which compacts the gold fillings in teeth ; so that the instrument need only be placed in position, and the work usually done by the dentist's assistant with a mallet is automatically accomplished. An instrument containing a minute platinum wire, rendered white hot by the current, is employed as a substitute for the needle in the destruction of nerves. A truly diabolical contrivance of an English dentist is an arrangement of extracting-forceps and a battery, so contrived, that, as the tooth is removed, a severe shock is administered to the victim. The peculiar benefit of this device appears to reside in the fact that the patient is hurt so much by the shock, that he fails to notice the less pain involved in the actual extraction of the tooth. The electric light is a valuable aid to the dentist. Miniature incandescent lamps are arranged with mirrors, so that they can be inserted in the mouth, and their rays directed at will. The oral cavity is illuminated so brilliantly that any departure from normality can easily be detected, while the light transmitted through the teeth reveals with much clearness any evidence of unsoundness.

As dental fillings often consist of different metals, — such as silver, tin amalgam, and gold, — electrical currents are frequently set up between them, the natural liquids of the mouth forming the conducting fluid. In such cases, gradual wearing-away of the attacked metal follows; and instances have been known where unaccountable aches in filled teeth have been cured by removing a filling of one metal, and substituting an inert substance or a metal of different electrical character.

In surgery, fine platinum wires highly heated by the current are used for cauterizing purposes, and for the removal of abnormal growths. The gastroscope consists of a rigid horizontal tube, terminating in one direction in an eyepiece, and in the other prolonged into a partially flexible tube which can be passed down the œsophagus until its end reaches the stomach. At the end of the tube is a tiny glass lantern, in which is a piece of platinum wire which is rendered brilliantly incandescent by the current. From this, light radiates freely on all sides, and illuminates the interior of the stomach. In the tube above the lantern is a little window. Into this a portion of the rays from the lantern are reflected back by the sides of the stomach. Finally there is a very ingenious arrangement of lenses and prisms, whereby the image of the side of the stomach is reflected back to the observer's eye at the eye-piece of the tube. The extremity of the gullet tube, with its little window, can be made to revolve, so that, after the instrument is once adjusted, the operator can easily inspect the different parts of the interior of the stomach.

The laryngoscope consists simply of a tongue depresser, on the end of which is mounted a small incandescent lamp. It is used for examining the interior cavities of the nose and mouth. The light has also been usefully employed in photographing the larynx. The photographic apparatus, which is quite small, is brought into position, and, by the pressure of the finger on a button, the electric circuit is closed through both a small lamp and an electro-magnet. The lamp illuminates the parts to be photographed, and the magnet opens the objective, so that the photograph is instantly taken on very sensitive prepared plates.

Trouvé's electric probe consists of three distinct parts, — a battery, a probe, and an indicator. The probe proper is a pipe, flexible or rigid, constructed so that the preliminary probing may be effected, and then the stylets of the indicating apparatus introduced. The indicator contains in its interior a very small electro-magnet with a vibrator in connection with two steel rods which pass into the body of the probe tube. These rods are insulated from each other, so that, as soon as they touch any metallic body in the wound, circuit is thereby established through them, and the vibrator moves, thus revealing the fact.

The induction balance has also been applied to the detection of metallic substances in the body. It was used, it will be remembered, unsuccessfully in the case of President Garfield. Professor Bell has devised another method of ball-finding, which involves the insertion of a needle near where the ball is supposed to be. This needle being connected by wire with one terminal of a telephone, while a metallic plate laid on the skin is connected with the other terminal, when the point of the needle reaches the ball a current arises (the ball and metallic plate naturally forming a couple), and a sound is heard in the telephone. The needle may be inserted in several places, with little pain, and even this may be reduced by ether spray.

It has been proposed to use the thermo-pile for measuring bodily temperatures with accuracy; and a system has even been suggested, whereby a physician sitting in his office can observe the temperature of his entire circle of fever-patients successively, by simply connecting by tele-graph-lines each one in turn with a galvanometer suitably disposed on his desk, — after which he might telephone back his instructions or prescriptions to the several attend-ants. It is not without the bounds of probability, that some one will yet devise an alarm contrivance which will automatically call up the physician whenever a patient's temperature reaches a certain danger point.

The applications of electricity to military uses bid fair to do much toward the revolution of modern systems of warfare. The electric light is of great utility, both afloat and ashore. Its beam swept around the horizon reveals the approach of an enemy, or lights up fortifications so that a bombardment may be unerringly directed upon them. Flashed in the faces of an attacking force, it is bewildering. On board of vessels of war, it is of espe-cial utility in illuminating the sea around the ship, thus revealing the approach of torpedo-boats. It may be car-ried up by balloons and thus employed for reconnoitring. Incandescent lights have been used for night signalling, the signals being indicated by rapid extinctions and illu-minations according to some predetermined code.

Great guns are now fired by means of the electric fuse, and this has been found of great value on board ship. It eliminates the inaccuracies of fire due to the rolling of the vessel during the necessary movement of the arm in pulling the usual lock-string. The gun can be discharged by electricity the instant a good sight of the object is obtained. So also the use of electricity allows of an absolutely simultaneous broadside, which may produce tremendous effects when several powerful guns are trained

upon a single point. On board of war-vessels, the firing
of the guns is now controlled by the captain from the
bridge, by means of a so-called annunciator, whereby
either individual guns or the entire battery may be fired
as desired. It also shows at a glance what guns are ready
for firing, and, by means of a tell-tale arrangement, indicates to the crews of the guns just when the latter are
about to be discharged.

Heavy guns are now trained by means of electro-
motors; and in England, mechanism of this description
has been adapted to the great cannon in the Spithead
forts.

It is probable that in the future, electricity will entirely
supersede the dangerous and unreliable fulminating substances now used as the means of igniting the charges in
fire-arms. Tests have recently been made with a rifle
fired by electricity, in which a small primary galvanic
battery is set in the stock of the gun, and connected with
the cartridge, which contains a fine wire which is heated
by the passage of the current, and in this way the powder
is ignited. As it is necessary merely to press a trigger
or button, to establish the circuit, this arrangement does
away with much of the ordinary lock mechanism.

It has been proposed to use the gases generated by the
decomposition of water, as a means of projecting shot
and shell, in lieu of gunpowder or other explosive; and
an electrolytic cartridge has been contrived, which consists
simply of a sealed glass tube containing water, into which
the ends of wires from a battery enter. The water is
supposed to be decomposed by the passage of the current,
and then a spark passing between the terminals fires the
evolved gases. The practicability of this device is by no
means assured.

The electric sight is an ingenious substitute for the bit

of white cotton, or other easily visible material, often fastened by sportsmen on the front sights of their weapons when hunting at night. It is simply a thread of platinum wire enclosed in a glass tube, and rendered white hot at will by a current from a small galvanic battery arranged in the stock of the piece. A larger incandescent lamp may be arranged near the breech and upon the barrel, and provided with lenses so that its beam is thrown directly upon the object aimed at.

Many very ingenious instruments have been devised, wherein electricity is employed for measuring the velocity of projectiles, by the aid of which some of the most difficult problems in gunnery have been solved. One of these contrivances registers, by means of electric currents upon a recording surface travelling at a uniform and very high speed, the precise instant at which a projectile passes certain defined points in the bore of the gun. Another, which determines the initial velocity of projectiles in the proof of gunpowder, is capable of correctly measuring periods of time as short as $\frac{1}{5000}$ part of a second.

For the explosion of mines or counter-mines, in siege operations, the electric fuse is now indispensable. So, also, submarine mines, or fixed torpedoes as they are termed, are not only exploded by electricity, but the ease with which the current can be controlled allows of their being blown up exactly at the moment when an attacking vessel is in range. A harbor to be protected, for example, is completely studded with these torpedoes sunk out of sight, but all connected in electric circuit with certain firing-stations ashore. By means of lenses, an image of the whole harbor, or all of it within a certain range, is thrown upon a whitened table in a dark chamber, well protected by bomb-proofs, so that the progress of the devoted ship is easily watched without danger until she has become hopelessly entangled. The positions of the submerged mines being accurately known, and in fact marked upon the whitened table, it simply remains to watch the instant that the image of a vessel comes over a marked point; and then the simple pressure of a key transmits the current which explodes the mine. Friendly vessels may thus be allowed to pass in safety, while hostile ships can be promptly destroyed. Some submarine torpedoes are so arranged, that, when a vessel strikes them, a weight is thrown across two contact points, one of which is in connection with the fuse and the other with the battery, so that the current is thus led to the fuse, and the mine automatically exploded. Another arrangement is such, that, when the torpedo is struck, the effect is simply the establishment of a weak current, not sufficient to blow up the torpedo, but enough to make a signal on shore. This shows that the apparatus is in order, and that the exploding current can be sent or not as the shore operator desires. In order to detect the presence of fixed torpedoes in an enemy's harbor, an instrument has been invented by Capt. McEvoy, called the "torpedo detector," of which the action is somewhat similar to that of the induction balance; the iron of a torpedo-case having the effect of increasing the number of lines of force embraced by one of two opposing coils, so that a current induced in one coil overpowers that induced in the other, and a distinct sound is heard in a telephone-receiver in circuit.

There are two kinds of torpedoes now in use by nearly all nations: namely, defensive torpedoes, which are stationary, and are moored in harbors and channels; and offensive torpedoes, which seek the enemy's ship, and either explode on striking it, or are blown up at the will of the controlling operator on shore. One of the earliest suggestions of exploding a moving torpedo by electricity was made by Lieutenant Henry Moor, U.S.N., who in 1846 addressed a long memorial to President Polk, asking for means wherewith to experiment upon his notion of attaching electric wires to shells so that, after these missiles had been projected, they could be exploded whenever desired. The idea being obviously impracticable in the form presented, it does not appear that the desired experiments were made. Since then, however, the idea has been over and over again suggested, of dropping torpedoes upon cities and fortifications, from balloons sent aloft by the besieging force. There is a very fatal possibility in the suggestion. Great damage might be done by letting fall a "dejectile" anywhere within such a large area of populated country as exists in and around New York City, for instance; and there seems to be no practical reason why a current sent over a wire connected to the balloon could not easily control mechanism which would determine the fall of the torpedo at any desired instant.

Without doubt, however, the most terribly effective and dangerous application of electricity to war purposes is that which has now reached an advanced state of development in the so-called fish torpedo. The Sims electric torpedo, which has already been adopted by the Government of the United States, is a submarine boat with a cylindrical hull of copper, pointed at both ends, and some twenty-eight feet in length by eighteen inches in diameter. This hull, in which is placed the four hundred pounds of explosive (dynamite) is submerged, and is supported at a certain depth by a float. Both hull and float are protected from obstructions by a sharp steel blade which runs from the bow of the hull to the top of the float, and from the stern of the float to the stern of the hull. The blade is set at such an angle as to make the torpedo dive under or cut through any obstacle. Within the hull is an electro-

MAN OF WAR DESTROYED BY THE FISH TORPEDO.

motor which drives the propelling screw. To this motor, electric current is supplied by a cable leading from a dynamo on shore, or on the ship from which the boat is despatched. By means of this current, the operator from his station on shore or on shipboard can at will start, stop, or steer the torpedo, and explode the charge, which can also be arranged to explode by contact of the boat with the attacked object.

The terrible potency of this weapon can hardly be over-estimated. In time of war these deadly " fish " will lurk in bomb-proof canals adjacent to harbors and water-ways, ready to slip out the moment a hostile ship comes within range ; or they will be anchored in different parts of the port, prepared to move on their fearful errand on the pressure of a key. No signs of them will be visible. They shoot along like huge sharks under the surface ; and, if the water be a little rough, nothing betrays their where-abouts. The first knowledge an enemy has of his peril is the frightful explosion beneath his very feet, which hurls his ship aloft in shattered fragments.

Conflicts between war-vessels, when thus armed, will be narrowed down simply to a question of which vessel first renders her torpedo effective. Guns and armor will count for nothing in such a battle, which will be more like a duel across a pocket-handkerchief, where the odds, slight as they are, favor the man who first raises his pistol to cover a vital point on his adversary. The torpedo, supplied with current from the dynamo on board the war-ship, will run ahead of its huge consort, and be propelled by its own power. Electric snap cables attach it to the vessel. The enemy may be far ahead, but the torpedo can travel at the rate of eleven miles an hour. The attacking vessel waits only to get within a mile or so of her adversary, and then she " lets slip the " fish " of war." The operator on board ship watches the two little balls which are fastened above the float, just visible above the waves, — visible, however, only when one knows where to look for them, — and has a good glass handy. He keeps these balls in line ; this enables him to see where the " fish " is going, and a touch on a button steers the torpedo in either direction. The enemy, anticipating perhaps some such attack, encompasses himself with floating booms. No matter : the fish goes under them. Suddenly a galvanometer-needle, which the operator is intently watching, moves : the " fish " thus signals back word that it has met its prey. The exploding button is pressed. A column of spray

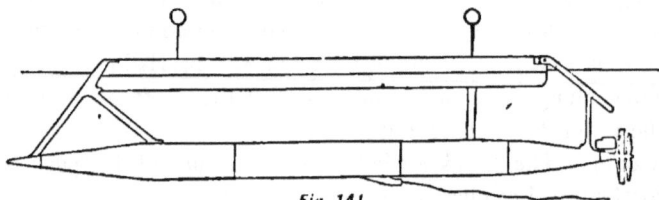

Fig. 141.

leaps into the air ; a dull explosion is heard ; a great black monster rolls over on its side, and then the waves break above the huge iron-clad and its crew of hundreds of souls.

Fig. 141 represents the " fish." The electric cable is shown passing into the lower portion of its submerged hull ; and at the stern is the propelling-screw which is protected by a guard-ring from chance entanglement with ropes, nets, or other obstructions. The rudder is on the upper part of the hull, just forward of the screw. In order to show just what this apparatus has actually done, we append (Fig. 142) a facsimile of a chart of an experimental trial made by General Abbot, U.S.A., at the Willet's Point torpedo-station. Here the course of the fish as it was guided from the shore is accurately plotted, so as to show all its windings. Note the curve on the left, indicating the doublings of the torpedo in its sinuous course, as if it were chasing some victim vainly attempting in this way to escape; and note also how it can be sent out to run two or three thousand feet, and then caused to return like a falcon to the hand of its controller. Even if an enemy does sight the partly submerged

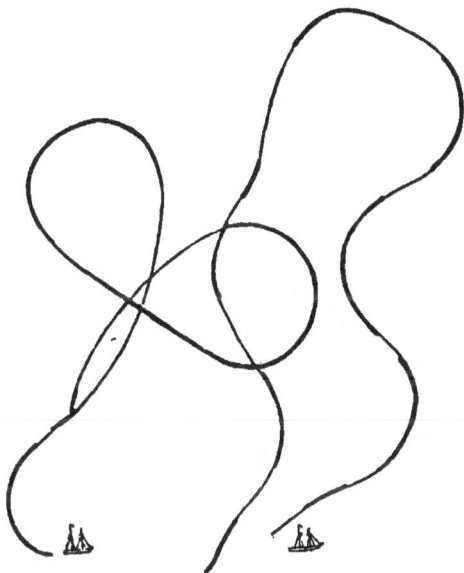

Fig. 142.

float, it will do him no good to fire at it. It is filled with cork or like light material, and more than half of it might be torn away without much impairing its buoyancy.

How to defend against a torpedo of this sort, is an unsolved problem. Heavy nettings around a vessel might stop one fish; but if the immediate explosion did not sink the ship itself, it would tear the netting, however strong, to pieces, and there would be an open way for another fish, sent immediately on the heels of the first. The telephone bids fair to be a good means of detecting the approach of a submarine torpedo ; for, if one of its terminal wires is connected with a submerged plate, the sound of the rapidly approaching fish can easily be heard. This would be of little avail, however, unless some sort of dredging-craft could run quickly in behind the fish, and cut the electric cable ; but in the time which it would take to recognize the approaching danger, and to notify the cutting vessel, — supposing the latter to be in perfect readiness, — the torpedo would probably get alongside and do its work. The problem is one of great importance, and many inventors are hard at work upon it.

Military telegraphs are now indispensable to armies in the field. Miles of wire are carried on reels, in specially constructed wagons, which hold also batteries and instruments. Some of the wire is insulated so that it can rest on the ground, and thus be laid out with great speed ; while other wire is bare, and is intended to be strung up wherever conveniently possible. For mountain service, the wires and implements are carried by pack-animals ; and often, for reconnoitring, reels of wire are carried like knapsacks on the backs of the men. All modern armies now have a regularly drilled telegraph-corps ; and telegraphic communication is constantly maintained between an advance-guard and the main body of an army, or between different divisions or brigades on the field. During the English operations in Egypt, the advance-guard was not only kept in communication with head-quarters, but with England ; so that, after the battle of Tel-el Kebir, news of the victory was telegraphed to the Queen, and her answer received, within forty-five minutes.

The telephone in its various forms is also of great military value. It enables constant communication to be held between pickets, skirmish-lines, scouting parties, and the officer in general command. It has been proposed to bury sensitive microphones in the earth along roads, around forts and camps, so that the approach or movements of a hostile force could instantly be detected. Actual experiment has proved that a delicate apparatus of this sort will render audible the sound of a spade scraping upon the earth, when digging is going on some five hundred feet away from the buried instrument; and the footfalls of men and horses, and the rumble of wheels, occurring at even greater distances, can easily be recognized.

The most noted of the early experiments in electrical blasting was the destruction of the submerged hull of the ill-fated "Royal George" man-of-war, in 1840. The most famous of recent electrical blasts was the destruction of Flood Rock in the East River, near New-York City, in the fall of 1885. Some idea of the immensity of this work may be derived from the fact that the total area undermined was over nine acres, and that 21,670 feet of galleries honeycombed the solid rock. In the roof and tops of the piers left to support it, over thirteen thousand holes were made. The explosives used were dynamite and rack-a-rock, a mixture of chlorate of potash and di-nitro-benzole. Into each dynamite cartridge, an electric fuse was placed, filled with fulminate of mercury, and containing a small platinum bridge, which, when the current passes, is heated to redness, and the fulminate thus exploded. The entire mine was divided into twenty-four independent circuits, each circuit representing or covering a certain section. Within each circuit were twenty-five fuses or mine-exploders. Each of the twenty-four circuits had its own wire, and the like ends of all the wires were brought together; the positive ends, for example, being dipped into one cup of mercury, and the negative ends into another and a separate cup. It was simply necessary to unite the two cups of mercury by a single wire in circuit with a battery, to send a current through all the circuits simultaneously. The cartridges in the drill-holes were not electrically connected, nor were any fuses arranged in them. The current simply exploded the six hundred "mine-exploders" distributed through the galleries; and the forty thousand cartridges, containing seventy-five thousand pounds of dynamite and two hundred and forty thousand pounds of rack-a-rock, detonated "by sympathy."

For marine use, electric lights are employed for the running lights of vessels. Electric telegraphs are utilized to signal directions from the bridges of steamers to the engine-room and helm; and numerous devices have been contrived, whereby the compass-needle in moving is caused to control an electric circuit which through suitable mechanism governs the rudder, so that a vessel can be made to steer herself upon any given course. Various forms of electric logs have been invented, which provide for a continuous registration, on board the ship, of the actual distance travelled through the water. The great English iron-clad "Colossus" was launched by the aid of electricity; a weight, which in falling removed the dog-shores, being controlled by a large electro-magnet, so that at the proper moment the simple pressure of a button allowed the huge craft to move freely into the water. The propulsion of small vessels by electro-motors has already been referred to. It is probable that these engines will come into more and more extended use afloat for the hoisting and bracing of yards, the lifting of heavy weights, and other work, for which manual labor on sailing-vessels, or steam on steamships, is now employed.

For any one who has been to sea, it is not hard to realize the terrible odds against any unfortunate who falls into the black darkness of the waves at night from the rigging of a fast vessel. The ship may leave the swimmer a mile or more astern before her speed can even be checked ; and to reverse her course involves sweeping around a circle miles in length. And then how is the man to be found, amid the multitudinous and ever-changing hills and valleys of the waves? Here, however, the electric light has proved of splendid utility. A British man-of-war recently was steaming at moderate speed one very dark night, when suddenly the always appalling cry of " Man overboard ! " was raised. Two of the officers, who had seen the sailor fall from the rigging, heroically leaped into the water to his rescue. Almost instantly the electric light on the lofty deck flashed out its great beam, revealing the three men clinging to a life-buoy. As the ship lost her way, and then came about, the brilliant ray followed them ; and so, when the life-boat was lowered, it was simply necessary to steer in the path of the beam to reach the buoy. In six minutes after the alarm was given, the men were saved, the boat hoisted, and the ship once more on her course.

Among the more important applications of electricity to railway purposes, is that of working automatic signals, which guard the road, and give warning of danger, without the intervention of man. It is a requisite of any signal-system, that the normal condition of its signals should indicate danger ; so that in case of any derangement of apparatus, accidental or intentional, warning will be given. Thus failure to act will at most stop or check the movement of a train. In Hall's system, an open circuit is employed, and the current which keeps the signals set at " safety " is transmitted over wires. This current being broken by an engine entering a block-section, and touching a circuit-closer, sets the signal at "danger." The so-called Union system uses a closed circuit, with an electric current moving through the rails. When a section of road is guarded by this device, the entrance of a locomotive breaks the current simply by placing its wheels upon the conducting rails, and thereupon visible signals of danger are given ; and when a train approaches a station or crossing, a warning bell is rung. To electric railways and railway telegraphs, reference has already been made. The electric lighting of railway-trains is now accomplished by the aid of storage-batteries and incandescent lamps ; the batteries being supplied by a small dynamo carried on the locomotive. Electric brakes, which depend upon the attractive energy of electro-magnets being exerted to press the "shoes" against the wheels, are used on some European railways.

The earliest application of electricity to music was probably that made by Père Laborde in 1755, in his so-called *clavecin électrique*. This curious instrument is described in Sigaud de la Fond's treatise of 1767, as follows : " A bar of iron insulated on a silken cord carries bells of different sizes for the different notes, two bells being supplied for each note. One of the two bells is suspended by a brass wire, the other by a thread of silk. The hammer, held by a silken cord, hangs between the two. From the bell suspended by the silk, extends a brass wire, the end of which is fastened by a second cord, and terminates in a ring which receives a small iron lever, which rests on an insulated iron bar. By this arrangement the bell suspended by the brass wire is electrified from the iron bar which carries it ; and the other, which is hung from this bar by the silk thread, is electrified by the other iron bar, on which the lever rests. When a key is pressed down, the lever is raised, and caused to touch the non-insulated bar. At the same instant the hammer is set in motion, and strikes the two bells with such rapidity that a single undulating [*sic*] sound is produced, which imitates very closely the tremolo effect of the organ. As soon as the lever falls on the electrified rod, the hammer stops. Thus each key controls a lever, and each lever a pair of bells; and in this way airs may be played as on any other clavecin."

The idea of controlling the hammers of a piano by electro-magnets, which should be energized and de-energized from a distant station, was suggested several years ago; and a glowing prospectus was issued by an electro-musical company which proposed to play any one's piano — after a few alterations in its inner mechanism — by electricity. There was to be a central station, in which was to be located the single controlling keyboard which governed all the pianos of the various subscribers; and here noted artists were to play between stated hours. When any subscriber desired music in his parlor, he had only to consult the programme, distributed daily, to learn what *morceau* was in process of performance, and then turn his switch, when his piano would instantly begin; so that in the humblest dwelling the choicest productions of the great masters, executed by the Von Bulows and the Liszts and the Rubinsteins of the day, were to be as readily available and as familiar as the "Maiden's Prayer" and "Monastery Bells." Of course there were some obvious difficulties attending this scheme; such, for example, as that of the possibility of receiving the wrong tunes, — the "Dead March in Saul," for example, at a dancing-party, or the last minstrel ditty at a funeral: but the addition of an electric annunciator which would automatically exhibit the name of the piece, it was believed, would prevent this trouble. So far as is known, the plan never went into practical effect, although some electro-musical concerts were given, in which half a dozen pianos were played in unison, making much noise but little music. In the explosive concert-performances, such as delight the ears of the throngs at Coney Island and other popular resorts, electricity is an indispensable assistant. To Mr. Patrick Gilmore is probably due the credit of discharging a whole battery of cannon in strict accentuation, with the "Anvil Chorus," by means of electric fuses and wires leading from the conductor's desk; the effect being, both metaphorically and literally, "stunning."

The harmonic telegraph, whereby musical sounds can be transmitted between distant points, has already been explained. Electric organs have been constructed, in which the action and stops are entirely controlled by the closing of circuits by the keys, etc. In Grace Church, New York, the chancel organ is placed in a chamber built for the purpose at the angle formed by the east wall of the south transept and the chancel wall. The gallery organ stands at the west end of the church, over the main entrance. The echo organ is situated on the roof, over the intersection of nave and transept. These organs are connected with the keyboards in the chancel, and are thus under the complete control of one performer. A curious contrivance, called a melograph, has been devised by Mr. Carpenter, which both registers and reproduces music. The operator manipulates keys like those of a piano, which control currents which operate perforators in an endless strip of paper, cutting long or short slits according to the duration of the note struck. This paper proceeds to a second apparatus, where circuit is made only through the openings in the paper strip, and thus only certain reeds are set in operation, to reproduce the original melody. An electrical recording device has also been invented, designed to rescue the fugitive improvisations of musical genuises from oblivion. Whenever a key is struck, a note is marked telegraphically on a moving strip of paper.

Possibly the reader, while seated in a theatre or opera-house, and waiting for the curtain to rise, has devoted a few minutes to wondering how the innumerable burners of the great chandelier which hangs from the dome are lighted; or how, even by the longest of poles, a match can be carried to gas-jets located apparently in the most inaccessible places. Then suddenly there is a succession of sharp cracks; and, before one's eyelids can rise after the involuntary wink, every burner is aflame. This is electrical gas-lighting. Electricity is a generous rival. Perhaps because of the inapproachable superiority of its own light, it can afford to help its weaker antagonist. Closer or nearer inspection of the myriad gas-burners of a theatre will show that they are all connected by delicate wires, and that at the tip of every one of them are a couple of metal points, between which the circuit is interrupted. Now, when a powerful electric current is sent into the wire, it travels over the conductor until it reaches one of these breaks, over which it jumps from point to point; and in its leap a spark appears. The gas is first turned on to all the burners. No matter how many they may be, the passage of the current is so infinitely swift that the spark at the tip of every one of them is made at the same instant, and every outgoing stream of gas is thus ignited at once. This is a very old invention. It appears to have been first made public by one Joseph Beck, in an English scientific paper, in 1839. At the same time it is perhaps the simplest, as well as most commonly used, arrangement of electrical gas-lighting apparatus. There are many more modern contrivances for the same purpose, which display exceptional ingenuity. For example, there are several forms of so-called automatic lighters, which on the first pressure of a button, no matter how far distant from the burner, a communicating wire being present, not only light the gas, but before doing so turn it on. Then, on a second pressure of the same button, the gas is turned off. This has been applied to street-lights, so that all the gas-lamps in a large district can thus be automatically lighted and extinguished without any help from the traditional lamp-lighter and his ladder. Then there are simple little contrivances connected to individual burners, so that it is necessary simply to pull down a hanging wire, or merely to turn on the gas by the cock in the ordinary way, when a little spring is wiped past a metal point on the burner-tip, a spark made, and the gas lighted. Of course it is a great convenience, on going into a dark room, to be saved the hunt for fugitive matches, and to have nothing to do but find the fixture, and turn on the gas; and it is even a greater comfort for paterfamilias to know that when strange noises in the lower part of the house arouse him in the middle of the night, he has not to descend into the darkness to meet an unknown fate, but simply to touch a button by his bedside, when every burner in every room, if he so desires, will blaze, and render his further investigation — whether it be for cats or burglars — at least free from nameless fears of an unseen and hence mysterious intruder.

The number of varieties of electric alarms, indicators, and annunciators, is simply legion. Most of them are automatic in their action. Others — like the hotel annunciators, which, when a button is pressed in a room, cause a bell to sound in the office, and reveal the number of the apartment whence the signal comes — require a closing or breaking of the circuit by hand. The mechanism of all of these contrivances embodies an electro-magnet, which, when the current is established by pressing the button, attracts a metal shutter bearing the number, and thus moves it so that the number becomes visible through an opening in a screen ; or else the magnet acts to release a catch so that the shutter is allowed to fall into view. The automatic contrivances either simply give an alarm as by ringing a bell or exhibiting a signal, or else actually control the power of some contrivance which does certain work. Sometimes an alarm is given, and mechanism operated at the same time. Thus electrical low-water regulators have been devised for steam boilers, which, when the water falls below a certain level, turn on the steam to sound the whistle, and also open the feed valve to let in a supply of water. Other electrical regulators have been arranged in connection with the dampers of furnaces, to open and close them at the proper time. So also, in connection with steam-engines, electrical governors have been adopted, which control the slide-valves and the admission of steam. Nearly all the electrical heat-regulators depend upon the elongation or contraction of a so-called thermostatic bar, made of metals very sensitive to differences in temperature ; or upon the movement of the mercury in a thermometer-tube. When the heat of an apartment exceeds a certain limit, the bar expands, or the mercury in the thermometer rises, and establishes a circuit, through which the current, being free to pass, actuates mechanism for opening a ventilator or damper, and so letting cool air into and hot air out of the chamber. This idea has been very successfully applied to artificial incubators, in which it is

necessary to maintain a temperature of about 102° Fah.
very uniformly during the long incubating period.   One
contrivance of this class is arranged to regulate the
temperature of an incubator heated by hot water from a
small boiler, with great accuracy.   The damper opens and
shuts responsive to even a fraction of a degree difference
in temperature, and the proportion of eggs hatched — often
as high as eighty-two per cent — shows how perfectly the
sentinel current does its work.

In some cases the body to be expanded by heat is made

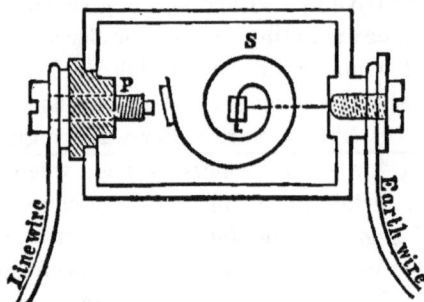

Fig. 143.

in the form of a spring as at S, in Fig. 143.   When the
temperature rises, the end of the spring makes contact
with the point P, and thus establishes the electrical circuit
from one wire to another.

Burglar-alarms are now in every-day use.   Some of
them depend upon the bringing into contact of two pieces
of metal by the opening of a door or window, thus establishing the circuit from a battery to an alarm-bell and
to an annunciator showing the location of the place of
attempted entry.   Others depend upon the breaking of a
closed circuit, releasing some form of alarm.   Others are
especially adapted to safes, so that in event of a burglar
breaking in, or even tampering with the receptacle, the

alarm is caused to sound. Door-mats and matting are also constructed with contact plates brought together by the pressure of the foot of a person stepping on them, and thus establishing a current to a bell which thus gives warning of any one entering or moving about a protected room. In large cities where district telegraph companies are in existence, arrangements are made whereby all the doors and windows of a residence can be connected with an alarm at a central station; so that the occupant can leave the house untenanted, with confidence that any burglar attempting to enter will at the same time, and indeed without his own knowledge, signal his own proceedings to the station, whence a policeman will be sent after him long before he can do any mischief.

In brief, there are almost as many alarms, regulators, and indicators, as there are special circumstances needing them. One of the most ingenious contrivers of apparatus of this sort was the famous French conjuror Robert Houdin, who retired, after his eventful career, to a charming mansion called the "Priory," in the village of St. Gervais. There he amused himself by devising a variety of ingenious electrical contrivances, many of which are graphically described in the following extract published several years ago : —

"The main entrance to the Priory is a carriage-way closed by a gate. Upon the left of this is a door for the admission of visitors on foot: on the right is placed a letter-box. The mansion is situated a quarter of a mile distant, and is approached by a broad and winding road well shaded with trees.

"The visitor presenting himself before the door on the left sees a gilt plate bearing the name of Robert Houdin, below which is a small gilt knocker. He raises this according to his fancy; but, no matter how feeble the blow, a delicately tuned chime of bells sounding through the mansion announces his presence. When the attendant touches a button placed in the hall, the chime ceases, the bolt at the entrance is thrown back, the name of Robert Houdin disappears from the door, and in its place appears the word '*entrez*' in white enamel. The visitor pushes open the door, and enters ; it closes with a spring behind him, and he cannot depart without permission.

"This door in opening sounds two distinct chimes, which are repeated in the inverse order in closing. Four distinct sounds then, separated by equal intervals, are produced. In this way a single visitor is announced. If many come together, as each holds the door open for the next the intervals between the first two and the last two strokes indicate with great accuracy, especially to a practised ear, the number who have entered ; and the preparation for the reception is made accordingly. A resident of the place is readily distinguished ; for, knowing in advance what is to occur, he knocks, and at the instant when the bolt slips back he enters. The equidistant strokes follow immediately the pressing of the button. But a new visitor, surprised at the appearance of the word '*entrez*,' hesitates a second or two, then presses open the door gradually, and enters slowly. The four strokes, now separated by a short interval, succeed the pressing of the button by quite an appreciable time ; and the host makes ready to receive a stranger. The travelling beggar, fearful of committing some indiscretion, raises timidly the knocker; he hesitates to enter, and when he does it is only with great slowness and caution. This the chimes unerringly announce. It seems to persons at the house as if they actually saw the poor mendicant pass the entrance; and in going to meet him they are never mistaken.

"When a carriage arrives at the Priory, the driver descends from his box, enters the door by the method now described, and is directed to the key of the gate by a suitable inscription. He unlocks the gate, and swings open its two parts; the movement is announced at the house, and on a table in the hall bearing the words, 'The gate is ——,' appears the word 'open' or 'closed,' according to the fact.

"The letter-box, too, has an electric communication with the house. The carrier, previously instructed, drops in first all the printed matter together; then he adds the letters one by one. Each addition sounds the chimes; and the owner, even if he has not yet risen, is apprised of the character of his despatches. To avoid sending letters to the village, they are written in the evening; and a commutator is so arranged, that, when the carrier drops the mail into the box the next morning, the electricity, in place of sounding the chimes in the house, sounds one over his head. Thus warned, he comes up to the house to leave what he has brought, and to take away the letters ready for mailing.

"'My electric doorkeeper then [says Houdin] leaves me nothing to be desired. His service is most exact; his fidelity is thoroughly proven; his discretion is unequalled; and as to his salary, I doubt the possibility of obtaining an equal service for a smaller remuneration.'

"M. Houdin possesses a young mare whom he has named Fanchette. To this animal he is much attached, and cares for her with the greatest assiduity. A former hostler, who was an active, intelligent man, had become devoted to the art so successfully practised by his employer in previous years. His knowledge, however, was confined to a single trick; but this he executed with rare ability. This trick consisted in changing the oats of his master into five-franc pieces. To prevent this peculation, the stable, distant from the house seven or eight rods, is connected with it by electricity so that by means of a clock fixed in the study the necessary quantity of food is supplied to the horse, at a fixed hour, three times a day. The distributing apparatus is very simple, consisting of a square box, funnel-shaped, which discharges the oats in the proportion previously regulated. Since the oats are allowed to fall only when the stable-door is locked, the hostler cannot remove them after they are supplied; nor can he shut himself in the stable, and thus get the oats, as the door locks only upon the outside. Moreover he cannot re-enter, and abstract them, because an alarm is caused to sound in the house if the door be open before the oats are consumed.

"This study clock transmits the time to two dial-plates. One, placed upon the front of the house, gives the hour of the day to the neighborhood; the other, fastened to the gardener's lodge facing the house, gives the time to its inmates. Several smaller dials, operated similarly, are placed in various apartments. They all, however, have but a single striking part; but this is powerful enough to be heard over the entire village. Upon the top of the house is a tower containing a bell on which the hours of meals are announced. Below this is a train of wheel-work to raise the hammer. To avoid the necessity of winding up the weight every day, an automatic arrangement is employed which utilizes a force ordinarily lost. Between the kitchen, situated upon the ground-floor, and the clock-work in the garret, there is a contrivance so arranged that the servants in going to and fro about their work wind up the weight without being conscious of it. An electric current, set in motion by the study regulator, raises the detent, and permits the number of strokes indicated by the dial. The manner of distributing the time from the study, Houdin finds very useful. When, for any reason, he wishes the meals hurried or retarded, he presses a secret key, and the time upon all the dials is altered to suit his convenience. The cook finds often that the time passes very rapidly; while a quarter of an hour or more, not otherwise attainable, is gained by M. Houdin.

"Every morning this clock sends, at different hours, electric impulses to awaken three persons, the first of whom is the gardener. But, in addition, this apparatus forces them to rise, by continuing to sound until the circuit is broken by moving a small key placed at the farther end of the room. To do this, the sleeper must rise, and then the object sought is accomplished.

"The poor gardener is almost tormented by this electricity. The greenhouse is so arranged that he cannot raise its temperature above 50° F., or let it fall below 37° F., without a record in the study. The next morning Houdin says to him, 'Jean, you had too much heat last night; you will scorch my geraniums;' or, 'Jean, you are in danger of freezing my orange-trees; the thermometer descended to three degrees below zero (29° F.) last night.' Jean scratches his head, and says nothing; but he evidently regards Houdin as a sorcerer.

"A similar thermo-electric apparatus placed in the woodhouse gives warning of the first beginning of an incendiary fire. As a protection against robbers, all the doors and windows of the house have an electric attachment. This so connects them with the chimes, that the bells continue to sound as long as the door or window remains open. During the day-time the electric communication is interrupted; but at midnight, the hour of crime, it is re-established by the study clock. When the owner is absent, however, the connection is permanent. Then the opening of the door or window causes the great bell to sound like a tocsin. Everybody is aroused, and the robber is easily captured.

"A pistol-gallery is upon the grounds, and Houdin often amuses himself in shooting. But in place of the ordinary methods of announcing a successful shot, a crown of laurels is caused to appear suddenly above the head of the marksman. A deep road passes through the park, which it is sometimes necessary to cross. On reaching it, no bridge is to be seen; but upon the edge of the ravine a little car appears, upon which the person desiring to cross places himself. No sooner is he seated than he is rapidly transported to the opposite bank. As he steps out, the car returns again to the other side. This being a double-acting arrangement, the same aërial method is made use of in returning.

"I finish here my description," says Houdin. "Ought I not to reserve some few and unexpected details for the visitor who comes to raise the mysterious knocker below which, it will be remembered, is engraved the name of Robert Houdin?"

Electricity is employed in timepieces in three ways. Thus it is made use of as a motive-power, to swing a pendulum, and replace the springs or weights of an ordinary clock. Or, it is employed for transmission: a central clock sends an electric current every second, half-minute, or minute, to one or more dials placed at a distance, which cause the hands to advance respectively a second, a half-minute, or a minute. Or, electricity is used to regulate clocks and dials propelled by ordinary weights and springs, and adjusts the hands every hour, every six hours, or every twenty-four hours. It is this system of synchronism which has been adopted by the city of Paris for the public clocks. It was first invented by Dr. Locke of Cincinnati in 1848; and Congress awarded him a premium of ten thousand dollars for his invention, designing to use it in astronomical researches and in determining longitude.

Time-signals are now transmitted to every important city and to all railroads in Great Britain, from the Greenwich Observatory. In other parts of Europe, especially in Germany and France, electric clocks are everywhere used. In Paris, the standard clock of the National Observatory is connected by special lines with about thirty "horary centres." At these points are placed clocks, the pendulums of which are continuously controlled by impulses sent every second from the observatory; and they, in their turn, distribute their beats to numerous stations in the vicinity. The whole city is thus supplied with time uniform and correct to a second.

In the United States, time-signals are sent from the standard clock in Cambridge Observatory to many stations in Boston, and at intervals are transmitted over the telephone-lines. Standard time is also marked on the tapes of the stock-exchange tickers. From the National Observatory in Washington, time-signals are sent to New York; and the operator at this station despatches the current which drops the time-ball on the Western Union Telegraph Building in the metropolis, two hundred and forty miles distant. The ball, after being hoisted, is held by a simple catch mechanism which is controlled by an electromagnet. At the moment of noon, New-York time, the officer in charge at Washington closes the circuit, the magnet retracts its armature, the catch is slipped, and the ball drops. The instant the ball reaches the base of the pole, the fact is automatically telegraphed to Washington. Owing to the great height of the ball when raised, it is visible for many miles around; and directly or indirectly the clocks and watches of nearly three millions of people are thereby kept from straying very far from the true time.

In referring to some military uses of electricity, we have mentioned the very remarkable apparatus which records minute intervals of time. This is the electro-chronograph; and by its aid not only is time measured with wonderful exactitude, but by its recording apparatus it enables us to note the precise instant when an event occurs. This is of great value to astronomers in securing a record, for example, of the transit of a heavenly body across the meridian; for the observer has only to keep his eye on the object, and tap with his finger a button or key at the proper moments.

Who, in his youthful days, has not read the story of Aladdin and that wonderful lamp which procured such marvellous things for its lucky owner? The fervid imagination of the Oriental romancer fairly runs riot in describing the "forty basins of massy gold;" and the beautiful slaves "bearing large golden basins filled with all sorts of jewels, each basin being covered with a silver stuff embroidered with flowers of gold;" and the gorgeous edifice with "its treasury filled with bags of money, the palace with the most costly furniture, and the stables with the finest horses in the world." And all this from the happy thought of a thrifty dame to rub the lamp clean; for it is only when the lamp is rubbed, that the "genie of gigantic size" appears, and the feast of wonders begins. No doubt we think in our boyish wisdom, that such things are all very well to read about, and a great many times too; but of course we know that such marvels are not to be taken in sober earnest.

But, O reader of maturer years, did not a "genie of gigantic size," whom we have named Electricity, come to us — if not at the rubbing of a lamp, certainly at the rubbing of a bit of amber? And what did Aladdin's genie do half as wonderful as ours has done? If Aladdin's sprite could transport him from place to place, cannot ours do as much for us? and very much more, for it can carry our very thoughts, even our spoken words, perhaps some day our faces. And as for the wealth it has showered upon us, who can estimate the value to humanity of the telegraph alone, all its other works aside? The rash request to seek the "roc's egg of the Caucasus" marked a limit to the power of the fabled Afrite. Who will set metes and bounds to the new power and potency which comes to answer our

> "best pleasure: be't to fly,
> To swim, to dive into the fire, to ride
> On the curled clouds"?

"It may be said," writes Priestley, "that there is a *ne plus ultra* in every thing, and therefore in electricity. It is true, but what reason is there to think that we have arrived at it?"

And to-day, entering as we are upon the very Age of Electricity, surrounded on all sides by its marvels, familiar with them when the mere fact of such familiarity in itself surprises us, that question asked one hundred and twenty years ago, in the feeblest infancy of the science, is as unanswerable now as then.

INDEX.

www.ingramcontent.com/pod-product-compliance
Lightning Source LLC
Chambersburg PA
CBHW031351290326
41932CB00044B/882